D1542605

SWINDOLL
LEADERSHIP
LIBRARY

WOMEN

AND THE

CHURCH

Reaching, Teaching, and
Developing Women for Christ

LUCY MABERY-FOSTER

WORD PUBLISHING
NASHVILLE
A Thomas Nelson Company

WOMEN AND THE CHURCH
Swindoll Leadership Library

Unless otherwise indicated, Scripture quotations used in this book are from
the *Holy Bible: New International Version* (NIV), copyright © 1978 by the
New York International Bible Society.
Used by permission of Zondervan Bible Publishers.

Scripture quotations identified KJV are from the *King James Version* of the Bible.
Scripture quotations identified NRSV are from The *New Revised Standard Version,*
copyright © 1976 by the Division of Christian Education of the National Council of the
Churches of Christ in the U.S.A. Used by permission.

Published in association with Dallas Theological Seminary (DTS):
General Editor: Charles R. Swindoll
Managing Editor: Roy B. Zuck
The theological opinions expressed by the author are not necessarily the official
position of Dallas Theological Seminary.

Library of Congress Cataloging in Publication Data:

Mabery-Foster, Lucy.
Women and the church : reaching, teaching, and developing women for Christ /
by Lucy Mabery-Foster.
p. cm.— (Swindoll leadership library)
Includes bibliographical references and indexes.

ISBN 0-8499-1360-8

1. Church work with women. I. Title.
II. Series.

BV445.M33   1999   99-24524
259'.082–dc21   CIP

Printed in the United States of America
99 00 01 02 03 04 05 06 BVG 9 8 7 6 5 4 3 2 1

To my four granddaughters,

Catharine Elizabeth Fulmer,
Lauren Elise Fulmer,
Madeline Renae Mabery,
Miranda Grace Mabery,

to whom I am passing the torch of Christian womanhood.
May you walk closely in the footsteps of our Lord Jesus Christ.

Contents

Foreword

 W henever I search books on a particular topic, I always look for one clue that stands out above all the rest. I don't look for a particular style of writing or even who has endorsed a certain work. After poking around a bit I check for the telltale sign that announces whether I should keep on reading. It is this: *Has the writer spent time actually doing what he or she is advocating?* When I find a writer has spent sufficient time "in the trenches," I'm more inclined to consider his or her work.

Lucy Mabery-Foster has devoted much of her adult life to working on the front lines of women's ministry. She has discipled literally hundreds of women throughout her steadfast ministry. When women sign up to learn from Lucy, they know she's going to shoot straight with them. She practices what has come to be known as "tough love."

She's also a pioneer woman! Lucy was the first female faculty member appointed to teach at Dallas Theological Seminary. In other words, she's not afraid to take on new challenges and move into uncharted waters. In both her personal and private life, she has stood tall under unusually difficult circumstances, some of which you will read about in her volume.

In addition to all of these fine characteristics Lucy is a devoted biblicist. She has pored over the Scriptures in coming to her conclusions. In an age of superficial answers I always appreciate reading from those who base their findings on the eternal Word of God. From start to finish, that's what Lucy has done. Let me add, this work will not leave you in the realm of the theoretical. This seminary professor works with women both in-side and outside of the classroom. Prepare to read about how you can minister more effectively to women from all walks of life. Dr. Mabery-Foster will lead you through a mini-course covering all aspects of ministry to women . . . each with scriptural justification.

There is a key phrase in this volume's subtitle. Did you notice it? It's true, this book is all about reaching, teaching, and developing women. The key phrase, however, to which I refer is *for Christ.* All our ministry efforts are in vain if they are not carried out for Him. May this fine work spur you on in your own ministry to women—for the glory of Christ our Lord.

—CHARLES R. SWINDOLL
General Editor

Acknowledgments

I have had a heart for ministering to women for as long as I can remember. For twenty years I taught the "Through the Bible" *Scofield Correspondence Course* produced by Moody Bible Institute. The first time I taught it, it took me nine years, but the one hundred women who started with me stayed with me through those years. They had such a hunger to learn God's Word and His ways that I never tired of our times together. We became good friends, and many of those friendships have lasted until now. My mind often returns to a warm scene with my youngest son in an infant-seat at my feet, while I taught God's Word to these dear women. Years have passed, my son is now grown and working in the business world, and I am deeply entrenched in academia, but nostalgia sneaks in now and again.

For many years God has been preparing me for writing this book. I learned long ago that Christianity is a relationship with a person—not a philosophy of life, a code of moral ethics, or a list of don'ts. And I knew that if I was to impact others, I had to become intimately associated with the person of Christ, for you can't impart to others what you yourself don't possess. And Christ Himself has indeed walked with me through the deep valleys of death and the mountaintops of joy.

My daughter, Janet Fulmer, and my sons, Daniel Mabery and Stephen Mabery, have given me support and encouragement in whatever avenues of life I have pursued. They all suffered with me through the death of my husband and their father, Trevor Mabery, and they encouraged me to pick up the pieces of my life and once again pursue my love of teaching. They supported me as I struggled through my doctoral work and the writing of my dissertation, and they encouraged me as I walked through the uncharted waters of becoming the first woman on the faculty of Dallas Theological Seminary. Most recently, I appreciate their support of my choice of a new companion in life.

I would like to especially acknowledge my new husband, C. L. Foster, who came into my life in 1996 and brought a new joy to my spirit—a joy that only another coheir with Christ could bring. He has patiently supported my writing of this book and given me constructive feedback along the way. When I have felt discouraged, he has been there to lift my spirit and remind me that it is not my strength but the Lord's that is behind the writing of this book.

My best friend, Glo Stegall, has been my greatest encourager for more than a decade. She has listened to and helped me formulate my thoughts through the years that went into this book, and she waded through my manuscript with encouraging words.

I also acknowledge my editor, Roy B. Zuck, who has written me notes of encouragement that have kept me going. His skill in editing manuscripts certainly shows through in his tireless efforts to make this series of books the best possible.

Part One

The Challenges
of Women's Ministries

Chapter One

Why Minister to Women?

S uppose Boston, Los Angeles, and Philadelphia—with their cumulative total populations of 5.5 million—were populated with only females. That's how many more female children, youth, and adults there are than males in our nation.[1] Are the unique needs of women, who constitute more than half our population, being adequately addressed by our churches? Can we view men and women alike when it comes to leading them to Christ and helping them reach their full potential in Him?

WOMEN'S MANY CHALLENGES AND ADJUSTMENTS

The more we understand the unique nature of women, the more we can see how essential it is to tailor-make some of our church ministries to target this vast constituency. We cannot assume that they will be adequately nourished spiritually if we lump them together with men in every church program. We must search out their needs and let them know that we understand their differences and are willing to help them with their various challenges.

Women adjust to life's situations differently from the ways men adjust. Take singleness, for example. The stigma attached to singleness for women often carries a heavy burden, adding to the loneliness that already exists within local churches that promote marriage and families as God's ultimate ideal. Women have fewer avenues than single men to reach out and choose their relationships. And then women's "biological clocks" always seem to be ticking away.

If women do marry, they will usually face the unique challenges of childbearing and child rearing. They desperately need mentors who can understand these challenges. Assuring words from other women who have been down similar paths are tremendous sources of strength. Men, although well-meaning, are often at a loss for words when it comes to identifying with this uniquely female situation. When my husband was driving me to the hospital to have our first child, he was trying to be comforting when he said, "Having a baby is just like having a tooth filled." The added problem accompanying that particular statement was the fact that he had never even had a tooth filled!

A godly woman mentor can often troubleshoot many uncharted courses young mothers must take. In our mobile society, having a mentor is especially beneficial because many young mothers live long distances from their parents.

The environments of widowhood and divorce are vastly different for men and women. Here again women are often burdened by having to raise children by themselves. In the United States children of divorced parents are usually awarded to the mother, especially if the children are young. The courts will place children in the father's care only if they have convincing evidence that the mother is unfit to care for the children adequately. Being a single mom in today's society has many challenges— finances being not the least of them. Working long hours to make ends meet, feeling guilty for lack of available time to invest in quality interaction with their children, and constant feelings of inadequacy and exhaustion— these are among the many problems single mothers face. These elements often force them into isolation and loneliness. The church definitely needs to enter the worlds of these women. Here again, widowed or divorced men have considerably more freedom.

Then there's the dating and remarriage scene. Men usually pursue women, and so women must sit back and wait to be asked. The word "awkward" well describes the situation when divorced or widowed women must reenter this arena. Should they date? Should they remarry? Many women are left to decide these questions alone, and this, too, adds to their feelings of aloneness. Age is again a factor—more of a consideration for women than for men. Men traditionally marry women younger than themselves, and so there are more available choices for them.

Women also face some physical challenges that men never experience—PMS and menopause being the two most common. Ironically, when the first of these disappears, the second begins. Medical attention has stimulated vast research and help in these areas, but understanding the problems that accompany them can help women along the paths of relief and acceptance. Women in the church can understand some of the troubling complications that plague some women, and as a result they can be of great support and comfort.

Many marital problems could be avoided if godly older women fulfilled the biblical mandate in Titus 2:4–5. "Then they can train the younger women to love their husbands and children, to be self-controlled and pure, to be busy at home, to be kind, and to be subject to their husbands." Two extremely demanding and influential tasks we choose in this life—marriage and parenting—require no formal training. Yet God is concerned enough about our marriages and parenting that he told older women to teach younger women how to develop good marriages and be good parents. Many of the problems our society faces today are the direct result of our failure to fulfill this divine mandate. It's time for church leaders to bring up younger women to be well-equipped for the tasks at hand.

Another great challenge for women in the work force involves harassment. Statistics validating female harassment are astounding, and we need to learn how to address this ever-increasing problem. For years, issues of harassment have been neglected, and women in our churches have often felt isolated, unheard, and unsupported. They have often borne these insults in silence, not knowing where to turn. Women who understand these problems can assist tremendously in guiding other women to the proper channels for help.

WOMEN'S MANY SPIRITUAL GIFTS

I have worked with women for years, and the majority of them have not yet discovered their spiritual gifts, or if they know them, they don't know how to find appropriate ways in which to exercise those gifts. Men and women alike receive gifts from the Holy Spirit, but how these gifts are to be exercised differs. Can we guide women in discovering how they are gifted, and then help them find the right places in the church to exercise those gifts?

WOMEN'S SPIRITUAL SENSITIVITY

For twenty-five years I taught "Through the Bible" classes to women, and I never tired of their enthusiasm to learn God's Word. I remember one young woman who never missed a single lesson in ten years. She even showed up one Monday morning after giving birth to a healthy baby boy on the previous Friday! I never cease to be amazed at women's spiritual receptivity. One year I let the women vote on the length of the classtime they wanted to attend—one hour or one and a half hours. They voted unanimously for the longer time. Many church services and prayer meetings have more women than men in attendance. In many unsaved homes the wife is more responsive to the gospel than her husband.

Biological Distinctives

Some people today maintain that men and women are equal and that no differences exist between them. However, the basic facts of biology show that they are indeed different. The chromosomal arrangements differ in males and females. In every cell in her body (with the exception of the sex cells we call eggs), every woman has a pair of X chromosomes. In every cell of his body (with the exception of sperm cells), every man has an X chromosome and a Y chromosome. A normal human embryo inherits twenty-three chromosomes from the mother and twenty-three from the father. The twenty-third pair determines what sex the baby will be. If the twenty-third pair are both X chromosomes, the embryo is a female; if the pair are an X and Y chromosome, the embryo is a male. When the egg cell is fertilized, the gender is determined instantly; and as differentiation of the various types of cells occurs, each cell in the body will have an XX (female) or an XY (male) pair of chromosomes. Hormones cannot change

6

the chromosomal makeup of the cells, but they do determine many secondary sexual characteristics.

Gender Distinctives

A popular view since the 1970s is that though men and women differ biologically, they are the same psychologically, emotionally, and intellectually. Many people claim that the seeming differences between the sexes in abilities, emotions, attitudes, and that even skills are merely the product of centuries of male domination and male-dominated interpretation.[2] However, extensive scientific research is suggesting otherwise. And the Scriptures present gender-specific social roles for marriage and the church. The masculine role typically involves leadership in the church and home, and the feminine role involves submission, which does not imply inferiority. God has designated role distinctions to help us live efficiently here on earth. Yet God clearly provides equal dignity and worth for both men and women. Both are created in the image of God.

A biblical view of sexuality involves the total person. Men must sense their God-given competence and be able to give whatever is required to lead lovingly in the home and the church. Women must sense their God-given security, knowing they are able to take their place of ministry with confidence—submitting to their husbands' loving leadership, following the spiritual leadership of men in the church assembly, and functioning with assuredness in appropriate areas of responsibility. Proverbs 31:10–31 gives us a beautiful picture of a very capable wife who was encouraged by her husband to reach her potential, and his confidence in her gave her room to be all she could be.

Research reveals that one of the areas of greatest gender difference is in male and female personalities. Unity exists in a woman's personality, so that she responds to situations with her heart, intellect, and temperament. When my husband was killed in a plane crash in 1987, it affected every part of my being—the way I thought and felt about things, the way I reacted to every one of life's situations. I remember asking God to let me focus for just one hour on the Bible lesson I was teaching without having my mind race over to my emotional pain.

Studies suggest that a man has the specific capacity with his intellect to free himself from his present circumstances for a time in order to accomplish certain things because his emotions, intellect, and body can be more readily differentiated. Of course, I have to take a man's word for it, but a number of men have told me their personalities tend to be separated into intellectual, physical, and emotional components.[3]

Research conducted in the United States has shown that men and women also differ intellectually. Women display a greater sensitivity to the concrete and personal dimensions of their environments, whereas men show a greater tendency to abstraction and a sensitivity to structure. Studies sponsored by Harvard University show that boys in the United States are far more likely than girls to be mathematically gifted. This was confirmed by Johns Hopkins University researchers Camilla Benbow and Julian Stanley, who did a seven-year study of the Scholastic Aptitude Test (SAT) scores of 10,200 gifted junior-high students and found that boys surpassed girls in their mathematical scores.[4] Those who want to disprove these findings claim that boys have always been expected to do better in math, so they get more support from parents and teachers. However, this cannot be substantiated universally. Males also hold an undisputed edge in visual-spatial ability.[5] Genetic research is presently attempting to link these abilities to specific genes. Is it possible that God designed us to serve different roles in life?

Women are usually better at verbal skills. Studies conducted with infants have shown that girl babies are usually more attracted to people and boy babies are more attracted to objects.[6]

Differences also exist in orientation. Man's social behavior is more goal-oriented; and the woman's is oriented more toward caring for personal needs. However, these studies are not saying that men can achieve goals more effectively than women and that women can care for personal needs better than men.

Studies also show that men seem to be more aggressive than women. This is seen in two-year-olds and continues on into adulthood.[7] Not long ago I was driving home behind two cars. The man in the front car failed to start off quickly enough from the stop sign to suit the man in the car in front of me. So at the next stop sign the impatient man bumped him and started pushing him through the intersection, enveloping his car in the smoke of burning tire rubber. This triggered a chain of reactions that ended with the man in the front car getting out of his car with a baseball bat and bashing in the hood of his intimidator's car. At that moment I pulled around both cars to avoid being involved in their conflict.

Women are usually more nurturing than men. This does not imply that all men are aggressive and all women are nurturing. Instead, it says that these traits are more frequently found in men and women, respectively. This aggression-nurturing gulf shows up in many areas but is hotly contested by some feminists. They have argued that the nurturing nature of women is not biological in origin, but has been drummed into women by a society that wants to keep them in the home.[8] But the signs that a woman's tendency to nurture is partly inborn are too numerous to ignore. These differences, now being recognized by modern scientists, have been implied in Scripture all along.

Emotionally men and women differ in the way they experience and exhibit fear, anxiety, and frustration. Men apparently tend to respond more emotionally to certain situations than women do.[9] Before his death, my husband, who was a surgeon, was always thought of as the epitome of calmness. He had one speed—calm and deliberate. But one day our small son stuck his foot into the spokes of my bike wheel, while I was biking with him seated in the basket attached to the handlebars. By the time I got him to the emergency room of the hospital where my husband was working, our son's foot was black. My husband met me at the door, grabbed him out of my arms, raced down the corridor, shouting, "Nurse! Nurse! I have a broken leg!" The nurse replied calmly, "Doctor, do you have a broken leg, or does your son?"

Areas of physical difference are often more obvious—especially in size, strength, and certain sex characteristics. The "weaker partner" (1 Pet. 3:7) probably implies physical strength, but present research is showing men are more susceptible to certain serious physical disorders.

As scientists are beginning to develop ways of viewing the brains of men and women, they are uncovering numerous differences. Women apparently transfer interactions between the right and left halves of their brains at a more rapid rate than do men. Women's brains remain in more active states even when resting than do the brains of men.[10]

Daniel Levinson's theory concerning seasons of life shows differences between men and women. To achieve complete entry into adulthood, according to Levinson, a young man must master four developmental tasks. First, he must define a "dream" of what he hopes to accomplish as an adult. Second, he must find a mentor. Third, he needs to develop a career. And fourth, he must establish intimacy.[11]

Follow-up studies found that there are seasons of a woman's life as well. The same four developmental tasks were found to apply to women, with some exceptions. Perhaps the most striking gender difference is in men's and women's dreams of the future. For both, the vision is of central importance, but men tend to have a unified vision of their futures focused on their jobs, while women tend to incorporate both careers and marriage in their ideas of their future. Less than 18 percent of the women in a research project focused exclusively on career achievement, and a bit more than 15 percent restricted their visions of the future to the traditional roles of wife, mother, and helper. Even those women who anticipated both career and marriage moderated their dreams in the context of their husbands' goals, fulfilling traditional expectations within a more contemporary lifestyle. Approximately 41 percent of these women expressed dissatisfaction with some aspect of their split dreams. Careers and marriages tend to be incompatible for many women. Although colleagues and family members felt these women were successful, the women themselves felt they had sacrificed career to family or family to career.[12] However, men sense little dichotomy between career and family life.

Another area in which men's and women's experiences differ is in the mentoring relationship. Although relations with mentors are considered important to the career and life development of young adults, women enter into this kind of relationship less frequently than men do. Part of the problem is that there are fewer women in positions to guide, counsel, or sponsor young women in the workplace. Women have greater difficulty than men in finding that special person who will not only help them as they enter early adulthood, but will also continue to support their development into middle adulthood. As a result, women do not cease being beginners in the world of work. Men may make changes in their careers or lifestyles, but they do not change their focus on their jobs and careers.

Women, in contrast, do. Around age thirty women usually reverse their earlier priorities. Women who were oriented toward marriage and child rearing tend to shift more toward occupational goals, while women who were career-centered generally move toward marriage and the family. Levinson's studies indicate that men and women have differing views of themselves and different concerns, as they cope with similar developmental tasks during their transitional period around age thirty.

God-designed differences should be viewed through the lens of compatibility between men and women, knowing that His design is always perfect. As David wrote, "For you created my inmost being; you knit me together in my mother's womb. I praise you because I am fearfully and wonderfully made; your works are wonderful, I know that full well. My frame was not hidden from you when I was made in the secret place. When I was woven together in the depths of the earth, your eyes saw my unformed body. All the days ordained for me were written in your book before one of them came to be" (Ps. 139:13–16).

Since men and women are equally precious and unique in God's sight, it is important for us to understand each other and how we can fit into His plans. Christian leaders need to understand women well enough to minister to them in a way that will point them to fulfilling relationships— first with their Lord and Savior Jesus Christ, and then with people around them in their homes, churches, or communities.

Chapter Two

Are Churches in Touch with Women's Needs?

*A*s I was listening to a young assistant pastor preach a Sunday morning message, I was personally supportive of him because I had watched him mature during his years at seminary. He began his sermon by stating that God has given every believer a gift for serving Him. The assistant pastor said these gifts have been given by the Holy Spirit at the moment of salvation and are to be used in the church for edifying believers. The preacher then read 1 Corinthians 12:7, "Now to each one the manifestation of the Spirit is given for the common good." Then he read verses 11–14.

The young pastor stressed how important it is for believers to exercise their spiritual gifts. After about ten minutes of this general admonition, he then said, "So, in light of this, each one of you wives should cross-stitch your husband's spiritual gifts and frame them for his desk." At that moment, without his knowing it, this young pastor lost more than half of his audience. He unwittingly excluded the women in the congregation as receipients of spiritual gifts.

We might make excuses for this young preacher and say that if we questioned him, he could clear up the problem, and most assuredly he would. But the fact remains that many women, because of this kind of teaching, become dissatisfied and begin to listen with a keener ear to the voice of the feminist cry of "inferiority."

When I was a seminary student, a man approached me after class one day and said, "Well, all I can say is that for a woman, you certainly do ask deep theological questions."

On one of my exegetical papers, the grader, giving me an almost perfect score, made the following comment: "I need to tell you that this is the best exegetical paper I have ever read written by a woman." Was that a compliment, or was he telling me that he had graded my paper by a different standard from those written by the men in the class? After all, how many papers written by women could he have read, since there were only two women in that degree program at that time?

ADAPTING TO CHANGE

We are living in an age in which there is much uneasiness within the church. Many are feeling that their needs are not being met, and that their churches are not willing to meet them where they are. Take, for example, the baby boomers. In the late 1980s they returned to the churches in large numbers because they wanted to teach proper values and beliefs to their children. But many became disillusioned and left again. Statements like this were often heard: "I admit that I need help raising my kids. Once I came to that realization, I fell back on what was familiar to me—the church. So we went back. Big mistake. Lots of my friends and coworkers have gone through the same disappointment over what the church has for us."[1]

Many evangelical churches are growing to such large numbers that they are no longer conducive to intimate fellowship. Sunday school, midweek services, and evangelistic crusades are being replaced by more intimate gatherings, such as small groups that meet for discussion, Bible study, and prayer; house churches; and worship festivals.[2]

In many evangelical churches across the country the percentage of female attendance and membership has exceeded that of males. If this is the trend for the future, then how should pastors minister most effectively to such a large constituency of their congregations? How should we as women in leadership prepare for ministering to other women? We need to consider prayerfully how we can meet the needs of the people in our churches—both men and women. How can we encourage men to be all they should be in the body of Christ, and how can we encourage women to exercise their spiritual gifts?

After age eighteen, there are consistently more women than men in churches, and after the age of sixty, the ratio increases dramatically. In our evangelical churches there are more women than men with high-school degrees; but when graduate levels are reached, there are more men than women. More than half of most congregations are made up of people who have full-time jobs—about 35 percent are men, and 20 percent are women. Over half of the women in our churches stay at home, and over 40 percent are mothers who work outside the home.[3]

Some women work because they want to pursue a career, and others work because they need to support their families, either in their marriages or as single mothers. Some women work in businesses at their homes, and some women work outside of their homes. Women are marrying at a later age than in years gone by, which sets up a whole new dimension for study—the single woman. Are we meeting their needs? Because couples are marrying at later ages, many individuals entering those marriages are committed to lifestyles that dictate that the wives continue working outside the home. Divorcées are another large group of people in our churches. Are we addressing the needs of those who have been thrust into singleness by divorce? And are we ministering to women who have been thrust into singleness through the death of their husbands?

The "Singles and Singles Again" classes are some of the fastest growing in our churches. In the past there was less need for networks because extended families were close by in surrounding communities. But that is no longer the case in our society. Thousands of young adults move away from home after college, sometimes hundreds of miles away. This creates a sense of isolation and feelings of aloneness that sometimes prompt women to marry hastily.

ROLE MODELS

Where are the role models for our young women in our churches today? Many older women have retired from work and from their nurturing roles in the home and are in "empty nests." How can we get these older women involved in mentoring younger women? How can we help empty nesters realize the satisfaction and fulfillment that comes from heeding Paul's admonition in Titus 2:3–5?

This passage also opens up another issue: that of marital dissatisfaction. There are many hurting marriages within our churches. Until recently it was not popular to admit having problems, whether individual, family, or marital. Dolores Curran lists the top fifteen traits people name as characteristics of a healthy family. In order of priority the traits are these: "communicates and listens, affirms and supports, teaches respect, develops trust, plays and laughs, shares responsibility, teaches right from wrong, values kinship, interacts in balance, shares a religious core, respects privacy, values service to others, values family mealtimes, shares leisure time, and admits to problems and seeks help."[4] This last trait is so different from our families of the past—especially Christian families. In the past, marital problems have been closely guarded secrets. Even today people usually seek help as a last resort and when they face feelings of overwhelming helplessness. Often the reason for this slow disclosure is that they seem to equate stoicism with spirituality. They reason that if they don't let people know they're hurting or having trouble, then the problems will disappear. We pat on the back those couples who "stay together" and who portray an image of "togetherness," and yet they may have been emotionally divorced for many years.

KNOWING WOMEN'S NEEDS

In a nationwide survey of evangelical churches people were asked to respond to the statement, "I feel some of my greatest individual needs are not presently being met by my church." One out of three—exactly 33 percent—responded that their greatest individual needs were not being met.[5]

When asked how much time couples spend talking with each other each week, the results were surprising. Eight percent of the couples said they spend about twelve minutes—a minute and a half per day. Fifteen percent said they talk one hour each week—about ten minutes each day. Sixteen percent said they spend two hours—about seventeen minutes per day. Only 8 percent said they spent twelve hours a week—a little over one and a half hours per day.[6]

When asked about relationships, only 25 percent of the men and 22 percent of the women said they had any intimacy in their marriages. Only 15 percent of men and 12 percent of women said their mates are their best friends.[7]

Single adults are a fast-growing body of believers. In many churches this group constitutes as much as 30 percent of the congregation. How are we addressing their needs? How involved are we with them? For a number of years my husband was the elder in charge of singles at the church we attended. It was such a fast-growing group that we had to meet off the main church campus in a rented building. Many of those singles never went to the main service across the street. Many singles stay to themselves because they don't feel comfortable in churches that consist mainly of families. How can we get singles involved in the church? How can we integrate them into the congregation and give them space to grow spiritually?

A national survey asked evangelicals to list in order the top ten subjects they want addressed from the pulpit. They listed the Book of Revelation, prophecy in the Bible, prayer, Bible character studies, Christian home, Christian child rearing, Proverbs, Bible walk-through, family worship, and the Book of Psalms. When the leaders in those same churches were asked what they thought their congregations would like to have taught, they listed this order: Genesis, Exodus, Leviticus, Numbers, Deuteronomy, Joshua, Judges, Ruth, 1 Samuel, and 2 Samuel.[8] What's so interesting about these lists is that the leaders did not mention even one of the preferred topics. These disparities tend to make us wonder if we have ever taken time to know those in our care—whether in the congregation, or Sunday school classes, or parachurch settings. Or do we follow a preconceived agenda?

When asked about family worship, 56 percent of the people surveyed said they felt inadequate in initiating good family worship. And yet church leaders felt that wasn't a concern; they listed it last. Again, are we ministering with the right target in focus? How can we get to know our people better so we can find out what they really need for spiritual growth?

Of significance is the fact that a growing number of women are enrolled in seminaries all across the United States. "Twenty years ago, there were almost no women in seminary. Now women make up 30 percent of students in the almost three-hundred-member Association of Theological Schools. At prestigious Yale Divinity School, nearly half the students are women, while at Harvard Divinity School women make up 60 percent."[9] Enrollment of women in conservative seminaries has also increased significantly in the last two decades. This suggests that womean are intensely interested in spiritual issues and in training for ministry.

Patricia Aburdene and John Naisbitt point out numerous changes among women today. Surveys show that thousands of Catholic and Protestant women worship in all-female groups. These authors have located more than 150 of these groups who are worshiping in private homes and on college campuses. Collectively this network calls itself "Women-Church." Three thousand women attended an international conference in Cincinnati in 1987, with the goal of reinterpreting the language, symbols, and texts of Christianity to serve women's spirituality. They also found that many non-Orthodox Jewish women are embracing the traditional Orthodox *mikva* (ritual bath) as a "spiritual and women's rights" ritual. The Episcopal Church has elected its first female bishop.[10]

Have we missed opportunities to minister to the women in our churches, so that they feel unfulfilled within the body of Christ? How can we become sensitive to the issues at hand, while staying true to the Scriptures, before women in our evangelical churches are drawn away into doubting the goodness of God?

Chapter Three

What Has Happened to the Traditional Family?

*U*nfortunately Christian women are getting more input from the world than they are from churches. Where are they learning about themselves, their relationships, and their cultures? According to George Barna, the strongest "schoolteacher" today is mass media. From television you would probably conclude that most people aren't married anymore, and their children are suffering no ill effects from the breakup of their families. Soap operas suggest that if you're not having an affair with someone else's mate, you must be the only one who is not, and you ought to be ashamed of such prudishness. If television pictures the traditional family at all, it is usually in an unfavorable or embarrassing light.

Many media psychologists and talk-show hosts, on both radio and television, give the impression that most families are dysfunctional and that happiness comes from taking care of oneself "at all costs."[1] Media personnel apparently feel that portraying strong families is neither news nor entertaining. So ironically, the exceptions—dysfunctional families, extramarital affairs, weak fathers—look like the norm. This imagery carries over into our churches, and we think all women are unhappy with where God has placed them and are looking for something "better." Unfortunately some of our leaders have bought into this mind-set. Once we start looking negatively at something, other things are colored with the same brush—everything becomes negative. But are we as unhappy as our society is saying we are? It's almost like going back to the days of Betty

Friedan, founder of NOW (National Organization of Women), when she claimed that American housewives were terribly dissatisfied but didn't know it.

However, most Americans believe that the health of our families is vitally important. Regardless of their particular inclinations or beliefs, the vast majority of Americans care about the family.[2]

Yet ample evidence shows that families are in transition. The coming decade promises to bring even more sweeping changes in the way we think about the family. Those transitions will, of course, have a substantial impact on the future of our nation, the strength of our religious institutions, and our fulfillment as individuals. Are we as church leaders being prepared for such a task? Are we willing to investigate other approaches to reaching people for Christ?

I attended a national leadership conference in which there were many pastors and leaders of church and parachurch ministries across the country. The topic of discussion was, "Can church congregations be shared between church and parachurch ministries, or are pastors too possessive of the people in their churches, claiming that they are 'their flocks'?" Are not believers God's people who can be used in many different areas of service, both in church and outside the church? Are we tapping into these great resources? For example, are we engaging our retired men and women into service where they can use their spiritual gifts? Many retirees have ample time on their hands; yet churches often fail to use them to the best of their potential. How can we better tap into these tremendous resources?

An area of concern in our churches is how to define "family." Generally speaking, the "traditional family" refers to people who are related to each other by marriage, birth, or adoption. This includes married couples without children and married couples with adopted or natural children. The "extended family" includes grandparents, aunts, uncles, nephews, and cousins.

THE NOUVEAU FAMILY

A significant shift has occurred in people's thinking over the last twenty years. Most Americans feel that describing family simply in terms of married people, their children, and perhaps their close relatives, is too restrictive and old-fashioned. In fact two-thirds of all adults describe their families in ways that can be called to some degree "nouveau"[3] or alternative. Also nearly half of all adults have some notion of family that draws on both traditional and noveau ideas. In other words adults whose definition of family can be called traditional have also embraced some alternative descriptions of family.

The nouveau family can be defined as "two or more people who care about each other."[4] The individuals need not be related by marriage or other legal bonds, nor even be living together. Because the definition includes no requirements or assumptions of permanence, the boundaries of "family" are fluid. For some this means marriage and possibly children; for others it means any relationship in which people care about or intimately relate to each other. In the minds of many Americans the essence of "family" is a shared experience or emotion. Many lawsuits are being filed over this very issue. The stakes are high for many groups, and it's no longer a simple issue.

People's views of family are closely related to their circumstances and their cultural upbringing. For instance, adults who have never been married are unlikely to describe a family as consisting of married adults, regardless of whether children are present in the home. "Baby busters" (people born between 1965 and 1983), who have been exposed to alternative families more than any prior generation, are more likely than older Americans to express nontraditional ideas in describing their families.[5] Today's young people, like the generations that went before them, clearly reflect the environmental conditioning of their time. When people have never been associated with a traditional family structure, they begin to base their definition of "family" on their own experiences.

Recently I was talking with a young woman who was assisting me in a store. She seemed so sad, so I asked her if something was wrong. She said, "Yes, I recently lost one of my closest family members, and I'm having a difficult time getting over my loss." I sympathetically responded by sharing comforting words from Scripture. Then I asked her whom she had lost—expecting to hear "mother," "father," "sister," or "brother." Instead she replied, "Oh, my dear cat died. She was a real member of my family."

I have heard others describe their families as "all the people whom I really care about, and who really care about me." Another said, "My family is actually my circle of close friends, the people who know me and accept me and look out for me."

Of married people surveyed by George Barna, 69 percent held to a nouveau view. Of single women 67 percent held to such a view; of divorced couples 67 percent held this view; and of widowed women 64 percent held this concept.[6]

How will this nouveau view of family impact the way we minister? On the surface we might think this is a harmless debate, but the rising acceptance of this view of the family has some important—and frightening—implications for our society.

This view suggests that family is not a permanent relationship. At any time, as soon as one of the people involved in the "family" feels that he or she is not adequately being cared for or feels drawn to other individuals, the definition of that person's family instantly changes.

The nouveau definition dilutes the distinctive character of the family. Ultimately, any person or group of people may be referred to as family. Family becomes synonymous with friendship. Street gangs become a family. A softball team that plays together after work may be a family. Even people who may never have met each other but who possess an intense, common desire to protect whales, for example, are referred to as a family. With this open view, "family" will cease to have a fixed meaning.

The inevitable result of the nouveau definition of family is the disintegration of trust in the permanence and reliability of love. In fact love is made to mean whatever the individuals involved say it is. For instance in the nouveau family a unit composed of a married adult and a lover (of the same or opposite gender) qualifies as a family. So each individual may have a variety of sexual relationships, all of which supposedly qualify as "family" relationships. The logical progression of this philosophy would be to remove the barriers to aberrant lifestyles, such as polygamy, bisexual relations, and group sex.

The nouveau perspective undermines many of the legal protections now given the traditional family. If our laws are revised to extend rights to nouveau families, the effects will be far-reaching. Those who are pushing alternative family agendas will gain greater access to government services, increased legal rights, and wider influence in the media and schools.[7] More than this, if homosexuals can change the laws defining family, then they may seek to undermine the scriptural mandates against adultery and homosexuality as well.

COMBATING TRENDS

How can our churches combat these trends attacking the traditional view of the family? Lasting, stable families are possible only if society is willing to restrict its definition of family in order to combat threats to its existence.[8] Despite the willingness of government statisticians and social scientists to accept nouveau definitions of the family, we must keep in mind that they are merely responding to the ways in which people think and behave. As long as the American people tolerate the equal status of alternative family arrangements, they can expect only increasing confusion and discord in their personal relationships. When the definition of family becomes so broad that it includes everything, it generally ceases to have significance. When it is clearly and narrowly defined, the family retains its strength and influence. But we are living in an age when people say truth is relative, and we are often afraid of imposing our views (even when based on the Word of God) on others. In the 1970s I began to see Christian young people take the view, "I personally wouldn't agree to this or that, but whatever you want to do is up to you." We have entered an age of tolerance.

For America to embrace the more conservative or biblical view of family will take strong compelling leadership at multiple levels: national, state, community, and family. Unfortunately this does not seem to be a trend in our churches today. And our courts may uphold nouveau family arrangements more and more. We are likely to witness a decade in which millions of Americans suffer the consequences of family relationships where "freedom outweighs responsibility, self-centered need overpowers mutual trust, and the reigning cultural values replace traditional, Bible-based perspectives."[9]

Christians are in for a battle to define the family in a manner com-

23

mensurate with Scripture. We must hold to the standards set forth in God's Word as the basis for family policies, systems, and teaching. From a biblical perspective the casual way in which many Americans regard their families is harmful. Christian leaders must believe these issues are important and worth fighting for. We also need to examine our own lives to see if we are conforming in any way to nouveau-family concepts. If we are tolerating situations that clearly contradict God's Word, we must turn from those circumstances and recommit ourselves to families that are grounded in biblically based principles.

Just because many of our church members don't fit within the traditional view anymore, we are not free to cast that ideal aside. Many Americans feel that if the traditional family unit falls, the nation will do likewise. "The American family has always stood as a central foundation in our nation's development. On the basis of the love, trust and stability provided by the traditional family, America has been able to move forward while nations lacking such a bedrock of stability and continuity have struggled to keep pace."[10]

Many women in this generation and beyond will not marry. Since most Americans now accept and even condone premarital sex between consenting adults, the option of having a child without being married, and the legality of cohabitation, much of the pressure for women to get married at a young age no longer exists.

How will we as Christian leaders minister effectively to this new generation? How will we model biblical standards before women today? Statistics show that those who view religion as important in their lives are more likely to be satisfied in marriage than those who give lesser value to religion. If we are married, are our marriages modeling Christ's relationship with His church, as Ephesians 5:22–23 instructs?

Marriage works because God created it to enable men and women to relate to each other in the most intimate and enduring ways. When marriage does not work, it is not because the institution is flawed, but because the people involved have flaws. We must be well versed in the passages of Scripture that address marriage, and we must be able to present them in a positive manner to those women under our leadership. And we should be equally prepared to encourage singleness if a woman feels gifted by God to be single.

Ministering to divorced people is becoming a much greater task for Christian leaders. America now has the highest divorce rate of any nation in the world. For Americans, the allure of divorce is that it appears to offer the simplest solution to what typically amounts to a complex web of problems. But it often shatters spouses emotionally and financially. In fact the consequences can be more devastating than the troubled marriage. Many divorced people say that fellow believers were quick to judge and slow to support them during the course of their marital problems. One woman said:

> What hurt me, though, and it hurt deeply, was how quickly the people who I thought were my friends felt they had to distance themselves from me once we announced that we were getting divorced. What turned me off was that there was such a pompous, holier-than-thou attitude about my suffering. I turned to the church, and my friends in it, for support—not asking them to condone the separation, but to at least help me through the toughest time of my life. What I got was a lot of mini-sermons about the sanctity of marriage and the sin of divorce. Do they really think I was unaware of that? Were they just trying to score points with God as His defenders? Anyway, their rejection of me has led me to leave active church life. I love God and know He loves me, in spite of the divorce. I'm just ashamed that the church couldn't reflect His love in the same way.[11]

We Christian leaders must know what we believe God's Word teaches on divorce—but we must also know how to reach out to hurting people who need the love of God expressed through His people. But for the grace of God, we might be in the same situation. How can we help these hurting people find forgiveness and a place to feel safe in the body of Christ? A divorced Christian has not lost his or her salvation, and yet we often treat divorced people as if they are unbelievers.

We will be ministering to women in various walks of life, in various times of change, loss, trouble, and growth. Women in our churches need to feel a part of that ministry. We need to encourage them to grow spiritually. We need to walk with them in their pain and to comfort them.[12]

Part Two

The Bible and
Women's Ministries

Chapter Four

The Consequences of the Fall
on Men and Women

When God created Eve, she shared a life of total union with Adam—spiritually, physically, emotionally, socially, and psychologically—with complete honesty and without shame. But now pain, disharmony, and distance characterize marital relationships. Genesis 3 records how such a drastic change came about, how sin entered the human race.

Was Eve more responsible than Adam for the Fall? How did the Fall affect Eve and all women after her? What consequences came to Adam and Eve's relationship because of the Fall? Are women to be dominated by men? Answers to these questions are crucial to understanding what the Bible says about women. The passages that tell of Satan's temptation of Eve give us timeless principles that affect both men and women today. As we become aware of Satan's schemes, as revealed in the Book of Genesis, we can avoid his taking advantage of us (2 Cor. 2:11).

Four principles involved in Satan's temptation of Eve may be noted.

First, Satan's temptation came in disguise (Gen. 3:1).[1] Eve did not know the serpent was Satan, but we know from the New Testament that he is "that ancient serpent called the devil or Satan" (Rev. 12:9). Satan deceived Eve by "cunning" (2 Cor. 11:3). In fact, the serpent was "more crafty than any of the wild animals" (Gen. 3:1) God had made. The word *crafty* means "skillful in underhand or evil schemes; cunning; deceitful; sly."[2] The devil seeks to "outwit us" by "his schemes" (2 Cor. 2:11).

Second, in Satan's temptation of Eve he questioned God's word.[3] The serpent said to Eve, "Did God really say, 'You must not eat from any tree in the garden'?" She responded, "We may eat fruit from the trees in the garden, but God did say, 'You must not eat fruit from the tree that is in the middle of the garden, and you must not touch it, or you will die'" (Gen. 3:1–3). The tempter took a clear-cut commandment from God and turned it into a debate. By asking Eve, "Did God really say . . . ?" he questioned God's word, though he didn't actually deny it—at least not yet.

The serpent's questioning led her to respond in two ways. (1) She minimized the Lord's provision.[4] Though the Lord had said they could eat of any tree except one, she highlighted the one exception, thereby overlooking God's provision of all the other trees. (2) Then she added to the prohibition.[5] The Lord had said nothing about not touching the tree of the knowledge of good and evil (2:16–17), but Eve said that He commanded them not to touch it (3:3). People still expand on God's prohibitions, viewing them as if He's holding back something wonderful.

It is not clear what led Eve to minimize the Lord's provision and add to His prohibition. Perhaps her concentrating on such a forbidden object easily led her to make these modifications. Where was Adam when this was happening? Presumably he was nearby because immediately after the words, "she took some and ate it," we read, "She also gave some to her husband, *who was with her*, and he ate it" (3:6, italics added).

Third, in tempting Eve the devil doubted God's integrity (3:4–5).[6] When the serpent saw that the woman did not have an exact knowledge of God's words, he flatly denied what God had said. The Lord said that if they ate of that one tree, they would surely die (2:17). But Satan said, "You will *not* surely die" (3:4). What was at first a question about the prohibition ("Did God really say . . . ?") now became a denial of the consequences of disobedience. The lie that there is no punishment for sin has deceived the human race from the beginning. As Jesus said, the devil "is a liar, and the father of lies" (John 8:44).

Satan explained that God gave the prohibition about the tree because He was jealous and was holding them back from their destiny. The serpent said God knew that they would become like Him, knowing good and evil. Satan was holding out to them the prospect of their becoming divine. But we never become like God by disobeying His commands!

Fourth, Satan's temptation of Eve appealed to her senses.[7] "When the woman saw that the fruit of the tree was good for food and pleasing to the eye, and also desirable for gaining wisdom, she took some and ate it" (Gen. 3:6). These compare with the three sinful attractions the apostle John wrote about in 1 John 2:16: "the cravings of sinful man, the lust of his eyes and the boasting of what he has and does." The tempter had now removed the barrier to Eve and Adam's eating—Eve was no longer convinced that God would punish them for it. Now the appeal of the forbidden fruit itself was sufficient to draw her into sin.

Even though the woman was deceived, the Scriptures do not place the blame for the Fall on her. The comment that the man "ate it" (Gen. 3:6) is significant. Allen Ross notes that Adam apparently needed no clever words of temptation—he simply went along with the disobedience, being led by Eve to eat. His response was a willful conformity.[8] While the New Testament says that Eve was beguiled and sinned ("the woman . . . was deceived and became a sinner," 1 Tim. 2:14), it also affirms that man sinned willfully (Rom. 5:12).

Some theologians have asserted from Genesis 3 that women are more easily deceived than men. Martin Luther, for example, said, "The subtlety of Satan showed itself also when he attacked human nature where it was weakest, namely, in Eve, and not in Adam. I believe that had Satan first tempted the man, Adam would have gained the victory."[9] Thomas Schreiner says that women "are more prone to introduce deception into the church since they are more nurturing and relational than men. It is not that they do not have the capacity to teach doctrine or the ability to understand it. Women are less likely to perceive the need to take a stand on doctrinal non-negotiables since they prize harmonious relationships more than men do."[10] However, Romans 5:12 states that "sin entered the world through one *man*" (italics added).

Satan's temptations to both men and women often follow the same four steps he used with Eve: He brings temptation in disguise, he questions God's Word, he gets us to doubt God's integrity, and he appeals to our senses.

Many women today have been led to doubt God's goodness. They feel God is holding out on them. Christian women must remember that spiritual, physical, and mental fulfillment do not come by disobeying God. Godlikeness in character and ability does not come by opposing God; it comes by knowing and obeying His Word.

CONSEQUENCES OF SIN

"Then the man and his wife heard the sound of the LORD God as he was walking in the garden in the cool of the day, and they hid from the LORD God among the trees of the garden" (Gen. 3:8). One effect of sin is that fear replaces close fellowship. Just as Adam and Eve hid from God, so people today hide from each other emotionally, fearing the deep intimacy God intended.

Another effect of sin is shame, "a painful emotion caused by a strong sense of guilt, embarrassment, unworthiness, or disgrace."[11] Adam and Eve covered themselves because they were no longer at ease with each other. Shame reveals itself today in many marriages. Husbands and wives lack trust in each other, and so they miss out on the blessings God intended for them.

When God asked Adam, "Have you eaten from the tree that I commanded you not to eat from?" (3:11), He of course knew what Adam had done. But His question was designed to encourage him to confess his sin. Adam and Eve did confess their sin, but not before blaming each other first. Adam responded, "The woman you put here with me—she gave me some fruit from the tree, and I ate it" (3:12). Besides blaming Eve, he also blamed God for giving her to him. In essence he said, "God, if you hadn't created Eve, then I wouldn't have disobeyed your command." Finally, he did confess ("and I ate it," 3:12). When God confronted Eve, again seeking confession, she, too, rationalized her actions by blaming the serpent before she admitted her sin ("and I ate," 3:13).

We too may admit to God that we have sinned, but we often want to inform Him of the circumstances surrounding our sin in order to soften the load of our responsibility and guilt. Passing responsibility on to others, we believe our lives result from what others have done to us directly through their actions or indirectly through genetics.

Besides the first man and woman seeking to place blame elsewhere for their wrongdoings, God announced several other consequences (3:14–20). He declared what life would now be like, since sin entered the world and contaminated it. There are always consequences of disobedience.

One consequence of the Fall is a perpetual struggle between good and evil. God told the serpent that He would "put enmity between you and the woman, and between your offspring and hers; he will crush your head, and you will strike his heel" (3:15). Continuous conflict would occur between the serpent and Eve, and between the serpent's "offspring" (demons and all who follow Satan and oppose the Lord) and her offspring (humanity at large and ultimately Christ). One day Christ would deliver the crushing blow to Satan's head, after receiving the strike on His heel at the cross.

Another result of our first parents' sin is that women's pain in childbirth would be increased (3:16). Still another consequence pertains to husband-wife relations. God said, "Your desire will be for your husband, and he will rule over you" (3:16). The first clause "Your desire will be for your husband" has often been misunderstood as meaning that wives will desire to be with their husbands. However, the word "desire" has an entirely different sense, as seen in Genesis 4:7 in relation to Cain: "sin is crouching at your door; it desires to have you." Therefore, as Ross suggests, 3:16 should be rendered, "Your desire was to your husband, but he shall have the mastery over you."[12]

Because Eve desired to get her husband to sin by eating forbidden fruit, he would rule over her (not her over him). So as a result of the Fall, man would rule over the woman. The Hebrew word for rule *(māšal)* describes dominion, mastery, and lordship, and sometimes has a harsh application.[13] Jewish scholar Umberto Cassuto explains it this way: "Measure for measure: you influenced your husband and caused him to do what you wished; henceforth, you and your female descendants will be subservient to your husbands."[14] In other words, as a result of the Fall, man at his worst, in his fallen state, is a domineering tyrant. And as a result of the Fall, woman at her worst, in her fallen state, constantly wants to take away that control. And so we have fallen humanity with gender battles fighting for control. Evil will always surface in the battle over who is to be in control. Of course, God's design for husbands is that they provide loving leadership, as spelled out elsewhere in Scriptures, but that is not the meaning in 3:16.

God cursed the ground because of Adam's sin, and so another effect of their sin is that by painful toil people would have to scratch out an existence from the ground (3:17–19), but not in the lush garden as God intended. Also death would reign over the entire race (Rom. 5:12). God said that because we are dust (not divine, as Satan had promised), we will return to dust (Gen. 3:19).[15] As Ross commented, "So much for ambitions for divinity! Man may attempt to be like God, but he is dust from the ground."[16]

For believers in Christ, life in the Spirit removes the sting of the curse so that a more harmonious and loving husband-wife relationship is envisioned than what is declared to be a result of evil in the human race. Regeneration does not yet remove the curse—there is still death, pain, and conflict; but new life in Christ changes how people live in a fallen world. So the lesson from Genesis 3 is clear: Sin brings pain, disharmony, and separation. The way to correct these problems in life is not by disobeying God. That is how they got here in the first place!

Once sin entered the world, there was great need for headship, so that life could run smoothly. God's order includes the headship of God the Father over God the Son; the headship of Christ over the man, and the headship of the husband over the wife (1 Cor. 11:3). The husband's headship is to be one of loving leadership, guided by the indwelling power of the Holy Spirit. It is totally opposite the domination that characterizes fallen humanity.

Unfortunately many Christians fail to make the distinction between domination and loving leadership. Women have been controlled and dominated under the pretense that this domination is a God-given capacity for men. Women have fought against this domination, wanting to be the ones in control. No wonder women have cried out against many of these painful conditions.

The world looks at any type of hierarchy as a sign of inferiority. But submission to leadership is not a sign of inferiority; it is a recognition that God is ultimately in control and that He has a purpose for the order He has established. The husband's leadership described in the New Testament is not one that can demand submission, because a woman controlled by the Holy Spirit is to submit willingly to the loving leadership of her husband. Christ is our example of willing submission, for He submitted to the Father in all things, and He is not inferior to the Father, for they are one. The sacrificial love of Christ models our submission to Him, and the sacrificial love of a husband for his wife opens the door for her willing submission to him.

The New Testament shows how this hierarchical arrangement fits within God's design for fulfilling His will on the earth. God through His Holy Spirit has gifted men and women to be His representatives to a lost and dying world. But that giftedness is certainly not displayed by disobeying God's Word. God is not trying to hold us back; instead He is seeking to conform us to the image of His Son, Jesus Christ, as coheirs with Him.

Chapter Five

What Is the Role of Women according to the New Testament?

We saw in Genesis 3 what life is like because of the Fall. The picture is rather bleak—fear, guilt, shame, isolation, domination, pain, toil, death. In addition the Fall led to the need for hierarchy—an order for living life for God's glory. Just as there is a hierarchy within the Godhead, so God introduced a hierarchy on the earth. Hierarchy does not imply inferiority, for women are not inferior to men any more than God the Son is inferior to God the Father.

Several New Testament passages address the role of women: 1 Corinthians 11:3, 8–9, 11; 14:34; 1 Timothy 2:9–15; Ephesians 5:21–33; Colossians 3:18–19; and 1 Peter 3:1–7.

1 CORINTHIANS 11:3, 8–9, 11–12

Verse 3

"Now I want you to realize that the head of every man is Christ, and the head of the woman is man, and the head of Christ is God." In this verse and in Ephesians 5:23 ("the husband is the head of the wife as Christ is the head of the church"), Christians have usually understood the word *head* (Greek, *kephalē*) to mean "authority over." Christ is the authority over the church, and a husband is the authority over his wife. However, this interpretation has been challenged in recent years by those who claim that, at least in some passages, the word *head* means "source" or "origin" rather than "authority over." They say Christ is the *source* of every man, Christ is the *source* of the church, and—referring to Adam and Eve—the man is the *source* of the woman.[1] Berkeley and Alvera Mickelsen, for example, argue that *kephalē* "does not mean 'boss' or 'final authority,'" but "source, or origin, as we use it in the 'head of the Mississippi River.'"[2] And Margaret Howe wrote, "The word *head* here must be understood not as 'ruler' but as 'source.' Christ came from God; he is 'the only Son from the Father' (John 1:14). As the agent of creation (John 1:3), Christ brought the man into being . . . and from the male of the species, the female came into being (Gen. 2:21–22)."[3]

Similarly, Letha Scanzoni and Nancy Hardesty suggest that "*kephalē* is used almost synonymously with *archē*, 'beginning,' somewhat similar to our use of 'the headwaters of a river' or 'fountain head.'"[4] So, when Ephesians 5:23 says, "Christ is the head of the church, his body," they take it to mean that He is the church's "life-Giver." And when Colossians 2:10 calls Christ "the head over every power and authority," they say, "'Head' here obviously means 'source.'"[5] Similarly, "Christ's headship over the church refers to His being the source of its life."[6]

These writers represent what may be called a "Christian feminist" perspective. But others who do not generally endorse the Christian feminist position support this view of *kephalē*. F. F. Bruce writes, "There is probably the same kind of oscillation between the literal sense of 'head' and its secondary sense of 'origin'. . . in 1 Corinthians 11:3, as well as in Colossians 1:18 and 2:10."[7] James Hurley retains the meaning of "authority over" in 1 Corinthians 11:3, but he says *kephalē* in Colossians 2:19 and Ephesians 4:15 means "source." "In English we speak of the 'head' of a river to refer to its point of origin. This was a typical usage of 'head'. . . in classical Greek. In Paul's day, therefore, the Greek word *head* . . . could mean a physical head, a person with authority, or the source of something. Head . . . was used in first-century Greek as a synonym for the more common words for 'ruler'. . . and for 'source.'"[8]

Do Greek sources actually use *kephalē* in the sense of "source"? No. "Source" is not listed as a possible meaning for *kephalē* in Bauer, Arndt, and Gingrich's standard New Testament Greek lexicon or in the older Greek lexicons by Thayer or Cremer. Nor does Moulton and Milligan's lexicon to the Greek papyri give that meaning.[9] Of course, that doesn't mean that the meaning of "source" is impossible, but it does mean that we are right in demanding some convincing citations from ancient Greek literature before "source" rather than "authority over" can be accepted as the meaning of *kephalē*.

None of the Christian feminists mentioned cite any evidence from ancient literature or from other scholars. F. F. Bruce and James Hurley[10] cite no evidence from ancient literature. Both authors refer to an article by Stephen Bedale.[11] Wayne Grudem makes these insightful comments about Bedale's article: "Upon reading the frequently cited article by Bedale, we are surprised to find that he does not cite even one text from ancient Greek literature outside the Bible. Thus the widely accepted argument for a 'common' use of κεφαλή to mean 'source' in extra-Biblical Greek literature has rested on only two occurrences of the word. Bedale cites no evidence—no results of word studies, no lexical authorities—to demonstrate his point; he simply assumes it to be true for the rest of the article."[12]

Bauer, Arndt, and Gingrich give this definition of *kephalē*, "in the case of living beings, to denote superior rank"[13] (not superior in essence), and they list nine examples of this meaning in Paul's epistles.

Using the computerized database system of the Thesaurus Linguae Graecae (TLG) project at the University of California at Irvine, Grudem surveyed the word *kephalē*. This resource has more than twenty million words from ancient Greek texts, with 2,336 instances of the word *kephalē* dating from the eighth century B.C. (Homer) onward, as used by thirty-six authors in all sorts of literature, including history, philosophy, drama, poetry, rhetoric, geography, and romantic writings. Grudem discovered that in *no* instance does *kephalē* have the meaning of source or origin.[14] He concluded that the use of *kephalē* in Greek literature to mean "of superior rank" at the time of the New Testament "was well-established and recognized, and it is the meaning that best suits the New Testament texts that speak of the relationship between men and women by saying that the man is the 'head' of a woman and the husband is the 'head' of the wife."[15]

Ephesians 1:22–23 gives support to the meaning of *kephalē* as headship: "And God placed all things under his feet and appointed him to be head over everything for the church, which is his body." The word "over" clearly suggests the idea of authority. As head of the church, Christ has authority over it.

Verses 8–9

"For man did not come from woman, but woman from man; neither was man created for woman, but woman for man." Paul was not saying here that the woman was created for the man to do with as he chooses, but that God created the woman because it was not good for man to be alone (see Gen. 2:18). The "helper" concept is in focus here. Lowery states it well: "Man . . . was God's authoritative representative who found in woman a divinely made ally in fulfilling this role (Gen. 2:18–24)."[16]

Verse 11

"In the Lord, however, woman is not independent of man, nor is man independent of woman." This verse reminds us of Galatians 3:28, "There is neither Jew nor Greek, slave nor free, male nor female, for you are all one in Christ Jesus," and Ephesians 5:21, "Submit to one another out of reverence for Christ." In 1 Corinthians 11:11 Paul was stating that in Christ men and women are subject to one another. Men and women are counterparts of each other, molded by God to fulfill the word of the ministry. Although there are role distinctions, there is no inequality. John MacArthur's statement is succinct: "Men and women serve each other, and they serve with each other. Although there is a difference in roles, there is an equality in nature, personhood, work, and spirit."[17]

Verse 12

In this verse Paul spoke of man and woman's mutuality of origin: "For as woman came from man, so also man is born of woman." Just as woman came from man in the creation, so man comes from woman by birth. They are "mutually dependent."[18] When Paul addressed one's position in Christ, he stressed mutuality. But when Paul addressed role distinctions, he pointed to headship—God's headship over Christ, Christ's headship over man, man's headship over the woman in the church and home. Within the body of Christ this hierarchy is necessary if we are to fulfill God's plan for us on earth. We must remember that Christ's headship is our example, and it is always one of loving leadership. It builds up, encourages, and edifies.

1 CORINTHIANS 14:34

This verse—"Women should remain silent in the churches. They are not allowed to speak, but must be in submission, as the Law says"—has been interpreted in various ways. One view is that Paul was forbidding women to ask questions in church meetings, and that as explained in verse 35, they should ask their husbands at home. A second view is that Paul was prohibiting women from speaking in "tongues." A third idea is that the ban is on the "discerning" of prophecies mentioned in verse 29. It is assumed in this option that women did prophesy, but they were now being excluded from the weighing of prophecies because that could possibly mean they would be exercising authority over their own husbands.

A fourth view is that Paul prohibited women from talking because they were acting in an unruly manner in church assemblies. Again verse 35 is seen as supporting this view. Perhaps, as in Jewish synagogues, women were seated on one side of the room and men on the other. The women could have been shouting out disruptive questions about what was being said, or possibly they were asking questions of men other than their own husbands. Or they were simply "chattering" so loudly that it had a disruptive effect. Their silence, on the other hand, would show their submissive relationship to their husbands.[19]

A fifth view is that Paul was advocating quietness (that is, not being unruly), rather than complete silence. This interpretation is suggested because being absolutely silent would seem to contradict the statements in 1 Corinthians 11:5 about women praying and prophesying. However, the Greek word Paul used in 14:34 (*sigaō*) does mean "to be silent." A different word (*hēsychia*) used in 1 Timothy 2:11–12 means "orderliness" or "absence of disorder." Some writers explain the alleged contradiction by suggesting that women could exercise their spiritual gift of prophesying in the local assembly, but if there was any question about how their prophecy was being evaluated, they were not to enter into this discussion. They could give the prophecy but not enter into the evaluation of that process.

1 TIMOTHY 2:9–15

Verses 9–10

"I also want women to dress modestly, with decency and propriety [or, 'discretion'], not with braided hair or gold or pearls or expensive clothes, but with good deeds, appropriate for women who profess to worship God." These verses tell women how they are to present themselves within a congregation for worship. Paul was not telling them that they shouldn't braid their hair or wear jewelry or nice clothes, but that these things were not to be the focus of their attention. Many women in the Greco-Roman world would spend hours fixing their hair, by braiding pearls and jewels into it in elaborate designs. They dressed for show; they wanted to be noticed for their finery. Paul was attacking excess. He was addressing the issue of a woman's heart before God—her attitude of worship and her desire to serve God.

Verse 11

Some Bible teachers say verse 11, "A woman should learn in quietness and full submission," is a culturally related mandate based on the limited education of women in Paul's day, and so it is not applicable today. "Women were less likely to be literate than men, were trained in philosophy far less often than men, were trained in rhetoric almost never, and in Judaism were far less likely to be educated in the law. Given the bias against instructing women in the law, it is Paul's advocacy of their learning the law, not his recognition that they started as novices and so had to learn quietly, that was radical and countercultural."[20]

42

Verse 12

"I do not permit a woman to teach or to have authority over a man; she must be silent." The word "or" (Greek, *oude*) in this verse is significant because it raises the question, Was Paul separating two distinct prohibitions (teaching and having authority over a man), or was he joining them (as in "teaching in a domineering way")?

Although the clause contains elements that may be distinctly identified, it is possible that Paul intended us to view these two elements together as a single whole. Philip Payne made an extensive study of this conjunction and concluded that the two elements in this verse are so closely related that they may best be viewed as a single coherent whole, not as two independent elements.[21] For example, he cites Romans 3:10, "There is no one righteous, not even one." "Not even one" gives an emphatic clarification that Paul intended "no one" to be without exception.[22] Payne suggests this rendering of 1 Timothy 2:12: "But I do not allow a woman to teach a man in a domineering way."[23]

Similarly, the church father Chrysostom (around 347–407), claimed that Paul was not forbidding women to teach at all. He was only prohibiting the headship of women in the Christian community.[24] He said a Christian woman's role differs from that of a man's. For example, women were not to be church elders.[25] As Foh comments, the command in 1 Timothy 2:12 does not exclude women from private instruction of men (Acts 18:26), teaching other women (Titus 2:3–4), and teaching children (Prov. 1:8; 2 Tim. 1:5; 3:15).[26] Instead, the command applies, she says, to the duties of an elder, whose teaching and exercising authority are inseparable. She adds that this leaves open the option for women to serve as church librarians, treasurers, Sunday-school superintendents, church-paper editors, choir directors, committee chairpersons, and other positions. A woman's authority in these positions "is not in the same category as the authority over individuals' doctrine and life that the elder has."[27]

Verses 13–14

"For Adam was formed first, then Eve. And Adam was not the one deceived; it was the woman who was deceived and became a sinner." Here

Paul made the comparison between the order of creation and his teaching on women to show that his teachings are in line with the way God created humanity. He warned against violating this ruling by reminding his readers of the temptation and the Fall, arguing that the church should not relive that kind of disorder and confusion, but should follow the initial ideal of creation. The apostle was not saying that his prohibition against women involved in teaching is found explicitly in Genesis. He was making his point by analogy.[28] Some argue that by connecting the prohibition to creation, Paul was saying that women are not to teach men anything anywhere, or at least nothing biblical or spiritual. But Paul did not say that. He said, instead, that women are not to teach men in the church assembly, for that would be exercising authority over them. Then he reasoned that this instruction is in harmony with the order of creation. If we accept a sweeping prohibition, how can we reconcile God's use of women down through the centuries to share His Word, to edify, exhort, instruct, and comfort, whether by instruction, song, celebration, or discipleship? Instead of dominating men in the church, "they are to receive instruction with an inner attitude of quietness and submission to the truth of God's Word (and His chosen teachers)."[29]

Verse 15

"But women will be saved through childbearing—if they continue in faith, love and holiness with propriety." The word "saved" does not carry the usual meaning of deliverance from sin, because then Paul would be saying that for a woman to be converted, she must bear children. However, as Douglas Moo claims, if women maintain their proper roles, "exemplified in motherhood, they will also insure participation in the eschatological salvation."[30] The apostle might be saying—especially in the first century when bearing and rearing children was the primary and constant activity of young women—that even though he had placed a prohibition on women, they should not think they will lack reward for faith in Christ. They, like Eve, can see God's provision of children as one important token of blessing, as well as one of the avenues of service that will be rewarding.[31]

44

EPHESIANS 5:21–33

In this passage Paul wrote: "Submit to one another out of reverence for Christ" (5:21). This command is actually a present participle, which means its action depends on the command "be filled with the Spirit" (5:18). Mutual submission to each other sets the stage for the following verses, because if husbands and wives desire to serve one another out of reverence for Christ, the role distinctions that follow will be in order.

Verse 22

Many people today abhor the command in this verse: "Wives, submit to your husbands as to the Lord." The notion of submission to authority is out of fashion and totally at variance with contemporary attitudes of permissiveness and freedom. And it's no wonder, because synonyms for the word "submission" include servility, prostration, abasement, bowing, scraping, cowering, cringing, crawling, toadying.[32] Ours is an age of liberation (for women, children, and workers), and anything hinting at oppression is deeply resented and strongly resisted. How are Christians to react to this modern mood?

We must agree that women in many cultures have been exploited, being treated like servants in their own homes. I was once asked to give mediation advice to a church elder and his wife. Claiming Genesis 3:16, the man would lay his wife over his lap and spank her in front of their children whenever he felt that she was not being obedient to him. If that didn't get the results he wanted, he would take her makeup away for a period of time. History bears out the fact that women (and children) have often been suppressed and mistreated. John Stott is correct when he says, "We who name Christ's name need to acknowledge with shame that we ourselves have often acquiesced in the status quo and so helped to perpetuate some forms of human oppression, instead of being in the vanguard of those seeking social change."[33]

Stott names three relevant truths that form an important preface to Paul's words in Ephesians 5. "(1) the dignity of womanhood, childhood and servanthood; (2) the equality before God of all human beings, irrespective of their race, rank, class, culture, gender or age, because all are made in His image; and (3) the unity of all Christian believers, as fellow members of God's family and of Christ's body."[34] Only when we keep these truths in the forefront of our minds can we begin to understand Ephesians 5:22–24 properly. The biblical concept of authority means responsibility, not tyranny. Wives are to submit and husbands are to love.

Several years ago I spoke in the Ukraine to a large group of pastors from all over that area. The topic of my first message was "Christ's relationship with His church," based on Ephesians 5. When I finished speaking, a pastor raised his hand and asked, "Why haven't you mentioned submission?" I replied, "I don't see in this audience any women so I chose to address a husband's responsibility through the picture of Christ." He asked another question, "But what should a man do if he has a rotten wife?" Quickly another pastor replied, "You beat her with a stick, of course!" After the laughter died down, I began, "Now help me to see this correctly. If a woman has a rotten husband, should she be submissive to him?" Lots of affirmation came from the faces before me. "Well, then, I would like for everyone here to tell me how a husband should respond to a rotten wife?" Total silence first filled the room, and then quiet murmuring began to invade the silence. My interpreter began to laugh. She said that the men knew what I wanted them to answer, but that they didn't want to do so. Finally, an elderly gentleman on the front row quietly rose to his feet and spoke in a hushed voice, "You are to love her as Christ loved the church."

Verse 23

"For the husband is the head of the wife as Christ is the head of the church, his body, of which he is the Savior." In Christ's headship over the church He expresses care rather than control, responsibility rather than rule. This truth is endorsed by the addition of the words concerning Christ's relationship to the church, "of which he is the Savior." The Head of the church is the Savior of the church; the characteristic of His headship is not so much lordship as saviorhood.[35]

Verse 24

"Now as the church submits to Christ, so also wives should submit to their husbands in everything." If the husband's headship of the wife resembles Christ's headship of His church, then the wife's submission to her husband will resemble the church's submission to Christ. There is nothing degrading about this, for *the wife's submission is not to be an unthinking obedience to her husband's harsh rule but rather a grateful acceptance of his care.* The husband-wife relationship is a voluntary, free, joyful, and thankful partnership, pictured by the relationship of the church to Christ. Whenever the husband's headship mirrors the headship of Christ, then the wife's submission to the protection and provision of his love, far from taking away from her womanhood, will positively enrich it.[36]

Verses 25–27

"Husbands, love your wives, just as Christ loved the church and gave himself up for her to make her holy, cleansing her by the washing with water through the word, and to present her to himself as a radiant church, without stain or wrinkle or any other blemish, but holy and blameless." If the word that characterizes the wife's duty is "submit," the word characterizing the husband's duty is "love." This is a love that loves even when there is no response. It's the same word used in John 3:16. The husband loves, not thinking about what he can get but what he can give.[37] He loved the church and sacrificed Himself on her behalf. His leadership over the church is a loving, selfless leadership. So husbands should be giving loving, selfless leadership to their wives. Ross reminds us that "Christ took the blame for something He didn't do—most men don't want to take the blame for what they do."[38]

In 5:25–27 Paul used five verbs to indicate the nature of Christ's commitment to His bride, the church. He *"loved"* her, *"gave himself up"* for her, to *"sanctify"* her, having *"cleansed"* her, that He might *"present"* her to Himself. The bride (the church) does not make herself presentable; it is the bridegroom (Christ) who labors to beautify her in order to present her to Himself. His love and self-sacrifice for her, His cleansing and sanctifying of her, are all designed for her liberation and her perfection, when at last He will present her to Himself in her full glory.[39]

Christ does not abuse or otherwise mistreat the church. He sacrificed Himself to save her, so that she might become everything He longs for her to be. Similarly, a husband should never use his headship to mistreat or stifle his wife, or frustrate her from being herself. His love for her will mean he gives himself for her, so she can develop her full potential under God and become more completely herself.

Verses 28–33

"In this same way husbands ought to love their wives as their own bodies. He who loves his wife loves himself. After all, no one ever hated his own body, but he feeds and cares for it, just as Christ does the church—for we are members of his body. 'For this reason a man will leave his father and mother and be united to his wife, and the two will become one flesh.' This is a profound mystery—but I am talking about Christ and the church. However, each one of you also must love his wife as he loves himself, and the wife must respect her husband."

In verse 25 Paul compared a husband's love for his wife to Christ's selfless, caring love. Then in verses 28–30 he compared a husband's love for his wife to his love for himself. "As Christ loves the church, his body (of which all believers are members), so should husbands . . . love their wives as their own bodies."[40] Just as Christ has made us part of Himself in a profound, indissoluble union, so husbands should love their wives as themselves.

The apostle began in verse 22 with the combination of submission and love. Now he ends with another combination: love and respect. When a husband loves his wife and sacrifices for her with a view to enabling her to become what God intends her to be, then she willingly submits to him and respects him. Responding to his love, she desires that he, too, will become what God intends him to be as the leader of their home. A husband can't demand submission and respect—it is a free choice the wife makes.

Certainly headship implies a degree of leadership and initiative, as when Christ came to pursue and win His bride. But more specifically it implies sacrifice, self-giving for the sake of the beloved, as when Christ gave Himself for His bride. If headship means power in any sense, then it is power to care, not to crush; power to serve, not to dominate; power to facilitate self-fulfillment, not to frustrate or destroy it.[41]

The wife's submission is actually an aspect of love, the giving of self that is foundational to an enduring and growing marriage. And we must keep in mind the fact that the husband and wife are both commanded to "submit to one another out of reverence for Christ" (5:21). Christ's leadership of the church is demonstrated in His servanthood.

Of course, a wife's submission to her husband does *not* exclude their making decisions together. Nor does it mean that women are to be treated, as they are in some countries, as if they are inadequate, incapable, inferior. Nor does it mean wives cannot excel in many areas of expertise in and outside the home.

COLOSSIANS 3:18–19

"Wives, submit to your husbands, as is fitting in the Lord. Husbands, love your wives and do not be harsh with them." When Paul wrote these words to the Colossians, he was again presenting the concept of the husband's loving leadership and the wife's willing submission. He had just encouraged them to edify each other. "Let the word of Christ dwell in you richly as you teach and admonish one another with all wisdom, and as you sing psalms, hymns and spiritual songs with gratitude in your hearts to God" (3:16). R. Kent Hughes points out that this admonition is given to free, responsible people and can only be heeded voluntarily. None is called to follow it into sin or irrationality or harm of any kind.[42] Many have used the story of Sarah's submission to Abraham (Genesis 12 and 20) to say that Christian wives must be submissive to their husbands, even if it means compromising their walk with the Lord. But this is not so, because Acts 5:29 clearly states that God is to be obeyed rather than man if a human order conflicts with God's standards.

I PETER 3:1–7

Verses 1–6

Peter wrote that a Christian woman is to be submissive to her husband, even if he is an unbeliever, because he might possibly be won to the Lord

49

through her Spirit-filled life. Peter was also implying that a Christian wife should not be guilty of nagging, which might occur in her zeal to win her husband to the Lord. Peter then added that a woman's outward appearance should not be her primary concern (3:3–4). I have a dear friend who prayed for her unbelieving Jewish husband for over thirty years, as she silently modeled Christ before him. She stayed at home with him on Sundays (with some criticism from Christian friends) and prayed for opportunities to witness. He enjoyed reading the Old Testament to her each morning at breakfast; and one day, when he finished Malachi, he asked if she wanted him to continue—into Matthew, of course. She said yes, and years later she had the privilege of leading him to the Lord a month before he died.

Verse 7

"Husbands, in the same way be considerate as you live with your wives, and treat them with respect as the weaker partner and as heirs with you of the gracious gift of life, so that nothing will hinder your prayers." Peter's reference to the woman as being the "weaker partner" has been a topic of much debate, especially in the context of our culture where any form of weakness suggests inferiority. In this passage he was probably referring to physical strength, certainly not emotional strength. Even in the area of physical strength, some women are not willing to concede. Some are offended when a man offers to open a door for them. "After all," they say, "I'm perfectly capable of opening my own door." But Peter was not talking about capability.

Husbands are instructed to treat their wives with respect as "heirs" with them "of the gracious gift of life," so that their prayers would not be hindered. Spiritually, a husband and wife are heirs together of the grace of God. They are one in Christ (Gal. 3:28) sharing spiritual fellowship with God. For this reason, they are to enter together into all that is theirs in this life, both physically and spiritually, so that the husband's prayers will not be hindered. Partnership in every area of life is important. Stott states that because God created men and women to be complementary to each other, they must recognize their differences and not try to eliminate them or take over each other's distinctives.[43]

CONCLUSIONS

As we reflect on these passages regarding a woman's role, we need to keep in mind that the spiritual service of men and women is to be carried out in the local church. "You will know how people ought to conduct themselves in God's household, which is the church of the living God, the pillar and foundation of the truth" (1 Tim. 3:15). Paul's instructions about women in 1 Corinthians 11; 14; and 1 Timothy 2 apply directly to the local church assembly (see, for example, 1 Cor. 11:18, 20, 33) and only indirectly to other related settings.

Although Christian organizations do many things that Christians do in a local assembly, they do not entirely match the distinctives of a local church. "When believers come together as a local assembly of the church there is a distinct organization, there are distinct purposes, and, therefore, there are specific rulings."[44] A local church is an organized assembly, with elders as leaders, who administer the ordinances, preach and teach the Word, and exercise church discipline. If a church-related ministry appropriates one or more of these activities or structures, it does not follow that it is a church, or that all of Paul's instructions about local churches apply.

Chapter Six

Are Some Practices for Women
Limited to Bible Times?

*C*ertain church practices in relation to women need not be followed today, according to some Bible students, because they relate only to cultures in biblical times. Other believers say these practices *are* applicable today as well as in Bible times. Still others take a moderate position, saying that certain standards apply only indirectly or only in some situations.

Some things in Scripture were clearly "cultural," that is, limited to a particular culture, time, and people. For example, Exodus 23:19 says, "Do not cook a young goat in its mother's milk." This mandate under the Law for Israel is no longer to be observed today because the Law was fulfilled in Christ. But Jewish people today say this command means they should not eat meat and dairy products in the same meal. However, neither Jews nor Christians would consider as binding the regulation about a man's duty to marry a childless widowed sister-in-law in order to produce an heir for his dead brother. On the other hand, some parts of the Law are timeless because Christ reinforced them when He was on the earth, namely, nine of the Ten Commandments (all except keeping the Sabbath). It is still wrong, for example, to kill, steal, covet, or take God's name in vain.

"If you want to be perfect, go, sell your possessions and give to the poor, and you will have treasure in heaven" (Matt. 19:21). Was that a universal command? If so, why was it not repeated to Lydia, the rich merchant woman of Philippi? Or to Philemon, the prosperous businessman and slave owner in Colosse?

Several issues confront Christians today regarding what is permissible (or required) biblically for women. Should women be ordained? Should women wear long hair? Should they wear head coverings? Should women engage in church planting? Should women lead in public prayer? Should women teach men in nonchurch settings? Answers to these questions relate to the issue of cultural-temporary situations not relevant for today versus universal-timeless situations that are applicable.

SHOULD WOMEN BE ORDAINED?

Evangelicals debate whether women should be ordained to the Christian ministry. What does ordination mean in the church? Is it a biblical concept? Is it applicable to women?

According to Walter Liefeld, the stand people take on ordaining women depends on two variables: "one's ecclesiology, particularly the definition and the significance of ordination with regard to the functions it permits, and the qualifications it requires, and one's interpretation of Scripture with regard to the ministries a woman is permitted to perform."[1]

In many churches today ordination means choosing and appointing certain qualified individuals to hold positions of pastoral leadership, including preaching, administering the ordinances, and supervising the affairs of congregation. On the other hand, in many evangelical churches ordination is simply a way of designating those whom God has called to minister. To this group, ordination does not grant an exclusive right to preside over certain rites or to exercise governing authority over the church.

In the Old Testament, the Hebrew priests, Levites, prophets, and kings were solemnly ordained or set apart for their special roles. Moses appointed Joshua as his successor by the laying on of hands (Deut. 34:9), which depicted Moses' bestowing of blessing on his successor.

Though Christ did not "ordain" any of His followers by a symbolic act or ceremony such as laying his hands on them, He did call, appoint, and commission twelve apostles (Mark 3:14). In electing Matthias to fill the place of Judas, the eleven apostles learned by prayer and casting of lots whom the Lord had chosen, and without ceremony they included him among them (Acts 1:21–26).

The apostolic church "set apart" seven men for service in the church, with the apostles praying and laying their hands on them (6:5–6). This is the first mention of this practice of "ordaining" others for ministry. Some, however, think this was not ordination as such but was a temporary measure for meeting a pressing need. Although Paul had been called and set apart for ministry by Christ, he submitted to the laying on of hands, as recorded in Acts 13:1–3. When the church at Antioch laid hands on Paul and Barnabas, these two leaders had already been in the Lord's work for some time. The fact that the church as a whole held a special service for this solemn purpose does not imply that authority was bestowed on these two men at that time. There is no indication that this "setting apart" by the church was more important than the original divine call; the ceremony merely blessed Barnabas and Saul for a special work, which was completed within three years.

Paul and Barnabas "appointed" elders in each of the churches they had established in Lystra, Iconium, and Pisidian Antioch (14:23), thereby committing them to the Lord. Later Paul laid hands on Timothy in appointing him to minister (2 Tim. 1:6). And the apostle encouraged Titus to appoint elders in the Cretan churches (Titus 1:5).

These appointments (which some call "ordination") in the early church seem to have been no more than formal confirmations of one's calling into service. Later in the first and second centuries more importance seems to have been invested in the ordination of leaders who were approved by an entire congregation. But the fact that ordination of presbyters or bishops was considered necessary seems to imply that the rite somehow contributed to their effectiveness. With the growing importance of the episcopal office, and the sanctity associated with it and the clergy in general, the rite of ordination assumed the character of the sacramental act, which could be performed only by a bishop. The ordination of clergymen was included as one of the sacraments as early as the fourth or fifth century.[2] Today the Roman Catholic and Greek Orthodox churches view ordination as a sacrament, but the Church of England and the Episcopal Church do not. Also the English Reformers did not believe that the laying on of hands conferred any grace.

Ordination of women is a recent topic in the church. A woman was first ordained to the ministry of a recognized Christian denomination in 1863, in the Universalist Church.[3] Until recent years most Protestant women leaders were in Pentecostal or Holiness churches.[4] Since the 1950s several Protestant denominations have ordained women to ministry positions. The November 1992 decision of the Church of England to ordain women meant that its thirteen hundred women deacons became eligible for the priesthood. The Vatican looked on with alarm at this change in the Church of England and vowed that Catholicism would never accept women for ordination.[5]

For a long time the Lutheran and Reformed churches have acknowledged and practiced ordination. Admission of women pastors in Sweden's Lutheran Church caused concern across Europe because its clergy claim common lineage with Anglican, Catholic, and Orthodox priests.[6] In the 1987 census of the 5.4 million-member Lutheran Church there were 821 ordained women clergy among the seventeen thousand total clergy.[7]

The Disciples of Christ, Quakers, and Plymouth Brethren do not recognize any human rite of ordination. The Methodist Church provides for the ordination of deacons by a bishop, while an elder is elected by the annual conference with a bishop and some elders laying on hands. In the United Methodist Church more than two thousand women serve congregations as pastors, several dozen are district superintendents, and a few are bishops.[8]

In 1976 the Episcopal Church officially authorized the ordination of women priests. By 1987 there were eight hundred among the 13,000 clergy for the 2.7 million-member Episcopal Church.[9]

Heated conflicts have occurred in the fifteen-million-member Southern Baptist Convention. Since local Baptist congregations have authority to ordain, there are a few women pastors and deacons in Southern Baptist churches; in 1987, 350 of the 60,000 total clergy were women.[10]

The Roman Catholic Church, with more than sixty million members, is firmly opposed to women becoming priests. But in 1983 the door was opened for parishes to be led by nuns or laity under the supervision of priests who visit to celebrate the sacraments. In the United States today, three-fourths of the three hundred Catholic parishes without priests are led by women. If present trends continue, the number of male Roman Catholic priests will have dropped 40 percent in the forty-

year period between 1966 and 2005.[11] The women serving these parishes preach, counsel, and administer the Mass. With this much exposure
to female leadership functioning as nonordained priests, how will
laypeople respond in future years?

Many churches that have barred women from leadership have changed
their governing rules in recent years and opened this possibility for women.
Some denominations, in a kind of affirmative action, have been pushing
women into places of leadership. As many as half of the students in some
mainline denominational seminaries are now female.

Some supporters of women's ordination give the impression that the
Bible is out of date and is no longer the infallible rule for faith and practice. They say contemporary culture and psychology have greater bearing
on women's rights than the biblical teachings that have been traditionally
understood as prohibitions.

Opponents of ordination of women have pointed to references in
Scripture that seem to limit women's roles in the church. Susan Foh states
that "there is only one sufficient argument against women's ordination:
scriptural prohibition" (1 Tim. 2:12).[12] Gretchen Hull argues for ordination of women from a "situational ethics" position. She describes the plea
for ordination of a woman who was a volunteer at a Presbyterian Home
for the Aged. Hull asks, "Who could question her proven love for those
who are often so unlovely? In light of Romans 14:4, who would deny her
call to serve them as their ordained pastor? Who would dare to say she
could not be in God's will?"[13]

The Bible and history alike indicate that certain types of senior leadership positions have normally been held by men. Overwhelmingly,
generals, prime ministers, presidents, preachers, evangelists, corporation
presidents, and seminary professors have been men; and when we look
carefully at the biblical record, we find notable exceptions to the general
rule. For example, Miriam is listed right along with her brothers, Moses
and Aaron, as playing an important role in Israel's life. Deborah was a
judge in Israel. Huldah was a prophetess during the reign of King Josiah.
Priscilla and her husband, Aquila, were prominent influences on the early
missionary movement, especially as they instructed Apollos more perfectly in the Christian faith. Yet it should not be surprising that leadership

in biblical times was always spoken of in masculine terms, because men were usually the leaders.[14]

It is fair to say that the Scriptures overwhelmingly favor male leadership in the church. Even most societies favor male leadership. But just as secular society has its exceptions, like Margaret Thatcher and Golda Meir, so the Bible indicates some exceptions to the norm.

John Piper and Wayne Grudem, who do not favor placing women in leadership positions in the church, were asked to explain why God endorsed women in the Old Testament who had prophetic or leadership roles. They responded that God did so because these instances did not call into question the primary order of role distinction. They said that in each case the women followed their unusual paths in a way that endorsed and honored the usual leadership of men, or indicted men's failures to lead.[15]

For example, Piper and Grudem refer to Miriam, a prophetess, who focused her ministry on the women of Israel (Exod. 15:20); Deborah, a prophetess and judge in Israel (Judg. 4:4; 5:7); Huldah, who evidently exercised her prophetic gift not in a public preaching ministry but by means of private consultation (2 Kings 22:14–20); and Anna, a prophetess who filled her days with fasting and prayer in the temple (Luke 2:36–37). They conclude that the fact that God may give power or revelation to a person is no sure sign that that person is an ideal model for us to follow in every respect, as illustrated by Abraham's and David's polygamy.[16]

Thomas Schreiner says Deborah's position as judge was a special case because she seems to be the only judge in the Book of Judges who had no military function. Her leadership was also an implied rebuke of Barak, because he was unwilling to go to battle without her (Judg. 4:8). Because of his unwillingness, the honor of the day went to a woman, namely, Jael (4:9, 22). Schreiner notes that women's participation in ministry in the Scriptures was always a complementary and supportive ministry which preserved male leadership.[17]

Clayton Bell, who favors women's ordination, argues that the only reason people should be ordained to office is to recognize them as having spiritual gifts for building up the body of Christ. And if the Holy Spirit has gifted a woman for helping build up the church, then the church should recognize those gifts and provide for their use in the church. He warns, however, that churches should not "push women in leadership roles just because they are female in order to rectify the imbalance built over the years. This would deny the New Testament principle of electing persons based on their qualifications for service and not because of their gender, and will result in the weakening of the church."[18]

In response to Bell's argument, however, I would say that a woman need not exercise a particular spiritual gift in the same way a man exercises that gift in order for her to be used by the Holy Spirit. All spiritual gifts do not have to be exercised in a local church. There are numerous opportunities to exercise our gifts outside that arena—areas where we can still help edify the body of Christ. The role distinctions designed by God do not limit the exercising of our spiritual gifts.

SHOULD WOMEN WEAR LONG HAIR?

To the Corinthians Paul wrote, "Does not the very nature of things teach you that if a man has long hair, it is a disgrace to him, but that if a woman has long hair, it is her glory?" (1 Cor. 11:14–15). Is this a cultural or timeless principle for us to follow?

In Israel a Nazirite was one who separated himself from others by consecration to God with a special vow. The rules for the Nazirite are presented in Numbers 6. One of the marks of his vow was letting his hair grow. At the end of his vow, he would cut his hair and present it on the altar to God. The inference was that he was totally set apart for God's service, not attending to his own person. Although the vow was for a fixed period of time, in at least two instances parents dedicated their children— Samson (Judg. 13:4–5) and Samuel (1 Sam. 1:11)—to be Nazirites for their entire lives.

In the 1960s some young men in Western cultures grew their hair long as a sign of rebellion against adult authority. Although some churches still hold rigidly to a literal interpretation of 1 Corinthians 11:14–15, most believe that these verses had cultural implications that are nontransferable to today. On the other hand, others maintain that when a woman's hair is longer than that of a man, it "gives visible expression to the differentiation of the sexes."[19]

SHOULD WOMEN WEAR HEAD COVERINGS?

Many churches say that women today should wear head coverings, based on 1 Corinthians 11:5: "And every woman who prays or prophesies with her head uncovered dishonors her head—it is just as though her head were shaved." They say this practice is timeless, not temporary, that it is for all Christian women today, not just women in Corinth. Was Paul saying that creation dictates that all women wear head coverings, or was he saying that they should use culturally appropriate expressions of femininity, which in Corinth was a head covering? Lowery suggests that in New Testament times it was the custom for women to wear head coverings. "It cannot be unequivocally asserted but the preponderance of evidence points toward the public head covering of women as a universal custom in the first century in both Jewish culture . . . and Greco-Roman culture. . . . The nature of the covering varied considerably . . . but it was commonly a portion of the outer garment drawn up over the head like a hood."[20]

Liefeld says that in 1 Corinthians 11:5 Paul was implying that Christian women should follow pre-Christian norms in order not to offend Jews (9:20), just as they followed conventional ethics not to offend pagans (9:21). Paul's principle, Liefeld says, was not the wearing of veils but rather conforming to Jewish and moralistic pagan norms for the sake of the gospel. Not to wear a head covering in public was considered a symbol of impropriety in biblical times.[21] Schreiner says Paul wanted the Corinthian women to adhere to the custom of not appearing in public with long hair flowing down their backs as did the adulteresses.[22]

Perhaps, then, wearing a head covering was a cultural practice which today would not have the significance it had in the first century. Not to wear a head covering was apparently an expression of insubordination.[23] Whether women wear hats today does not seem as important as the attitude of the heart.[24] Some people say a woman's literal hair anticipates the need for a head covering. Pointing to verse 15, "Long hair is given her as a covering," they say that since women have a natural covering, they should follow the custom of wearing a physical covering in public. Others, however, say the word translated "as" should be rendered "instead," so that verse 15 is saying that women need not wear a physical covering because the hair itself is a covering. The hair is in place of a physical covering. "This view, however, does not explain the women's act of covering or uncovering her head mentioned in 1 Corinthians 11:5–6."[25]

SHOULD WOMEN ENGAGE IN CHURCH PLANTING?

Some people claim that a society that accepts women as corporate executives and university presidents will find it difficult to listen to a church that silences them. The problem with this line of argument is that our society is not asking, "What does God say?" but rather, "What do we want in light of what our culture is doing?" But it is wrong to base our interpretation of Scripture on what society dictates.

What roles should Christian women in foreign cultures be allowed to assume? Many women in China are preachers because so few men are qualified to preach. Others question whether women missionaries should be church planters in other countries. Some students say, "You send us women to evangelize us and to establish churches, but in your own country you don't think this is right. Why?" These are difficult questions to answer.

When Piper and Grudem were asked how we can justify sending women missionaries to minister in ways that are forbidden at home, they responded this way: "We do not wish to impede the great cause of world evangelization by quibbling over which of the hundreds of roles might correspond so closely to pastor/elder as to be inappropriate for a woman to fill. It is manifest to us that women are fellow workers in the gospel and should strive side by side with men as Philippians 4:3: 'Yes, and I ask you, loyal yokefellow, help these women who have contended at my side in the cause of the gospel, along with Clement and the rest of my fellow workers, whose names are in the book of life.' And Romans 16:3: 'Greet Priscilla and Aquila, my fellow workers in Christ Jesus.' "[26]

In considering missionary work Schreiner states that "women can proclaim the gospel to men in those [foreign] cultures, for 1 Timothy 2:11–15 prohibits only authoritative teaching to a group of Christians within the church, not evangelism to those outside the church."[27] He adds that men should take the leadership roles of a church as soon as it is established.[28] (For more on how women are serving in missions see chapter 17.)

SHOULD WOMEN LEAD IN PUBLIC PRAYER?

For years in Wednesday night prayer meetings in conservative churches men would meet for prayer in one room and women in another. Tradition dictated that women should not pray publicly when men were present.

Even in Christian homes fathers led the family in prayer. In my own home my mother never prayed at the dinner table when my father was there (which was most of the time)—my father as head of our home always led in prayer. When I was a student in seminary there was one class in which I was the only woman—a class on Eschatological Problems, taught by John Walvoord. After several weeks went by, Dr. Walvoord asked me to open the class in prayer. When I hesitated, he quietly encouraged me, saying that I was, after all, next in line in his gradebook—it was my turn. So I prayed. When I finished, he said, "Well, that's the first time a woman has ever prayed in one of my classes." And I replied, "Well, that's the first time I have ever prayed in front of a group of men."

Was this wrong? What about Acts 1:13–14, which says, "When they arrived, they went upstairs to the room where they were staying. Those present were Peter, John, James and Andrew; Philip and Thomas, Bartholomew and Matthew; James son of Alphaeus and Simon the Zealot, and Judas son of James. They all joined together constantly in prayer, along with the women and Mary the mother of Jesus, and with his brothers"? And 1 Corinthians 11:5 refers to women praying, which presumably was in the main church assembly, not just in the presence of women only.

SHOULD WOMEN TEACH MEN
IN NONCHURCH SETTINGS?

Another area of consideration is that of women in leadership outside the church, for example, teaching in Bible colleges or seminaries, or teaching on the mission field. For many years women were excluded from these positions, but that is now changing. Is this change due to our bending to societal pressure, or to a different understanding of the Scripture passages related to women in certain ministries? The view of Dallas Theological Seminary (and presumably of other conservative seminaries, as well) is that the restrictions mentioned by Paul in his epistles are limited to the corporate body of the local church, and therefore cannot be superimposed on positions outside that arena. A Bible school or seminary is not a church; such schools are established to help equip men and women for ministries of various kinds. No longer are these educational institutions training only pastors for pulpit ministries; both men and women are being trained for a wide range of ministry opportunities. Furthermore, seminaries do not engage in ordaining men for the pastorate; that is the role of churches or denominations.

How then do we determine which practices were temporary, limited to cultures in Bible times, and which ones are permanent, applicable for all times? Allen Ross answers that Paul's rulings on practices related to women had the "assembly" of the church as their frame of reference. Only when we duplicate what Paul meant by the "church" can we be sure his mandates apply directly. The more an organization differs from a local church, the less we should seek to make Paul's ruling apply.[29] This seems to be a helpful guideline for this thorny issue.

Chapter Seven

Women in the New Testament
and in Church History

*I*n spite of the order of creation, Satan's temptation of Eve, and the Fall, God has been pleased to use women. He used them to give prophetic utterances and to declare His mighty works in song and in proclamation. He sent women as well as men to carry out the Great Commission, discipling, baptizing, and teaching. He sent them along with men to disciple new Christians by expounding the revelation of God and to pray and prophesy in the church so long as there was a sign of authority present.[1]

Women were just as actively involved in the life of the early church as were men. Women prayed with the men in the upper room (Acts 1:14). Both women and men received the Holy Spirit at Pentecost (2:1–4), and the Holy Spirit used Philip's daughters as they prophesied (21:8–9). Paul recognized that the Holy Spirit used women for prophetic speaking (1 Cor. 11:5). He instructed them to teach (Titus 2:3–5; 2 Tim. 1:5; 3:14–15; see also Prov. 1:8). He encouraged them to cultivate ministries of good works, service, and hospitality (1 Cor. 16:19; Col. 4:15; 1 Tim. 2:10; 5:9–10). Women, like men, according to the apostle, are to use their spiritual gifts to serve the Lord. In Romans 16, at least ten of the twenty-nine people Paul commended for their loyal service were women.

Paul affirmed the personal equality of men and women in Christ (Gal. 3:28). A woman obtains salvation exactly as a man does—by faith in Christ (Eph. 2:8–9; 1 Pet. 1:18–19). Christian women and men are coheirs with Christ (Rom. 8:17). The Holy Spirit indwells women and men alike (Rom. 8:9; 1 Cor. 6:19–20; 12:13). And women have equal standing before God as believers in Christ (Rom. 5:1–2).[2]

Also women and men have the same spiritual privileges and responsibilities. Women have access to God in prayer just as men do (1 Cor. 11:4–5). Women are matured by God's Word just as men are (1 Pet. 2:2). Women enjoy the privileges and responsibilities of the priesthood of all believers (2:5; 3:7; Rev. 1:6). And women are given the same spiritual gifts available to men today, including the gifts of pastor-teacher and evangelist (Rom. 12:3–8; 1 Cor. 12:11, 27; 1 Pet. 4:10).[3]

Paul encouraged men and women to remain single and devote themselves to the service of the Lord (1 Cor. 7:32–34). This is significant because it shows that marriage is not the highest goal for women—serving and glorifying the Lord is! Throughout the Old Testament and in the early church women shared in public ministry, often communicating the Word of God. Many of these passages are descriptive (and not prescriptive or instructive as were apostolic rulings), but they are still important for our learning. These descriptive reports of women's participation in ministry and service are favorable and positive.[4] So there should be no hesitation to draw from these passages to show how God has used women down through the ages.

As we examine the role of some marvelous women in the Scriptures and in history, learning wonderful lessons of servanthood from them, let's focus on what they did rather than on what they were not permitted to do.

WOMEN IN THE GOSPELS

It is no surprise to see that women were active in the early church. In Jesus' birth, ministry, death, and resurrection women were very much involved. The four Gospel writers record that a significant group of women had followed Jesus in His Galilean ministry and ministered to Him. Then when He was crucified, several women were there at the cross—when all but one of His male disciples were conspicuously absent![5]

Matthew, Mark, and Luke wrote that several women were present at Jesus' burial. Luke declared that the women who had followed Jesus from Galilee still followed along as His body was carried to the tomb. Mark detailed the care with which Mary Magdalene and Mary, the mother of Jesus, observed where He was laid, and Matthew noted how they kept watch over the sepulcher after the men had left. John alone recorded the garden interview between Mary Magdalene and the risen Christ.

The proclamation of the astounding Easter event was entrusted to these women. The angel reminded them that Jesus had already told them about His resurrection. The women remembered and hurried off to tell the apostles. Their witness remains an integral part of the gospel to this day. The early church considered Mary Magdalene an "apostle of the apostles," and Luke apparently relied heavily on the testimony of women as he wrote both the Gospel of Luke and the Book of Acts.

Mary, the Mother of Jesus

No female has been honored more than Mary. She was of the tribe of Judah and the line of David. "Her lineage made her a rightful candidate to bear God's Son, but it was her godly character that ultimately qualified her to be His mother."[6] As a virgin, probably a teenager, Mary conceived Christ in a miraculous way. Later she married Joseph, a carpenter, and had four sons—James, Joseph, Simon, and Judas—and several daughters, whom the Gospels do not name (Matt. 13:55–56). She was a devout, pious woman, so that one could easily see that the Lord was with her (Luke 1:28). But what is amazing is her simple submission to the plan of God (Luke 1:38).[7]

Mary is listed with the apostles who gathered in the upper room after Christ ascended (Acts 1:13–14). She was present not as an object of worship, but as a worshiper of Jesus Christ.

Elizabeth

When Elizabeth was six months pregnant with John the Baptist, Mary came to visit her, and at that moment Elizabeth was "filled with the Holy Spirit" (Luke 1:41), and she became the first to confess Jesus in the flesh ("Blessed is the child you will bear!" 1:42). She gave Mary the title "mother of my Lord" (1:43). This Spirit-filled greeting prompted Mary to respond with her song, recorded in Luke 1:46–55, which is sometimes called the Magnificat.[8] What an encouragement Elizabeth must have been to young Mary, who had to carry such a stigma in the midst of her people. Elizabeth was probably the first person who really understood Mary's unique pregnancy.[9]

Anna

When Mary brought the Baby Jesus to the temple, the elderly Anna, who had been widowed for many decades, spoke to everyone there about Jesus. She was renowned as a prophetess, one who proclaimed the Word of the Lord. God spoke through her. She had grown old in her service for the Lord in the temple, and now having seen Jesus, she gave the Lord thanks (Luke 2:36–38).

Mary Magdalene

Mary Magdalene was from the town of Magdala, a place which the Talmud says had an unsavory reputation and had been destroyed because of harlotry. The little town was on the western shore of the Sea of Galilee. Mary was introduced in Luke 8:2 right after the story of the sinful woman (7:36–50). This, plus the notoriety of her hometown, has led people to conclude that she had been a prostitute, but there is no evidence for that. Luke would probably have made the connection explicit if there had been any evidence linking the two women.[10] Mary was much aware of the powers of Satan because she had been possessed of seven demons, whom Jesus exorcised from her (8:2). Her life shows us that our past, no matter how dark, need not keep us from serving the Lord.[11]

In the dark days of Jesus' death and burial, Mary Magdalene was there. And on the morning of the Resurrection, she was there in the garden. What a great honor God gave this faithful woman, allowing her to be the first one to see the risen Savior. Then Christ commissioned her to be the first herald of His resurrection: "Go instead to my brothers and tell them, 'I am returning to my Father and your Father, to my God and your God'" (John 20:17).

Joanna

Joanna (Luke 8:1–3; 23:55; 24:10) was the wife of Cuza, the manager of Herod Antipas's household. Along with Mary Magdalene and Susanna, Joanna was healed of evil spirits and diseases. With other women, she traveled with Jesus and helped provide for him financially. She also was one of the women who announced the Resurrection to the apostles.

Martha of Bethany

Martha of Bethany was known as the more practical one of the two sisters of Lazarus. She and her sister, Mary, were important figures in the village of Bethany. Martha had a gift and love for serving in the practical things of life. John 11:5 tells us that "Jesus loved Martha and her sister and Lazarus." When Christ challenged Martha at Lazarus' death, she gave one of the most beautiful confessions of faith in the Gospels: "Yes, Lord, . . . I believe that you are the Christ, the Son of God, who was to come into the world" (11:27).

The last we read of Martha is at the supper given for the raised Lazarus (12:1–3). Mary sat at Jesus' feet and anointed them; and Martha, still serving, did not offer a word of objection. In fact, at that time only their actions were recorded. On one occasion Martha was distracted by obligations and cares (Luke 10:40), but now she simply served the Lord in her capacity and let others serve Him in theirs. Wouldn't this be a great lesson for us to learn?

Mary, Sister of Martha and Lazarus

Mary "sat at the Lord's feet listening to what he said" (Luke 10:39). Her posture teaches us that "only one thing is needed" (10:42). Service is not paramount—learning from the Lord is. We must learn from Him, and then He will teach us how to serve. We will have nothing to give if we don't first sit at His feet. She, along with her sister, Martha, witnessed Jesus' power in restoring their dead brother to life (John 11:17–55). Later she poured expensive perfume on Jesus' feet and wiped them with her hair (12:3). In response to this act Christ said that she was preparing Him for burial (12:7).

Peter's Mother-in-Law

Peter's mother-in-law is best known as the woman Jesus healed. Immediately after being freed of her fever, she got up and waited on the Lord (Matt. 8:14–18). Her servant's heart shines through as an example for us.

The Woman Subject to Bleeding

This woman had a physical condition that had rendered her ceremonially unclean (Mark 5:25–34). Her faith should certainly be a model for us, for she had said to herself, "If I only touch his cloak, I will be healed" (Matt. 9:21).

The Syrian Phoenicean Woman

A descendant of the ancient Canaanites, this gentile woman suffered tremendous grief over the demonic control of her daughter (Mark 7:24–30). Her response shows great humility and faith: "Even the dogs eat the crumbs that fall from their masters' table." Wouldn't you love to hear our Lord say to you, "Woman, you have great faith!" (Matt. 15:28)?

The Widow with the Fraction of a Penny

The widow with the two small copper coins (Mark 12:41–44; Luke 21:1–4) shows how the Lord evaluates giving; the proportion of the sacrifice and not the amount is what pleases God. Her offering also shows that what is given to God from the heart is what counts.

The Sinful Woman

A sinful woman came to the house where Jesus was eating with some Pharisees and stood behind Him, weeping, covering His feet with her tears. She wiped His feet with her hair and anointed them with perfume from an alabaster jar, and He accepted her devotion. Her faith saved her, and she expressed that faith in her love for Jesus (Luke 7:36–50).

The Woman at Jacob's Well

The Samaritan woman had the distinction of being the first one to witness to her people about Jesus (John 4:1–26). We don't even know her name—just her immoral lifestyle. She showed considerable knowledge about her own religion and was open to hearing what Jesus had to say. She was a "morally inept and unacceptable person, going to the well to draw water for her physical thirst," but she became a "discerning disciple, drawing people to Jesus, the source of living water."[12] Christ draws us to Himself while we are still lost in sin. He does the drawing—we do the responding. To think that He can use us is a wonderful revelation!

The Adulterous Woman

A woman caught in adultery was brought to Jesus by the teachers of the Law and the Pharisees (John 8:1–11). Jesus forgave her and in doing so, He was not condoning her sin. The Jewish leaders had already disregarded the Law by arresting the woman without the man (Lev. 20:10). This story shows us that salvation washes us clean, so that we can serve Him.

WOMEN IN THE BOOK OF ACTS

The involvement of women continued in the first few decades of the church, witnessed by both biblical and extrabiblical sources. A number of women served as leaders of the house churches that sprang up in the cities of the Roman Empire—the list includes Priscilla (Rom. 16:3–5; 1 Cor. 16:19), Chloe (1 Cor. 1:11), Lydia (Acts 16:40), Nympha (Col. 4:15), and possibly the "elect lady" of John's second epistle.[13]

Several women accompanied the apostles on their missionary journeys as their colleagues. Perhaps some of them were coworkers in presenting the gospel to other women. It was through them that the Lord's teaching penetrated also the women's quarters. Men were not allowed near these quarters, and so women would be needed to minister to them, thereby helping fulfill the Great Commission of Matthew 28:19–20.

Paul mentioned Phoebe in Romans 16:1–2: "I commend to you our sister Phoebe, a servant [*diakanon*] of the church in Cenchrea. I ask you to receive her in the Lord in a way worthy of the saints and to give her any help she may need from you, for she has been a great help to many people, including me." The word *diakanon,* translated "servant," is rendered "deacon" when used of male officers of the church (1 Tim. 3:10, 12). Some Bible students therefore feel that Phoebe was a deaconess. Others, however, prefer the rendering "servant."

The Four Daughters of Philip

Philip had four unmarried daughters who prophesied (Acts 21:8–9). This is all we know about them. Apparently they did not have what we would call the office of a prophet in the classical sense of Old Testament prophets, but they did communicate the Word of God in a fresh and meaningful way, demonstrating the reality of their faith.[14]

Rhoda

Rhoda was a young servant girl who excitedly told the many believers who had gathered at the house of Mary, the mother of John Mark, that God had answered their prayers and freed Peter from prison (Acts 12:1–19). Not believing her, they told her that she was out of her mind, and so Peter had to keep knocking until they let him in. She experienced what they would find in their ministry, that when they told people that Jesus is alive, they would often be met with disbelief.[15] God answers prayer, and strangely, we are often surprised.

Sapphira

Sapphira, along with her husband, Ananias, is an example of what we should not be like. The couple lied to the Holy Spirit concerning the land they sold because they wanted to appear committed to God when actually they weren't (Acts 5:1–11). Peter said they were led by Satan because he had filled their hearts. The term "fill" is an expression for "control," as in the command, "Be filled with the Spirit" (Eph. 5:18). Christ calls us to be truthful—with Him, with ourselves, and with others. We need to avoid teaching one way and then living another.

Lydia

Lydia (Acts 16:12–15, 40) was a prominent businesswoman who lived in Thyatira and dealt in purple cloth. She was head of a household and there-fore was either widowed or unmarried.[16] A devout Jewish proselyte, Lydia placed her faith in the Savior and was baptized. She and others who fol-lowed her became some of Paul's first Macedonian converts. Her genuine faith was shown by her willingness to show hospitality to Paul, Silas, and Luke. Continuing to sell her fabrics, she also served the Lord.

Dorcas

Dorcas, also known as Tabitha, was among the numerous disciples of the early church (Acts 9:36–43). She is the only woman referred to in the New Testament as a disciple (9:36). Since she lived in Joppa, she may have been an early convert of Philip the evangelist. She "was always doing good and helping the poor" (9:36). When she died, the believers in the town went to Peter, who came and raised her from the dead. "In her case, she would rise, literally, to the exact kind of lifestyle she had lived before: a continuation of her previous pattern of godly generosity."[17]

Priscilla

Priscilla and her husband, Aquila, are known for having a church in their home (Rom. 16:3–5; 1 Cor. 16:19) and for instructing Apollos (Acts 18:24–26). This husband-and-wife team was extremely dynamic. When they are first introduced (18:2) and when mention is made of a church in their home, Aquila is named first. By implication, we can assume that "while Priscilla is the more important figure, Aquila's authority, both as a Chris-tian leader and as the head of the home, is still very much recognized."[18]

The fact that Priscilla and Aquila "explained" to Apollos "the way of

God more adequately" (18:26) shows that they both were involved in teaching. The Greek verb for "explained" is *ektithemi,* which means "to set forth, expound." It speaks of expounding Scripture in an effort to evangelize and train disciples. It is used in Acts 28:23 for Paul's teaching on the kingdom of God. From Priscilla we learn that it is possible to be a spiritually gifted woman and also be a submissive and supportive wife.[19]

Eunice

Eunice, Timothy's mother, was a woman full of faith (2 Tim. 1:5). She was probably in a mixed marriage, because Acts 16:1 says that she lived in "Lystra, where a disciple named Timothy lived, whose mother was a Jewess and a believer, but whose father was a Greek." Yet she taught her son the Scriptures when he was in infancy (2 Tim. 3:15). She should be a tremendous encouragement to women today who live in unequally yoked marriages. Our families are fields in which to plant the seeds of the gospel. We need to help women in this type of marriage to stay true to God's calling as Eunice did.

OPTIONS FOR WOMEN IN THE EARLY CHURCH

In the first-century church specialized orders began to emerge for women: virgins, widows, deaconesses, elders, and priests. Some women in these orders were formally ordained and sat with clergy in front of their congregations. Yet as early as the second century the majority of Christian churches opposed this kind of equality.[20]

Virgins

In Ignatius's *Letter to the Smyrneans* we learn of virgins being supported by the church and obligated to it. The *Acts of Paul and Thekla* also present virginity as the most noble calling for Christian women. Early on, the model developed that if a woman wanted to be a good Christian and good teacher she must be a virgin, rejecting marriage. Clement of Alexandria balanced this picture by showing how wives too can achieve perfection and the blessing of God, but he did not relinquish the ideal of virginity.[21]

Widows

Widows in the early centuries of the church became part of the ordained clergy. In the *Testimony of Our Lord Jesus Christ,* a fifth-century work based on Himmolytus, there is evidence that the process of selecting and ordaining widows paralleled that of deacons and bishops. Widows were primarily charged with prayer, fasting, and ministering to the sick. They were to instruct learners, to gather for prayer and encouragement, and to rebuke and restore the wayward.[22]

Deaconesses

By the first half of the third century deaconesses formed a distinct order, with tasks more strenuous than those of the widows. They were to visit believing women in pagan houses (where ministers could not go), visit the sick and minister to the needy, assist with the baptism of women, give communion to women, and instruct women. The Council of Chalcedon set down rules for their ordination.[23] However, from the middle of the third century the *Didaskalia Apostolorum*—the first church order to reflect a major controversy surrounding women's leadership—placed many restrictions on women.[24]

Elders

The Greek word for "older woman" is *presbytis* (used in the New Testament only in Titus 2:3), but some say that in the early centuries of the church the plural form of the word referred to female clergy. The fourth-century church father Basil used the term for one who was a head of a religious community.[25]

Scholars differ over the gender of the name Junias (Rom. 16:7), a fellow prisoner of Paul. If the name is masculine, it is found only in this passage and is a short form for Junianus. Grammatically it might be feminine, but this raises questions because Paul referred to this person as an apostle.[26] It seems preferable to view the name as masculine.

Priests

A few scattered references refer to women as priests. Pseudo-Ignatius's *Letter to the Tarsians* says virgins are to be honored as priestesses. The catacombs in Rome, especially the Priscilla Catacomb, portray many women in prayer postures normally reserved for men. One fresco of the late first century shows a woman breaking bread in an observance of the Lord's Supper (most of the participants look like women). Another painting (from the second century) shows a woman veiled and praying, but this was probably in the context of taking the gospel to women. It is also affirmed from the *Didaskalia Apostolorum* that the practice of ordaining women priests was a pagan custom and that sacerdotal and teaching functions are limited to the ordained men of the church.[27]

OBSERVATIONS

From the middle of the third century on, controversies over women's ministries in the church orders teach us much about women's leadership. Women were evangelizing, baptizing, teaching, interpreting Scripture, involved in visitation, functioning as leaders of groups within the church, and speaking at assemblies. But the church orders from this time also indicate that such ministries brought great conflict. The difference was that during the first two centuries women would have exercised leadership in the private sphere, that is, in house assemblies. During the third and fourth centuries these ministries would have continued, but Christian worship began to be perceived as public and formal. Since Hellenistic women were not allowed to exercise authority in public, women's ministries would have been returned to the private sphere.[28]

As today, the ancient church presented a variety of opinions about women. Celsus, a second-century detractor of the faith, once taunted that the church attracted only "the silly and the mean and the stupid, with women and children." His contemporary, Cyprian of Carthage, acknowledged in his *Testimony* that "Christian maidens were very numerous" and that it was difficult to find Christian husbands for all of them. These comments give us a picture of a church disproportionately populated by women. Possibly this was the case because in that society unwanted female infants were abandoned to die, but Christians, of course, repudiated this practice and so they had more living females. Also in the upper echelons of society, women often converted to Christianity while their male relatives remained pagans, not wanting to lose their senatorial status. This also contributed to the inordinate number of women in the church, particularly upper-class women. Callistus, bishop of Rome (A.D. 220), attempted to resolve the marriage problem by giving women of the senatorial class an ecclesiastical sanction to marry slaves or freedmen, even though Roman law prohibited this.[29]

In a letter to his wife, Tertullian gives us a glimpse into some of the ministries of church women in his time. He speaks, for example, of his wife visiting the poor, visiting believers in jail, and bringing water to the saints for their foot washing.[30]

MINISTRY OF WOMEN IN THE MIDDLE AGES

Many remarkable Christian women lived in medieval times. Women's ministries then were generally associated with nunneries rather than with local churches. However, some women did have to serve in church ministries. In some situations these ministries by females created heated controversy, where the women served as "cohostesses" to itinerant priests celebrating the Mass in villages where there were no parish priests.[31]

There were five religious options for women in the medieval church: nuns, hermitesses, Beguines, tertiaries, and anchoresses.

Nuns

Women could either marry men their families chose for them or accept life in a convent as nuns. If a woman went to a convent, she took the three monastic vows of chastity, poverty, and obedience. Hildegard of Bingen (1098–1179), famous mystic, author, and adviser to popes, kings, and emperors, was sent to join a convent when she was only eight years old.

Hermitesses

Some women rejected communal life in the convent, choosing instead to live in isolation as hermitesses. Like many men of their time, these women lived alone in the forests, deserts, and marshes. Since most of the countries were rural, this lifestyle was possible, but by the thirteenth century, much of Europe was deforested because of new towns appearing. Thus new religious vocations for women arose in place of hermitesses.[32]

Beguines

A Beguine (religious woman) took temporary vows of chastity and simplicity of life, wore some type of identifying dress, and dedicated herself to good works. Since she wasn't bound to any order, she could live at home or with other women of similar values. Thus the Beguine need not withdraw from the world. Also, whenever she chose, she could end her vow and marry. An outstanding Beguine of that time was Mary of Oignies (1177–1213), who, though married at fourteen, convinced her husband that they should live in celibacy and share a religious vocation of caring for lepers. Ivette of Huy (1157–1228), who married at thirteen and was widowed at eighteen, gave the care of her children to her father and used her home as a haven for pilgrims and travelers, while she worked in a nearby leper colony.[33]

Tertiaries

After the success of Francis of Assisi there arose a number of communities with vows of poverty that depended on alms for their living. These groups were called tertiaries. They were organized into three orders. The first order included friars, wandering preachers sworn to absolute poverty. The second order was for women in nunneries and convents who also took vows of poverty. The third order consisted of laypersons, male and female, married and single, who identified with the reforms of Francis. Many women, both virgins and widows, entered this order, took vows (which were revocable), and led religious lives.[34]

Anchoresses

Anchoresses were women who took religious vows and lived in seclusion in small rooms attached to churches. They practiced total withdrawal and great self-denial. Many women who had previously been nuns, Beguines, or tertiaries chose to become anchoresses.[35]

HERESIES OF THE HISTORICAL CHURCH

One of the most surprising heresies adopted by women was that of false goddesses. The worship of Isis was a fashionable cult in ancient Rome, especially among women. Mystery religions invaded Christianity, mostly in the form of gnostic heresy, embraced by men and women alike. Gnosticism held strange views of women, deifying "the feminine principle" but generally denigrating their physical being. This feminine principle in gnostic thought was expressed frequently and under a variety of names, including "Mother," "Sound," "Thought of the Father," "Image of the Invisible Spirit," "Perfect Mind," "First and Last," "Thunder," "Mother of All," and the "Ineffable Mother who presides over heaven."[36] Interestingly some of these same heresies are embraced by radical feminists today.

Chapter Eight

Is Feminism Biblical?

Several years ago I attended a national conference whose keynote speaker was a radical feminist. I was astounded at the charisma with which she manipulated her audience of about two thousand people and I was appalled at her blatant heresy. Enthralled, the people were feverishly scribbling notes, anxious to write down everything she said.

Couldn't they see where she was leading? Why were they following her so blindly? I began praying that God would confuse this woman's speech because of her obvious swaying powers over so many people. As I prayed and she continued, I noticed increasing agitation in her voice. She stopped her lecture and asked, "If there's anyone in this audience who believes in Pauline theology, I want you to get up and walk out!"

I didn't move. I continued praying, now asking God to expose her for the heretic she was. She stopped her lecture a second time, exclaiming, "I don't understand it! I can't feel free to express myself." She returned to her now-blasphemous presentation of how traditional views of God as Father and Sovereign are too binding. I continued to pray, and she stopped her lecture a third time, shouting, "It must be the walls of this hotel, because I can't find the freedom to express myself fully!"

I found her confusion interesting, especially since she claimed to have mystical powers; she never was able to single me out of the audience, even though I was sitting in the second row directly in front of her. I began to wonder how so many people could be so mesmerized by obvious heresy.

The feminist movement has come a long way from the days when its parameters were easily defined.

TRADITIONALIST AND FEMINIST VIEWS

This chapter discusses the various camps within the feminist perspective and how each group uses, abuses, or misuses Scripture. To minister effectively to women today, we must know what is influencing their lives. Those influences are often subtle and sometimes blatant.

Feminism encompasses a broad spectrum of ideas, philosophies, and religious viewpoints. Some Christians have embraced the feminist cause entirely. Others reject it completely, angered by its heresies. Most Christians are somewhere in the middle, struggling to find a balance between the extremes, to separate the wheat of feminism from its abundant chaff. That search is especially difficult because of the volume and complexity of the issues and because of emotional overtones in the debate.

The term *feminist* designates those who wish to eliminate all gender-based roles in society. Their slogan is often, "Anatomy is not destiny." The term *traditionalist* refers to those who wish to maintain gender-based roles in society. "The traditionalist argues that gender is a valid basis for defining social (not to mention biological) roles, that males and females are not 'equal' in the sense of being interchangeable, and that society can and must observe gender differences."[1] The major organization of the traditionalist camp is the Council on Biblical Manhood and Womanhood (CBMW).[2]

Feminists can be divided into three groups. The first group, *secular feminists*, approaches feminism with a straightforward humanism that disavows God, revelation, and religion.

The second group, *liberal religious feminists*,[3] maintains various ties with the Judeo-Christian religious establishment. "Although their feminist agenda is virtually indistinguishable from that of their secular counterparts, it is usually couched in a liberal Jewish or Christian theological framework."[4] Rosemary Ruether says that contemporary liberal feminist theology rejects the idea of women's subordination based on natural inferiority, or order of creation, or priority in sin.[5]

82

Feminists in this group also say that since women are equal to men, they have a right to "equal access to education, professions, and political participation in society."[6] This group also assumes that the domination of men over women is sinful, and patriarchy is a sinful social system.[7] Originally all those who held feminist views supported an organization called the Evangelical Women's Caucus (EWC),[8] later called the Evangelical and Ecumenical Women's Caucus (EEWC). Its founding in 1974 marked the beginning of the contemporary biblical feminist movement.

A third group, *evangelical feminists*,[9] holds conservative views of the Bible and theology, but nevertheless embraces the feminist proposals to abolish gender-based roles in society, church, and home. Evangelical feminists believe that the Bible, which they consider authoritative, allows for feminist ideas when rightly understood. In 1986 a group of evangelical feminists resigned from the EWC and formed another biblical feminist group, Christians for Biblical Equality (CBE).[10]

The theological backbone of the evangelical feminist view is Galatians 3:28: "There is neither Jew nor Greek, slave nor free, male nor female, for you are all one in Christ Jesus." Paul Jewett, a prominent promoter of evangelical feminism, calls this verse "the Magna Carta of humanity."[11]

According to feminists, Galatians 3:28 teaches that God has created in Christ a whole new order of relationships, and that the hierarchical view of social relationships stems from the old order from the Fall. In the new order all discrimination based on race, economic status, or gender is to be eliminated. In Christ, relationships between men and women should transcend the male-female division, so that gender should be irrelevant in social roles and relationships.

Evangelical feminists insist that in Galatians 3:28 Paul was speaking about not only an equality of men and women in their standing before God, but also the practical outworking of that standing in society. Letha Scanzoni and Nancy Hardesty state, "Men and women do not lose their biological distinctives by becoming Christians, of course, but in the light of Galatians 3:28: 'All social distinctions between men and women should be erased in the church.'"[12]

Taking such a view of Galatians 3:28 places the feminists in apparent conflict with other passages in the New Testament that seem to teach that

Christians are to maintain gender-based roles. Evangelical feminists respond to this observation in one of three ways.

First, some feminists simply deny that the New Testament anywhere teaches a hierarchical model of male-female relationships. Evangelical feminists Herbert and Fern Miles write, "There is nothing in Ephesians 5 that would even remotely indicate that wives are responsible to submit to their husbands."[13] Most of the feminist writings handle biblical passages with a bit more subtlety and sophistication than this, but the basic impact remains the same: changing the meaning of the text from its traditional understanding to one that is more compatible with the feminist understanding of Galatians 3:28. Virginia Mollenkott maintains that the Bible was not wrong in recording Paul's thought processes, but that some of his statements are simply untrue, and some of his commands are obsolete.[14] Ruether suggests that Galatians 3:28 did not originate with Paul, but probably with a "pre-Pauline, Hellenistic Christian mission closely associated with the one Paul joined."[15]

Second, many feminists suggest that, although the New Testament writers sometimes taught a hierarchical model of male and female roles, those teachings are no longer binding on twentieth-century Christians. This approach attempts to separate the cultural and temporary in the New Testament from what is universal and timeless. Scanzoni and Hardesty claim that any interpretation of Scripture that attempts to "legitimate the power of a political ruler, a church authority, a husband, or any man on the basis of a descending hierarchy (God, man, woman, children, dogs, lizards, blueberries, thorns, rocks) are ignoring the thrust of Scripture."[16] Therefore, since feminists view the New Testament teaching of female subordination in the church and home as merely "a given historical social order," they dismiss it.

Third, a growing number of feminists—including some evangelicals—admit that Paul taught a hierarchical model of male-female relationships but believe he was simply wrong. Mollenkott says, "For Bible believers the problem is that the apostle Paul seems to contradict his own teachings and behavior concerning women, apparently because of inner conflicts between the rabbinical training he had received and the liberating insights of the gospel."[17] She adds that any passages that teach a hierarchy of men over women should be viewed as "distorted by the human instrument, reflecting merely Paul's rationalizations rather than God's truth."[18]

Galatians 3:28, however, says nothing explicitly whatsoever about how male-female relationships should be conducted in daily life. Paul was making a theological statement about the fundamental equality of male and female Christians in their standing before God. So any ideas about how this truth should work itself out in social relationships cannot be drawn from this verse.

Traditionalists do not claim that Galatians 3:28 is without social ramifications. They insist that the fundamental oneness in Christ of all Christians does carry profound implications for the way Christians are to relate to each other. Traditionalists depart from feminists, however, in specifying what those implications should be.

Feminists insist that the verse implies *all* gender-based roles must be eliminated. Traditionalists question this assumption, holding that this conclusion is not logically required. The arguments for equality and social hierarchy are not mutually exclusive. Just as equality roles coexist in the Trinity without conflict, so also may equality and hierarchy coexist in the church and the home. But, even in referring to the Trinity, changes in thinking have begun to appear. A National Council of Churches committee produced an *Inclusive Language Lectionary,* in which it attempted to eliminate gender identifications or restrictions in reference to either God or Jesus. For example, the title Son of Man is translated the "Human One," and Son of God is rendered "Child of God." The committee argued that these translations are defensible both linguistically and theologically.[19] But this change in the metaphor changes the meaning.

Traditionalists argue that the New Testament regulates, not eliminates, hierarchical roles, to prevent them from being abused. Wherever there is properly constituted authority, there is also the potential for abuse. As noted earlier, as a result of the Fall, men have tended to dominate women. With the coming of the Holy Spirit, this domineering situation is replaced by loving leadership. This authority is to be used in a way that honors Christ. So those in authority—husbands, elders, parents, employers—are instructed in how to use their God-given authority in a godly way. Conversely, those who find themselves under a properly constituted authority—wives, servants, children, members of the congregation, citizens, employees—are also told how to fulfill their roles in a godly way.

The result is not a society without authority/submission roles, but a social hierarchy, ordained by God and carried out in a manner that fulfills the teaching of Christ in Matthew 20:25–28: "You know that the rulers of the Gentiles lord it over them, and their high officials exercise authority over them. Not so with you. Instead, whoever wants to become great among you must be your servant, and whoever wants to be first must be your slave—just as the Son of Man did not come to be served, but to serve, and to give his life as a ransom for many."

Why do feminists insist on redrawing the pattern of New Testament teaching, despite the fact that it is unnecessary? Since Galatians 3:28 does not demand eliminating male-female roles in society, what does?[20]

Mary Kassian remarks that the feminist philosophy "adds a subtle, almost indiscernible twist to the basic Biblical truth of woman's worth. Feminism asserts that woman's worth is of such a nature that it gives her the right to discern, judge and govern that truth herself. It infuses women with the idea that God's teaching about the role of women must line up with their own perception and definition of equality and/or liberation."[21]

In 1963 Betty Friedan helped define modern feminism with her book *The Feminine Mystique*.[22] In 1968 Mary Daly wrote *The Church and the Second Sex*.[23] These were but parts of the current wave of a tide that has been encroaching on male dominion for over two hundred years. Yet that current wave is now broader and more powerful than any that went before, and it seems to be part of a worldwide trend. In the years ahead feminists will continue to seek to erase the distinctions between male and female. This creates a dilemma for modern Christians as to how to respond to feminism.

Some Christians sense that much in this movement should be embraced. We cannot deny that females have often been abused and oppressed at the hands of males. How could we not be angry at the prospect of a woman being paid a fraction of what a man earns for doing the very same work? We are all probably embarrassed at the words of Tertullian, who described woman with these words: "You are the devil's gateway; you are the unsealer of that (forbidden) tree; you are the first deserter of the divine law; you are she who persuaded him whom the devil was not valiant enough to attack. You destroyed so easily God's image, man. On account of your desert—that is, death—even the Son of God had to die."[24]

We are probably equally surprised when reminded that only since 1920, when the Nineteenth Amendment to the United States Constitution was adopted, have women in the United States had the right to vote. Most of us at one time or another have probably embraced unbiblical views that were harmful to women. Much of what feminists emphasize is to be praised and supported.

However, the worthy goals of the feminist movement are part of a structure of thought that is so antibiblical that the boundaries are difficult to determine.[25] Should Christians embrace the movement with its heresy, or reject it with its truth? Kassian calls it a "slippery slope," because a "provisional acceptance of a faulty presupposition will—if not for a certain individual, then certainly for the next generation—lead to its complete acceptance."[26]

DOCTRINAL ISSUES IN FEMINISM

Three important doctrines—Scripture, God, and humanity[27]—merit consideration in relation to feminism.

The Doctrine of Scripture

Our view of the Bible is crucial in determining how we approach the feminist debate today. Secular feminists, of course, disregard the Bible entirely, viewing it as an artifact of antiquity useful only in providing examples of how men have oppressed women through the years.[28] They rule out all attempts to appeal to the Bible.

Some liberal religious feminists differ greatly from the secular feminists' approach to the Bible. Some reject the Bible altogether as patriarchal. Separating herself from traditional biblical views, Mollenkott writes, "Gone are traditional Christianity's emphases on sin, guilt, and retribution; instead, we are empowered toward cocreatorship, welcomed to continual renewal on a continuous Great Non-Judgment Day."[29] Others attempt to keep some traditional biblical positions, but they interpret them from the feminist position.

Many liberal religious feminists say large portions of Scripture are irrelevant. And still others abandon the Scriptures altogether, like Mary Daly, who describes her departure as "the Self-Realizing of women who have broken free from the stranglehold of patriarchal religion, with its deadly symbols, its ill logic, its gynocidal laws and other poisonous paraphernalia."[30]

Modern concepts of biblical revelation lend themselves to a "pick-and-choose" approach that allows the interpreter to accept what seems compatible and to reject whatever seems extraneous. Liberal feminists usually do not base their arguments on biblical authority, since arguments from authority require the kind of Bible liberals do not accept.

To most modern liberal theologians, revelation must not be equated with the Bible. Rather, revelation is viewed as personal encounter with God's acts in history, preeminently in the act of God in Christ. The Bible may therefore be a fallible human witness to God's revelation in history, but it is not itself revelation. To the liberal all past Christian ideas, including those in the Bible, are open to evaluation, redefinition, or even rejection in light of fresh encounters with God's redemptive acts. Consequently revelation is never finished and complete; it is always continuous, unfolding, building out of the process of culture and experience.

With such a view of the Bible it should come as no surprise that liberal Christian feminists show little patience with attempts to establish biblical precepts or patterns as normative for contemporary Christians. The Bible is merely a human witness to God's dealings with His people in the past, not a "God-breathed" guidebook for the church today. To view the teachings of the Scriptures as God's will for all times is absurd, according to that view. Therefore liberal Christian feminists, although not ruling biblical arguments off limits, nevertheless set them aside as irrelevant whenever they contradict their own views.

Evangelical feminists typically take a much less critical approach to the Bible. Admittedly some are willing to question the Pauline genuineness of the Pastoral Epistles and the historicity of Genesis 2. For example, Paul Jewett raised doubts about Pauline authorship in some cases when he said, "All the Pauline texts supporting female subordination, both those that are directly from the apostle's pen and those that are indirectly so, appeal to the second creation narrative, Genesis 2:18–23, never to the first."[31]

Both Jewett and Mollenkott speak of the "story of Adam's rib" as "poetic narrative," "myth," or "saga," rather than history.

But the question remains, How do evangelical feminists line up their feminism with a commitment to the authority of the Bible? Since traditionalists, secular feminists, and most liberal religious feminists alike believe the Bible teaches submission of a wife to her husband and to male leadership in the church, how is it that evangelical feminists believe that the Bible, while authoritative, upholds feminism? They have proposed a variety of solutions.

First, some have attempted to solve the problem by arguing that both ancient and modern readers have been reading the subordination of women into the Bible rather than deriving it from the text.

Second, other evangelicals have suggested that the problems have to do with whether key biblical passages are relevant today. According to this argument, the cultural baggage of the Bible must be discarded rather than set up as normative. As David Scholer says, 1 Timothy "should be understood as an occasional ad hoc letter directed specifically toward enabling Timothy and the church to avoid and combat the false teachers and teaching in Ephesus."[32]

Third, some argue that even though the Bible does affirm the subordination of women, that aspect of biblical teaching is simply in error. This approach begins to blur the distinction between the evangelical and liberal feminists. In other words, not all the Bible is inerrant. Rather, God's Word is mingled with error contributed by human authors, and so the two must be sorted out.

Traditionally evangelicals have rejected such a view of the Bible, but evangelical feminists who resort to that means of lining up their feminism with conservative biblical commitments usually insist on retaining their evangelical credentials. Stanley Grenz takes the position that the biblical texts in question relate only to the culture of that day. He says that Paul placed no restrictions on women using their gifts in public worship, and that the apostle spoke only of the demeanor with which women were to serve. Grenz says that Paul did not want women who ministered to violate cultural norms and thereby bring the gospel under attack.[33]

Mary Evans also presents a cultural view of these passages when she says that just as the New Testament writers were deeply influenced by the Old, "it was inevitable that they, living in a particular cultural milieu, would be steeped in the concepts and conventions of their time which would thus govern the pattern of their thought and the meaning of their terminology."[34]

The Doctrine of God

For many feminists "the God of the ancient Christian creeds will not do."[35] Ruether says "an external redeemer is not necessary for this process of conversion, since we have not lost our true self rooted in God."[36]

To secular feminists, of course, egalitarianism—equality of men and women in every area of society—requires the elimination of God altogether. Since secular humanists believe individuals must be their own God, feminism flourishes in that environment. Mary Daly says that the courage to leave Christianity and all patriarchal religion is in fact a "living faith" that "propels women out of patriarchal religion, whereas blind faith in dead symbols keeps women lost/trapped inside its gynocidal, spirit-deadening maze."[37]

Liberal religious feminists, by contrast, are more interested in redefining God than in eliminating Him. But can God be redefined? In a "Re-imaging Conference" in 1993 women from various denominations all over the world met to talk and think about imagining God in different ways and to engage in worship that reflected such "re-imaging," specifically with regard to their understanding of deity.[38] To them God should not be thought of as "He." They say that thinking of God as masculine further evidences male-dominated patriarchal thinking. Feminists believe men have made God in their own image. Feminists resist thinking of God as "Father," "Master," "Lord," or "King."

With such open-ended pictures of deity the remaking of society is a constant priority for feminists.[39] God's purpose is always focused on liberating people from constraining stereotypes and from all forms of oppression. So according to this view the feminist movement is one of God's most noble causes. But there are no absolutes in a system of this kind. This is amazingly similar to Judges 21:25, which states, "In those days Israel had no king; everyone did as he saw fit." The relativistic society of the past is emerging once again.

The freedom to redefine God at will is a direct result of liberal views of revelation. How then do evangelical feminists, who claim they believe in the final authority of the Bible, manage the conflict between the biblical picture and their egalitarian views? The answer is that although evangelical feminists sometimes find their conservative view of God to be heavy baggage, their commitment to the inspiration of the Bible prevents them from casting it aside. Liberal feminists, on the other hand, find oppressive the biblical notion of a sovereign, immutable, personal God, whose design and will is to be obeyed by His creatures. They dismiss it as a typical projection of male domination.

A conservative view of Scripture, however, prevents such an easy dismissal, leaving evangelical feminists the uncertain task of balancing an ancient, biblical view of the Creator with a modern, egalitarian view of the creature. Since these two views do not mix easily, both the ancient writers and today's liberals seem more consistent in their assumptions than the evangelical feminists who attempt to blend the two.

In today's literature evangelical feminists usually ignore such doctrines as God's sovereignty, authority, and immutability, because those doctrines are less agreeable to their egalitarianism.[40] And, some of the more harsh egalitarian demands, such as the elimination of all authority/submission roles in society, are avoided or rejected. In this way the problems are minimized. But the main approach of evangelical feminists is to argue that in Christ a new order was instituted in which all roles based on gender were eliminated (Gal. 3:28). Egalitarianism, they say, is therefore a direct and necessary deduction from Christ's redemptive work, a deduction that transcends or supersedes whatever social patterns may have existed before. Jewett explains it this way: "The thought of the apostle, then, must be that in Christ the basic divisions which have threatened human fellowship, are done away."[41]

The Doctrine of Humanity

Psalm 8:4 asks, "What is man that you are mindful of him?" Secular feminists have little difficulty in responding to this question, but they can claim no authority but their own for the worth of their answer. People, they believe, can be whatever they want to be. But they insist that individuals be measured against no other yardstick than that of their own potential. And then there are those like Jenny Hammett, who claim that God can be defined by analyzing man: "If to be created in the image of God is to be created female and male, then one way to do a *logos* of God is by understanding what it is to be male and female. And perhaps then we might move beyond a God who is known for omnipotence."[42]

Liberal religious feminists often speak of people as God's creatures, made in the image of God, and even of God's work in history to bring people to their full potential. Yet beyond such God-language the views of the secular and religious feminists sound much the same.[43] What they share is a commitment to an egalitarian society that emphasizes unity rather than polarity, sameness rather than distinctiveness, wholeness (in their view) rather than dichotomy—a unisex community.

For both groups the goal is the transcendence of maleness and femaleness in the quest for a genderless ideal. All stereotypes in society that emphasize sexual differentiation are viewed as destructive and are to be resisted. According to feminists, the healthiest people—the ones most adaptable and capable of handling the fullest range of human experience—are those who can manifest both female and male responses. They draw from age-old ideas of mythology concerning Zeus, who split powerful male-female beings because they attacked the gods. Dualities represent disunion; they are unnatural and exist only to be overcome. Such crippling antitheses as object-subject, reason-emotion, male-female—each so indicative of the alienation of the human situation in general and of Western culture in particular—must be integrated and correlated to find the deeper wholeness and unity that undergirds them. Therefore feminists emphasize egalitarianism, interchangeability, and freedom from sex roles in the social realm. This results in attacks against traditional concepts of hierarchy, authority, and obedience.

The secular or liberal feminists' social views here are merely the visible manifestation of their deeper philosophical or theological commitments. The idea of God as Being and nonauthoritarian leads naturally to feminist conclusions. Even in the late 1970s radical feminists like Naomi Goldenberg predicted where feminism would take our culture once the Bible was discarded: "Surely new gods will be born. Since 'gods' always reflect the styles of behavior we see as possible . . . so must our pantheon [expand]."[44] In the words of Mollenkott, "After all, everyone else at their core is exactly who I am: undivided from God Herself, ultimately secure in a love that can never be broken. Whether or not we are able to recognize each other's holiness during this little life, I believe that eventually we all will rejoice together in the bliss of universal at-one-ment."[45]

Liberal feminists reject God as sovereign Father and Lord, saying that this concept leads to alienation, polarity, and hierarchy, and is responsible for much of the world's oppression.

Ruether says that Jesus' role in salvation becomes quite different in feminist theology. "Redemption cannot be done by one person for everyone else. No one person can become the 'collective human' whose actions accomplish a salvation that is then passively applied to everyone else. His story can model what we need to do, but it happens only when all of us do it for ourselves and with one another."[46] Of course, no one person can accomplish salvation for humanity—unless that person is God. The feminist perspective is fast approaching a denial of the deity of Christ.

So, how can evangelicals, who maintain traditional views of God, hold an unreserved feminism so deeply rooted in liberal ideas of God and reality? The answer must be that we cannot! Most evangelical feminists are not aware of the philosophical roots of their pleas for the elimination of gender-based roles. They have appropriated political and social goals uncritically and are now striving to overcome the resulting inconsistencies.

Jewett, an evangelical theologian, has attempted to avoid major inconsistencies by rejecting some of the more radical feminist ideas on the one hand and by straddling the fence on his evangelical views on the other. He rejects as unbiblical the concept of roles based on gender, but on the other hand, he states that some of Paul's teachings are in error. He says that "one can only suppose that the apostle's remarks in 1 Corinthians

14:34–35 reflect the rabbinic tradition which imposed silence on the woman in the synagogue as a sign of her subjection. The law enjoined silence upon the woman in public worship only in the sense that rabbinic authority so construed it by way of a general implication."[47]

The greatest difficulty for evangelical feminists is that in the end the Bible does teach sex roles, hierarchy, a husband's authority over his wife, and a wife's submission to her husband and to male church leadership. To be sure, the biblical versions of those concepts must be distinguished from both their sinful abuses throughout history and their representations as found in feminism. Liberals largely reject the biblical world-view and traditionalists largely embrace it. Only evangelical feminists attempt to have it both ways, pleading at once for a traditional theology and a feminist society.

The evangelical world-view, based on the Bible, includes the concepts of authority and hierarchy. God is the source of all authority (Rom. 13:1). This concept, woven throughout the entire Bible, is far from incidental. Most secular and liberal Christian feminists find this in the Bible as well, but they usually portray this biblical perspective as unattractively as possible and then reject it.

Humanistic society accepts a wide range of secular, humanistic, sometimes partially theological teachings that have one feature in common: the denial of the authority of a sovereign, personal Creator over man's existence. In this secularized society we have what Francis Schaeffer calls "sociological law" by which he means "law that has no fixed base but law in which a group of people decides what is sociologically good for society at the given moment; and what they arbitrarily decide becomes law."[48] In 1951, Frederick Moore Vinson, former Chief Justice of the U.S. Supreme Court, said, "Nothing is more certain in modern society than the principle that there are no absolutes."[49]

This humanistic rebellion against the authority of God is the cultural medium from which radical feminism springs and in which it thrives. Radical feminists do not want anyone to instruct them on who or what they ought to be. They want to define their existence for themselves. Dave Hunt and T. A. McMahon note that Arnold Toynbee, after studying civilizations across the whole span of history, concluded that self-worship was the paramount religion of mankind.[50] Historian Herbert Schlossberg said, "Exalting mankind to the status of deity therefore dates from the furthest reaches of antiquity, but its development into an ideology embracing the masses is a characteristic trait of modernity."[51]

A vivid reality of this is found in the so-called goddess movement. Its followers are encouraged to construct small altars in their homes to be used for meditation. At a Boston conference, women were told to use mirrors on their altars to represent the "Goddess." These mirrors would continually remind them that "they are the Goddess and that they have divine beauty, power and dignity."[52]

Results of These Doctrinal Views

Viewing the biblical picture of a divinely ordained male-female hierarchy as poisonous, secular feminists reject it with impassioned devotion. They cannot tolerate any concept of an original divine arrangement of roles to which humans are to conform. Instead, they are drawn to their own constructions of reality that conform more happily to their requirements, such as existentialism or Marxism. Holding to existentialism, Mary Daly insists that "the Deity can be better described as one's concept of ultimate reality and meaning; the power of being, as a process, not a person. We owe the church Nothing, since the church has given us precisely Nothing. We then see that we have Nothing to lose by Leaving."[53]

Likewise liberal Christian feminists reject the basic world-view of the Bible in favor of a more contemporary mind-set. Inevitably they, too, are drawn to theological assumptions that are more agreeable to their feminist ideologies.

To accept the radical feminist perspective of God, one must redefine Him—usually toward the impersonal. Revelation, if it exists, is viewed as an ongoing thing, discovered in the unfolding of human experience. The concept of an original divine will for creation is rejected in favor of a more fluid, evolutionary vision of reality. Ideas of hierarchy, authority, and submission to authority are totally rejected, and in their place appear an appropriate set of "god words" that promote egalitarianism, human rights, and the transcendence of sexual distinctions. Changes appearing in the *Inclusive Language Lectionary* are said to be perfectly defensible both linguistically and theologically.[54]

Many traditionalists believe that evangelical feminists have unknowingly bought into this package. The feminists' pleas for the discarding of all gender-based roles indicate that they have adopted not simply the secular movement's mind-set but also some aspects of its basically nonbiblical world-view as well. Since evangelical feminists do not reject the Bible, they are forced to attempt massive efforts of reinterpretation, first, by eliminating those aspects of the Scriptures that are hostile to feminism, and second, by making it appear that their cause is sanctioned in the Bible.

Traditionalists are aware that the biblical outlook on life appears outmoded by present-day standards. They too feel the societal pressure to conform to a more modern mind-set. Yet they are also aware that the rise and fall of intellectual history demonstrates that the world-view of any given culture or generation provides an extraordinarily fickle standard by which to measure truth. People of every age believe their view of the world is most reliable, and the present generation is no exception. Christians need to remember that modern thinking merely continues the age-old human tradition of suppressing the truth about God, as stated in Romans 1:18–23.

In advocating the elimination of all gender-based roles the evangelical feminists go too far. They have embraced a profoundly unbiblical ideology and are pressing it on the church. Traditionalists are convinced that they cannot stand by and let this happen.

Evangelical feminists do not appear to slow down their efforts, nor will traditionalists concede. How, then, will the conflict be resolved? We can only pray that both sides of the confrontation will handle themselves and the issues with honesty, integrity, and the balance that comes from attempting to "speak the truth in love."

Chapter Nine

Where Is Feminism Headed?

My husband, Trevor, grew up in a small town in west Texas. The church he attended decided to have a forty-year celebration and the elders invited the five men who had pastored the church in those years to return for a day of preaching and fellowship. We attended the all-day service, listening to the five men preach in the order in which they had pastored the church. The first preacher delivered a wonderfully sound, biblically accurate message that really touched our hearts. When the fifth man stepped to the pulpit, the contrast was amazing. The Word of God was never mentioned, and the message was on social issues.

The whispers that circulated around were filled with questions: "Where did the change occur?" "Why weren't we aware of how far away from the Word we've strayed?" The changes were gradual, and I'm certain that if the fifth pastor had been called to that church right after the first one, he wouldn't have been allowed to stay. The changes through the forty years were gradual and caught the people off guard.

I wonder if feminism has caught us off guard? We've come a long way from Friedan's social concern to the present-day goddess movement. Let's trace the major players in this field to see where we're headed if we stay on this course.

LEADING VOICES IN FEMINISM

Betty Friedan

In 1963 Betty Friedan wrote *The Feminine Mystique*, a book that started a revolution. Her book advanced the theory that American women had been trapped by the feminine mystique, which was the belief that the only desirable role for them was that of wife, mother, and housekeeper. Friedan said that a woman could not reach her potential as a complete human being unless she identified her problem and broke free.[1]

"Each suburban wife struggled with it alone. As she made the beds, shopped for groceries, matched slipcover material, ate peanut butter sandwiches with her children, chauffeured Cub Scouts and Brownies, lay beside her husband at night—she was afraid to ask even of herself the silent question—'Is this all?'"[2]

Friedan suggested that women who seemed to feel comfortable in this state were only denying themselves their true identity and self-actualization. According to her, "equality and human dignity are not possible for women if they are not able to earn."[3] She also said that when women have economic freedom, they have choices—to marry for love or to leave intolerable situations. Of course, in her push for "freedom of choice," the next step was a "woman's right to birth control and safe abortion; [and] the right to maternity leave and child-care centers if women did not want to retreat completely from adult society during the childbearing years."[4]

When Friedan founded the National Organization for Women (NOW) in 1965, she felt education would alleviate problems American women face and would help them find their potential. Her solution to women's dilemmas has several problems. First, she defines a woman's identity in terms of her work. "Today, a sense of worth and purpose is derived from a person's job. Therefore, if our jobs are unimportant; or if we have no job, we feel unimportant, worthless, without purpose."[5]

Housework, she says, cannot give women a sense of identity.[6] Friedan seems to assume that work outside the home is fulfilling and worthwhile, whereas work within the home is unfulfilling and not worthwhile. She condemns housework because it is repetitive and boring; such a dull routine, she says, stifles a person's growth. She seems unaware that almost all jobs have boring, repetitive aspects.

When I was in China in 1985, I visited some factories where women sat for long periods of time at sewing machines, making one specific piece of a garment. I watched one woman make collars for shirts. Each collar, when finished, was still attached to the previous one by a string as it fell into a basket beneath the machine. At least a hundred collars were in her basket. As I watched, she never looked up, but continued her repetitious task. I wondered if she was ever permitted to see the finished garment. And yet, according to Friedan, this little woman was "free" because she was employed outside the home.

Feminism started with Friedan telling women they were dissatisfied with their lives (even though they might not have been aware if it), and that the unified voice within women was shouting, "I want something more than my husband and my children and my home."[7] Did they ever dream that they were shouting for a different god?

Letty Russell

Letty Russell said she spent her entire adult life "trying to figure out how to subvert the church into being the church."[8] She was one of the first women to be ordained by the Presbyterian church. She worked in the East Harlem Protestant Parish in the early 1960s, where she attempted to find a way to "make the church into an 'open circle' of those gathered in Christ's name for service to and with others."[9] She then became a professor of theology at Yale Divinity School. Her theological methodology is based on viewing everything from the "norm of the New Creation, by which we must judge the Bible, Christian theology, and social struggles."[10]

Mary Daly

Some, like Mary Daly, have switched camps entirely, going from a theologically liberal feminist perspective to a totally secular view. In the early 1960s Daly received two doctorates from the University of Fribourg, Switzerland, one in theology and one in philosophy. In 1971 she moved from classifying herself as a "radical Catholic" to a "postchristian feminist."[11] At that time she wrote her second book, *Beyond God the Father: Toward a Philosophy of Women's Liberation*. Because of this book Daly was fired from her faculty position at the Jesuit-run Boston College, but she was rehired and given tenure because of the pressure placed on the college from individuals in the feminist movement throughout the world.[12] Since that time she has written numerous books, totally separating herself from any pretense of clinging to the church.[13] Her latest book, *Outercourse: The Be-Dazzling Voyage*, presents her journey into radical feminism.[14] She has a tremendous following and is frequently a keynote speaker at conferences in support of the feminist perspective.

Rosemary Radford Ruether

Rosemary Ruether is Georgia Harkness Professor of Theology at Garrett-Evangelical Theological Seminary in Evanston, Illinois. Among her two dozen books are *Faith and Fratricide* (1974), *Sexism and God-Talk* (1983), *Women Church* (1986), *Gaia and God* (1992), and *Women Healing Earth* (1996).

Ruether has what she calls an "all-embracing" philosophy as a base for her theological assumptions. She says that she can see "both positive and negative aspects of the Jewish and Christian traditions and the ancient pagan traditions, and [is] skeptical of exclusivistic views on either side; that is, either Christians who see the biblical tradition as totally superior to inferior paganism, or feminist neo-pagans who regard the biblical traditions as totally evil, in contrast to a paganism imagined to be totally pro-woman in harmony with nature."[15] She says God is not a "being removed from creation, ruling it from outside in the manner of a patriarchal ruler; he is the source of being that underlies creation."[16] She also believes that some people may fail to reach their potential. It is this interpretation of "reality" that underlies her feminist ecological liberation theology.[17]

Carter Heyward

Carter Heyward was thrust into the American religious arena in 1974 when she and ten other Episcopalian women were ordained as priests by three retired bishops. This was accepted by the national convention of the Episcopalian Church in 1976, and now the American Episcopal Church has several thousand women priests and many bishops. She believes that male domination is "the primary systemic and ideological expression of sin."[18] Ruether explains that for Heyward, redemption encompasses "all expressions of human creativity that break through disconnecting and dominating relations and spark experiences of mutual relation, even if partially or momentarily."[19] She believes that this theology of "mutual relation" must ultimately "reshape the model of God and God's relation to us. God is not a separate power or being over against us, situated in some space outside of the world, disconnected from reciprocity with us. Rather, God is the ground of mutual relation."[20]

Delores Williams

Delores Williams is an African American woman who grew up in Kentucky and was active in the civil rights movement. She did her doctoral work at Union Theological Seminary, New York, where she now teaches as a professor of theology and culture. She questions "the manner in which the African-American community has accepted the Hebrew Bible as analogous to their own story, rather than writing their own story as canon or at least making their own story a more explicit norm for judging the adequacy of biblical models."[21] To Williams, redemption must be considered in terms of the experiences of black women's oppression and their struggle for survival and quality of life. Her basic theology can be summed up with these words: "Black women encounter a redeeming God, not through Christ's sufferings on the cross, but in wilderness experiences in which they find a God and a relationship with Jesus that has empowered them to embrace their own power and integrity."[22]

Paul K. Jewett

Paul Jewett, professor of systematic theology at Fuller Theological Seminary, considers himself an evangelical feminist. He rejects the argument for female subordination as being "incompatible with (a) the biblical narratives of Man's creation, (b) the revelation which is given us in the life of Jesus, and (c) Paul's fundamental statement of Christian liberty in the Epistle to the Galatians."[23] He claims that "any view which subordinates the woman to the man is not analogous to but incongruous with this fundamental teaching of both the Old and the New Testaments."[24]

Jewett says Paul's words in 1 Corinthians 14:34–35 mirror the rabbinic tradition, which imposed silence on women in the synagogue as a sign of their subjection. Jewett even considers plausible the suggestion that someone other than Paul wrote this section.[25] To resolve this apparent difficulty Jewett says that "one must recognize the human as well as the divine quality of Scripture."[26]

Virginia Ramey Mollenkott

Virginia Mollenkott is professor of English at William Paterson College of Wayne, New Jersey. She has authored numerous books, including *The Divine Feminine* (1983), *Is the Homosexual My Neighbor?* (1978), and *Women, Men, and the Bible* (1977), and she wrote the foreword to Jewett's book, *Man as Male and Female*. She has moved from calling herself a fundamentalist to embracing a totally secular view of feminism. She writes some shocking words in her book *Sensuous Spirituality*:

> So how does a fundamentalist who believes she is essentially and totally depraved become transformed into a person who knows she is an innocent spiritual being who is temporarily having human experiences? I experienced a reality that was even better than that: like my Elder Brother, Jesus, I am a sinless Self traveling through eternity and temporarily having human experiences in a body known as Virginia Ramey Mollenkott. After all, everyone else at their core is exactly who I am: undivided from God Herself, ultimately secure in a love that can never be broken. Whether or not we are able to recognize each other's holiness during this little life, I believe that eventually we all will rejoice together in the bliss of universal at-one-ment.[27]

Letha Dawson Scanzoni and Nancy A. Hardesty

Letha Scanzoni attended Moody Bible Institute, and Nancy Hardesty went to Wheaton College. They are two of the founders of the Evangelical

Women's Caucus. Three editions of their book, *All We're Meant to Be,* have been published (1974, 1986, 1992). In this book they say that the two accounts of creation (Gen. 1:1–2:3 and 2:4–3:24) are contradictory[28] and that in the past Christians have built theology on the second account while ignoring the first.[29] They assume that Paul based his views on only half of the story—Genesis 2. In addition, they say that Paul made a "theological leap from Genesis 2 to woman's subordination" in 1 Corinthians 11:8–9, which is not supported by the Genesis text.[30] They classify themselves as "evangelical," which means a commitment to the authority of Scripture and a belief in the importance of a personal relationship with Jesus Christ as Savior and Lord.[31] And yet they also claim that it is possible to speak of God without using male pronouns.[32] Hardesty wrote the book *Inclusive Language in the Church* (1986) to address this topic.

THE FEMINIST SPIRITUALITY MOVEMENT

In recent years a number of women in North America and Western Europe have become deeply involved in the so-called feminist spirituality movement. This new religious system began in the 1970s. As of yet, there are "no official sacred texts, no absolute leaders, no required affirmations of faith, no membership dues, and no undisputed agenda of beliefs and rituals."[33] Their theological and ritual focus is the celebration of womanhood.[34]

The women involved in this movement are fully aware that they are creating a new religion, and so one of their most important hurdles is the "search for authenticity," which they attempt to trace back to "archeology (status of ancient goddesses), anthropology (studies of primitive cultures in which women are less oppressed than in modern society), history (reports of persecution of women throughout the ages), literary analysis (of books by women authors), and psychology (Kristeva, Jung, Melanie Klein, and others)."[35] This was foreseen back in the 1970s when Naomi Goldenberg said, "A society that accepted large numbers of women as religious leaders would be too different from the biblical world to find the book [Scripture] relevant, let alone look to it for inspiration. God is going to change. We women are going to bring an end to God."[36]

Once a person walks away from the truths of God's Word, a whole gamut of options are open for a society in which there are no absolutes.

Many people today have embraced this movement.[37] A large core of spiritual feminists identify themselves as witches and belong to organized covens. Goldenberg notes that witchcraft is the first modern theistic religion to conceive of its deity mainly as an internal set of images and attitudes.[38] They practice a religion that places divinity within the person. (Wasn't this Satan's offer to Eve in the Garden?) Still other spiritual feminists belong to ritual or study groups that do not identify with Wicca (witch) religion.[39] What is troublesome about this movement is that many have retained affiliation with the Jewish or Christian group in which they were raised, in order to try to bring about feminist change within mainstream Jewish or Christian denominations.[40]

One name, prominent among feminist ranks, is that of Zsuzsanna Emese Budapest, the first witch in the United States to put feminism together with witchcraft. She began the "feminist spirituality movement," also known as the "Goddess Movement."[41] Her first book, published in 1976, *The Feminist Book of Lights and Shadows*, received wide readership and later was expanded into a larger volume called *The Holy Book of Women's Mysteries* (1984).

Budapest became the high priestess of the first feminist coven called the "Susan B. Anthony Coven Number 1," a role model for the country with many more feminist covens to follow. She chose to name her coven after Anthony, who said she wouldn't go to either heaven or hell at her death until the women's movement succeeded. "The Susan B. Anthony American coin (minted by the U.S. Department of the Treasury), puts Budapest's coven symbol in the pockets of every American."[42] She had the first "Goddess" cable TV show, entitled *Thirteenth Heaven*.

Her latest books are *The Grandmother of Time* (1989), *Grandmother Moon* (1990), and *The Goddess in the Office* (1992). Writers who promote this movement are usually prolific; their literature includes novels, diaries, descriptions of rituals, sacred histories, and philosophical treatises. Yet none of these writings is considered canonical.[43]

Margot Adler is a journalist at National Public Radio and the author of *Drawing Down the Moon: Witches, Druids, Goddess-Worshipers and Other Pagans in America Today* (1986). With more than 100,000 copies in print, the book still sells more than 10,000 copies a year. Granddaughter of psychoanalyst Alfred Adler, Margot Adler is an elder with Covenant of the Goddess. She says, "I think it would be fair to say that none of this would have happened to me if I hadn't been hit over the head in the seventh grade by studying the gods Artemis and Athena. This was the late 1950s, and there weren't a lot of powerful images of women. What was interesting was we studied Greece for a whole year, and this was my religion. But I think way down deep I didn't want to worship these goddesses—I wanted to BE them."[44]

Another strong voice is from a highly quoted priestess of the "Old Religion of the Goddess," Miriam Simos. She is a witch, a religious leader, a writer, counselor, and women's spirituality superstar known as "Starhawk."[45] She claims that those in the goddess movement highly value diversity because they see it evidenced in nature and in a polytheistic world-view which allows for many powers or images of divinity.[46] "Individual conscience—itself a manifestation of the Goddess—is the final court of appeals, above codified laws or hierarchical proclamations."[47] Many feminists look to Simos as a role model. Geela Raphael says, "Starhawk is a spiritual leader, a women's spirituality leader. As a potential rabbi wanting to be a spiritual leader, I want to see as many role models as I can. Her form of non-hierarchical religion can be used in more traditional practice."[48] In her book *The Spiral Dance* she presents an overview of the "re-emergence of witchcraft as a goddess-worshipping religion."[49]

Linda Pinty, minister at the First Parish Church of Unitarian Universalists in Cambridge and one of the cofounders of CUUPS (the Covenant of Unitarian Universalist Pagans), says she was brought up a Baptist in Michigan but left the church in her late teens. She said that the neopagan movement brought a lot of things together for her, and that it offered her a much healthier and holistic way of experiencing ecstasy about life and the goodness of creation. In neopaganism a need to "heal" the earth is prominent; adherents feel it is important to take care of Mother Earth.[50]

Diann Neu, a graduate of the Graduate School of Theology, Berkeley, is cofounder with Mary Hunt of WATER (Women's Alliance for Theology, Ethics, and Ritual).[51] Neu claims that this alliance of Christian and Jewish women can promote a feminist interpretation of religious rituals. This organization publishes a newsletter; presents workshops, conferences, and lectures; holds ecumenical monthly breakfasts for women in ministry; and serves as an all-purpose resource of information on feminism.

At the All Souls Church in the Washington, D.C., area a small group of women are currently investigating women's religious history each Sunday afternoon through "Cakes for the Queen of Heaven," a ten-part correspondence course available through the Unitarian Universalist Church. Their argument is this: "We do have a different perspective—it has to do with the human context and human relationships. If women are not cognizant of their spiritual history, they are missing out on a more complete identity that can help form our ideas of who we are and what we want to do in this world and how we're going to do it."[52]

The name "Cakes for the Queen of Heaven" comes from Jeremiah 7. God condemned Israel for worshiping false gods and then running to Him and crying, "'We are safe'—safe to do all these detestable things" (7:10). Then Jeremiah said, "The children gather wood, the fathers light the fire, and the women knead the dough and make cakes of bread for the Queen of Heaven" (7:18), the Assyrian pagan goddess Ishtar. When Jeremiah confronted them about this great sin, the men replied, "We will not listen to the message you have spoken to us in the name of the LORD! We will certainly do everything we said we would: We will burn incense to the Queen of Heaven and will pour out drink offerings to her just as we and our fathers, our kings and our officials did in the towns of Judah and in the streets of Jerusalem. At that time we had plenty of food and were well off and suffered no harm. But ever since we stopped burning incense to the Queen of Heaven and pouring out drink offerings to her, we have had nothing and have been perishing by sword and famine" (44:16–18).

Margot Adler says that present-day neopaganism "antedates Christianity and monotheism."[53]

Parallel to the feminist spirituality movement—which has attracted mostly white, middle-class women—the Womanist movement has developed among black women. Cheryl Sanders offers the following succinct definition: "The womanist is a black feminist who is audacious, willful and serious; loves and prefers women, but also may love men; is committed to the survival and wholeness of entire people, and is universalist, capable, all loving, and deep."[54]

Womanist theology draws on secular feminism, Christianity, the writings of Alice Walker (author of *The Color Purple*), and African-American folk culture. Unlike white feminist spirituality, which is often separatist and anti-male, the Womanist movement affirms black women's "historic connection with men through love and through a shared struggle for survival and for productive quality of life."[55]

Diana Hayes, professor of theology at Georgetown University, sees herself more as a womanist than a feminist. "Within Christianity, theology and spirituality have been male oriented, male dominated, because they are the ones articulating it. . . . So the challenge has been to . . . have the men who dominate theological circles realize that they cannot speak for the rest of the human race. Women do not think or act the way men do. Therefore our spirituality will not be the same as men's."[56]

Womanists are challenging the feminist movement in the same way feminists have been challenging the church.

Both feminist spirituality and womanism differ from contemporary mainstream Christianity and from American civil religion in several ways. These women's religions embrace nonmaterialistic value systems, decentralized organizations, ongoing revelation, and female images of divinity.[57]

Feminists "practice a religion that places divinity or supernatural power within the person."[58] Satan's promise of deity to Eve in the Garden is once again being offered to us, and many are accepting the offer. But rebellion against God brings death, not deity!

More than two decades ago radical feminist Naomi Goldenberg observed that "the feminist movement in Western culture is engaged in the slow execution of Christ and Yahweh. Yet very few of the women and men now working for sexual equality within Christianity and Judaism realize the extent of their heresy."[59]

Many things that radical feminists are advocating repeat what the surrounding nations of ancient Israel practiced. These things were abominable to the Lord. We need to heed God's warnings against the practices of heathen nations when He said to Israel, "If your very own brother, or your son or daughter, or the wife you love, or your closest friend secretly entices you, saying, 'Let us go and worship other gods' . . . do not yield to him or listen to him" (Deut. 13:6–8).

Part Three

Ministering to
Today's Women

Chapter Ten

Helping Women
Live Life to the Fullest

W omen are usually exposed to faster rates of change and instability in their lives than men, with the juggling of jobs, taking care of children, and tending to household needs. They tend to be more vulnerable to life-cycle stresses because of their greater emotional involvement in the lives of those around them. Many women are heavily involved in a wider network of people for whom they feel responsible. Their role overload leaves them burdened when faced with unpredictable stresses, such as illness, divorce, or unemployment. This means they are doubly stressed—they are exposed to more network stresses and are more emotionally responsive to them.

In recent years women have been marrying later because they are "less likely to see marriage as their central life experience."[1] Those with more education and income are more likely to divorce and least likely to remarry; this contrasts with men, among whom the wealthiest and best educated are the most likely to stay married or to remarry quickly. Women who are divorced suffer an average income drop of 40 percent, whereas the man's income rises on an average of 17 percent. National census surveys inform us that 75 percent of the poor in our country are women or children, mostly living in one-parent households. After divorce, men have a much larger pool of marriageable spouses from whom to choose another wife. In first marriages the average wife is two years younger than her husband; for second marriages the age difference is slightly over three years.[2]

Traditionally, women have been held responsible for the maintenance of family relationships and for all caretaking: for their husbands, their children, their parents, their husband's parents, and any other sick or dependent family members. Many women in their fifties and sixties are providing in-home care to an elderly relative. Usually one daughter or a daughter-in-law has the primary care of an elderly mother. Clearly, caregiving for the very old (who are mostly women) is primarily a woman's issue. As more women join the labor force, they are unavailable for caretaking without extreme difficulty. At present more than half of all women between the ages of forty-five and sixty-four are working outside the home, and most of them are employed full-time. With more and more four-generation families on the scene, the caregivers may themselves be elderly and struggling with declining functioning.[3] So today's middle-aged women are caught in a "dependency squeeze" between their parents and their children. We need to look at these variables in women's lives to determine how best to walk beside them when needed.

THE IMPORTANCE OF CONTEXTS

We all know how important it is to look at Scripture in context, that is, to look at a particular verse in relation to the verses immediately before and after it, in order to arrive at its true meaning. To interpret God's Word accurately we must consider each verse or group of verses in its historical, cultural, grammatical, and theological setting.

And so it is with people. We cannot fully understand their problems without considering the contexts of those problems. To get the whole picture we need to avoid seeing them in isolation. To counsel a woman well, it is important to understand her historical background. In what kind of family did she grow up? What were her parents like? How did they express affection to her? Did they experience conflicts? How did they resolve them? What kind of boundaries did her family have? To which parent would she go if she had a problem? Her cultural or social milieu should also be considered. In what predominant culture did she grow up? What was her social status? With whom does she associate? How does she perceive her world?

PRINCIPLES THAT GUIDE RELATIONSHIPS

In my counseling I have concluded that at least three factors influence a person's present relationships. *First, present relationships are influenced by how effectively we have resolved issues in our upbringing.* If a person still has unresolved problems with members of the family of his or her origin, that individual will have difficulty with relationships today. Paul encouraged us to put the past behind us. "But one thing I do: Forgetting what is behind [I strain] toward what is ahead" (Phil. 3:13).

Not dealing with unresolved issues usually narrows a person's capacity to be free from the past; those issues keep protruding into the present. I was once working with a couple who were experiencing some marital difficulty. Both husband and wife worked hard; they had several children, a limited budget, and very few discretionary minutes each day. One afternoon the husband came home from school a little early and looked around to see what he could do for his wife to show her his love for her. He decided that the kitchen floor, which was very dirty, would be the object of his labor; so he got out the mop, soaped it up, and scrubbed the floor until it was spotless. He then wrung out the mop, placed it in the kitchen sink, and began his studies.

When his tired wife came home from work, what do you think she saw? The mop in the kitchen sink! Her very words were, "No idiot would put a dirty mop in the kitchen sink where only dishes belong!" After some discussion we discovered that in her family her parents had rigid rules, one of which was "what went where"—and mops always went in the closet. Once she realized what had precipitated her anger, she was able to resolve it and accept her husband's kind gesture. It is truly amazing how genuine understanding of an issue can open the door to resolution.

Second, speaking words isn't the only way a person communicates. A person may not say anything, but that doesn't mean he or she isn't communicating. Much of our communication, in fact, is nonverbal. Our body language—facial expressions, frowning, smiling, glaring, shrugging the shoulders, sighing, slamming doors, showing other signs of disgust—communicates certain feelings.

Sometimes silence says much more than words ever could. When I am counseling a couple who have a strained relationship, they will usually come into my office and choose to sit as far away from each other as possible. When this happens, I can't look at both of them at the same time, so I usually ask them to sit together on the couch. Most often one of them (usually the woman) will grab a pillow and either hold it or place it between them. This communication is done without a word.

Third, we cannot act in isolation. What we do and who we are affects others. Our contexts include our parents and siblings, our spouse and children, business associates, friends at church and elsewhere, and neighbors. When we are acting within one arena, we are still affected by the other spheres of influence in our lives. If a husband or wife has problems at work, those frustrations are usually carried home and influence the family.

So stress comes into relationships from many directions as people interact within their various contexts. In the past, stress was viewed as an individual thing—something that appeared in isolation in one person's life. We used to label things as "his" problem or "her" problem—never looking at the "problem" as belonging to the entire system, their various contexts. We say, "My husband is anxious or stressed," or, "My wife is angry or depressed." We seldom stop to say, "*Our family* is stressed or in pain or full of anger." It's amazing how a person's stress level has the strangest way of showing up in his or her mate, or in the "bloodstream" of the children. Children have a wonderful way of being less inhibited, and they will often act out their parents' problems, sometimes harming themselves in the process. The more we can view our situations as part of a whole, the more we will be able to resolve and change some of the patterns that place stress on the family. This certainly does not eliminate individual responsibility, but it is saying that we cannot act in isolation.

A person's actions often don't make sense when viewed in isolation out of context. One of my favorite ways of demonstrating this point is to show students a four-frame cartoon script on an overhead projector with the first three frames covered and the fourth frame showing an older woman saying to a young woman, "I think *I'll* have myself another one of them." I ask my students to tell me what the old woman is talking about. They come up with all sorts of answers, from "another piece of pie or cake" to "another husband." After they have brainstormed on the possibilities, I put the cartoon on an overhead projector with the first three frames *un*covered. In the first frame the older woman says, "I think it's so wonderful that you're going to have a baby!" "Thank you, Miss Dolores!" Second frame: The older woman says, "I love babies." "Me too!" replies the young woman. Third frame: The older woman repeats, "I really, really love babies!" And then in the fourth frame she says, "I think *I'll* have myself another one of them."

The more you attempt to help others work through their problems, the more you see how they are involved in and influenced by various contexts. We need to think "systemically," that is, to see how one or more factors affect the total person and his or her environment. If you treat garden plants with a systemic insecticide or fertilizer, you know that it will come up through the roots and affect the entire plant—leaves, stems, and all. Similarly the problems of one family member can influence the entire family—systemically.

A husband once told me that he yelled at his wife because she pouted so much, and the wife said that she pouted because her husband yelled at her. Once the cycle started, it was difficult to determine which came first. The couple's actions are merely part of a pattern of interactions.

We rarely can see linear cause and effect, saying that because "A" happened, "B" will automatically result. But if this were the case, we could come up with grocery lists for a perfect marriage, raising perfect children, and living in a perfect environment.

Things happen because of a multiplicity of variables interacting within a given context. If we could return to a sinless state before the Fall in God's perfect environment, we could return to a simplistic cause-and-effect scenario. But sin is ever present, and we find ourselves saying with Paul in Romans 7:15, "I do not understand what I do. For what I want to do I do not do, but what I hate I do."

Looking at problems as the result of the way a whole system works is called circular causality. This works the same if we are looking at family problems like anorexia, bad study habits, obesity, or alcoholism. These symptoms develop within context. The individuals are still responsible for their own actions, but you can understand them better by looking at them in context. If you treat the individual problem in isolation without understanding what part it plays in the overall system, another problem will possibly appear somewhere else in the system. That's because families under stress will show that stress through many different channels.

Instead of viewing the family member with the "obvious" symptom as the "sick one," we need to see that person as the one in whom the *family's* problem has surfaced. In a child it could take the form of excessive bed-wetting, hyperactivity, school failures, drugs, or obesity; in a spouse it could be excessive drinking, depression, chronic ailments, or perhaps a heart condition; in an aged member of the family it could show up as confusion or senility.

One time a couple came to me for counseling because their youngest boy began to wet his pants at school in the first grade. The parents had tried everything to overcome this problem, and in frustration they came for help. After hearing their story and watching the family interact, I assigned the father the task of taking his wife out on a date once each week. He said, "My son is the problem; fix him." I told him he would have to trust me on this one, so he reluctantly followed my assignment.

My rationale behind the assignment was this: The little boy was the last in line of several children. The mother was sending unconscious messages to him that she was out of her "mom job" and didn't know what to do with herself. So he rescued her by returning to childish practices. Once he stopped receiving those messages, he could continue to grow up because Dad was caring for Mom.

When one part of the family is treated in isolation from its interconnections with another part, as though the problem were solely self-contained, fundamental change is difficult to introduce.[4] In the family emotional system, when an unresolved problem is isolated in one of its members and fixed there by diagnosis (labeling), it enables the rest of the family to "purify" itself by locating the source of its "disease" in the problem of the identified person. By keeping the focus on one of its members, the family denies the very issues that contributed to one of its members being symptomatic, even if it ultimately harms the entire family.

When looking at the family in its historical context, we are looking at the extended family system over several generations. The influence of a person's family of origin has significance for his or her present life. Specific patterns of behavior, perceptions, and thinking, as well as specific issues (for example, sex, money, drinking, health), have an uncanny way of reappearing.

The way we deal with issues started way back in our families while we were growing up. It's an interesting fact that as adults we are attracted to individuals who take us back to childhood. It's as though we are getting another opportunity to resolve some of those issues. If we find ourselves overreacting to present circumstances, it might be coming from some learned response from the past. The problem with this is that we usually don't think, "Oh, I'm reacting this way because of something from my childhood." Instead, we find ourselves feeling that we are right and our spouse is obviously wrong. And then the emotional distance begins, and distance in the marriage increases.

DEVELOPING GOOD COMMUNICATION SKILLS

Learning to communicate well in any relationship takes commitment, practice, understanding, patience, and the willingness to be vulnerable. Marriage partners need to model Christ's relationship with the church. The problem with most marriages is that many of these ingredients are missing. In Christian marriages we start with commitment to the marriage—but not commitment to change in order to make the marriage stronger. In many areas this is because we don't think there is a need for change; after all, we bring into a marriage our own preconceived ideas of ourselves, and how we respond to another individual is basically a learned mind-set from childhood and from, of course, our sin natures. Personalities are like printer's templates used to stamp letters on a page. We come with our unique template—but so do our mates. When those two templates are put together into the crucible called marriage, that's when the cycle of interaction in relationships starts, and I might add, the problems.

So we cannot excuse ourselves by saying we did a particular thing because our mates did something. Life doesn't work that way. Rather it's that we are responding to a situation, which in return was a response to another situation, which was also a response to a situation, and on and on. How problems persist is more important than how they originated, and their persistence depends mainly on social interaction, with the behavior of one person both stimulated and shaped by the response of others. What people do in order to control, prevent, or eliminate a problem usually plays a crucial role in perpetuating it. Thus knowing the problem helps in reaching the solution. A problem then consists of a vicious cycle between some behavior someone considers undesirable (the complaint) and some other behavior intended to modify or eliminate it (the attempted solution). In other words, individuals get stuck between a problem and another individual. If we can help people step away from this triangle, resolution is often possible. If you can get a married couple to respond differently, then the problem will often take care of itself.

In my counseling of couples I have found that the biggest threat to developing closeness between a couple—and the thing that is the greatest contributor to distance—is "time" commitment. It takes time to develop anything worthwhile. We say our mates are important, but when we have to choose between our work—especially when it's related to the Lord's work—and developing our marriage relationship, we usually choose our work. What we have failed to understand along the way is that our marriages are the Lord's work—and if we fail there, our public ministries will suffer also. Christian workers spend so much time giving to others that our families tend to get what's left of us, and often that is very little. Our emotional banks only have so much from which to draw, and we often choose to spend their contents in the public eye. Life is full of demands—whether those demands are built around preparation for one's ministry or actually participating in that ministry.

To make a difference in relationships it is necessary to set aside time with each other—time to learn what the other is like, how the other thinks, what the other desires. But then this requires that we become vulnerable, and that is often threatening. Talking "about" issues keeps us at a distance from personal involvement. It's easier to stand up in front of a woman's group and speak about good marriages than it is to be involved in working on our own marriages. In fact it's easier to talk about anything than to be personally involved. But if we are to be all God intended for us, we must make the effort, both in our marriages and in all our relationships.

Good communication skills are important for any healthy relationship. And of course, the most important relationship we have is with the Lord. Learn how to communicate on an intimate level with Him. Learn how to talk with Him and let Him communicate with you through His Word. If we really believe that the Scriptures are God's Word to us, we must spend more time there. You can't have good relationships with others until you have developed your relationship with God. From Him you can learn how to listen, how to seek forgiveness, how to praise, and how to put others' needs above your own. Here are eight important principles for communicating meaningfully with your spouse, your children, your coworkers, your friends.

First, set aside thirty minutes each day in which only you and your spouse are together, without any distractions. Sit and face each other, and allow fifteen minutes each to share what's important to you. As your partner shares, practice listening—really listening, without judgment, without criticism, without planning what you will say next—just listening. Then, as you take your turn, learn to share a part of yourself that's difficult to reveal—perhaps fears, longings, or areas of emptiness. Practice pointing out things you really enjoy about the relationship, staying away from negatives at this time.

Good marriages take time to develop—they don't just happen. Once I was counseling a young couple who were experiencing great difficulties in their marriage. I asked them to participate in a communicating exercise in my office, in which they were allowed to express whatever was on their hearts—positive or negative. I asked the wife to face her husband and tell him what was on her heart, what she was feeling, the areas in which she was feeling the most pain. With tears streaming down her face, she poured out her heart to him for about ten minutes. When she finished, I turned to the husband and said, "Now, I want you to look at your wife and tell her in your own words what she just said to you." He sat there with a stunned look on his face, unable to say a thing for a moment. Then he said, "I wasn't listening to her because I thought you were going to ask me to share what was on my heart, and I was formulating my thoughts while she was talking." The wife burst into tears again because her main complaint was, "You never listen to me!"

Second, learn how to handle anger appropriately. Ephesians 4:26–27 says,

"In your anger do not sin: Do not let the sun go down while you are still angry, and do not give the devil a foothold." This implies that anger of itself is not sin. It's how we handle that anger that makes it sin. If we harbor anger in our hearts, it becomes bitterness, and bitterness is sin (Heb. 12:15). A display of anger can be appropriate or inappropriate. Inappropriate anger is directed at another person and attempts to tear down character, rather than being directed at a particular situation. Some couples have told me that once they get into a heated argument, they often pull out all stops to "win the argument." But is there a winner in this kind of argument?

Words are powerful tools which can easily be used to harm. Once they are out there, they can't be retracted. The old saying, "Sticks and stones can break my bones, but words will never hurt me," couldn't be further from the truth. We don't forget words spoken in love or hate. "The tongue also is a fire, a world of evil among the parts of the body. It corrupts the whole person, sets the whole course of his life on fire, and is itself set on fire by hell. . . . Out of the same mouth come praise and cursing. My brothers, this should not be" (James 3:6, 10). We certainly need to teach women how to evidence self-control in matters of the tongue. So often, we women have resorted to verbal battles because sometimes we are more adept in this arena.

Third, learn to express yourself in the first person singular. We should express our feelings like this: "I am hurt by what happened today." "I feel left out." "I am angry at what happened." But what we usually say is, "You hurt me." "You left me out." "You make me mad." Whenever we say "you," we are attacking the other person, blaming him for our feelings or actions. This usually puts up a wall of defense to the attack, and nothing is solved. It is far more productive when we can reword our thoughts to say something like, "When you do this, I feel disappointed, angry, hurt." In saying this, we are taking responsibility for our own feelings.

After all, the statement "You make me mad" sounds as though the other person has total control over us, so that we are helpless individuals, just reacting to something out of our control. When another person acts in a particular way, we need to learn that we have choices. We can choose to get angry (sometimes what happens deserves this response). We can choose to disregard what was said, considering the source. We can reframe what was said to try to understand the other person's perspective. The problem is that we are so used to reacting to situations as if we are only victims, that we quickly get in touch with anger. We think there's no other recourse—but there is! We can allow the indwelling Holy Spirit to produce His fruit in us, which is love, joy, peace, patience, kindness, goodness, faithfulness, gentleness, and self-control (Gal. 5:22).

Fourth, when you find yourself welling up inside with sudden anger, stop and ask yourself, "Why am I angry?" What is the situation triggering in you, possibly from your family of origin? Remember that sometimes we overreact to a present situation because of something we learned in childhood. Everyone comes into a marriage with certain "family rules," which they think are "gospel" for the way life should work: "Always take your shoes off before coming into the house." "Never leave dishes in the sink." "Children don't have a voice in family matters." You can add your own family rules to this list.

Fifth, learn how to say "I'm sorry," "Will you forgive me?" and "Yes, I forgive you." Forgiving does not mean forgetting, as we have often been told. For instance Scripture says God forgets our sins, but we know that He is omniscient (knowing everything), so what He is actually saying is that He chooses to look at our sins through the blood of His Son, Jesus Christ. It's as if we never committed the sin, because when God looks at us, He sees us in His Son's righteousness. In marriages, when husbands and wives are practicing forgiveness, it means choosing to set something aside and not continuing to dredge it up for future use.

One of my most difficult tasks in dealing with couples is to get them to put the past behind, so that the present can be different. When one of my sons was a very young child, I was attempting to teach him the principle of forgiveness. He had misbehaved, and I had disciplined him, saying that we would now forget the situation. His reply to me was that I wouldn't really forget it because when Daddy came home, I would certainly tell him. When my husband came home, sure enough, one of the first questions he asked was, "Has Dan been a good boy today?" I remember the surprised look on Dan's face when he heard me say yes. Forgiving means choosing to place aside the wrong done and not return to it.

The reason so many of us have a hard time forgiving is because the issues are still unresolved, and we haven't really dealt with them. But God commands us to forgive in order to be forgiven: "For if you forgive men when they sin against you, your heavenly Father will also forgive you" (Matt. 6:14). We must forgive others, and then we can work on our emotions.

Sixth, don't expect your mate to be able to read your mind—only God can do that. Share what's on your mind! Much confusion develops because of a lack of verbal communication. Our preconceived expectations for the way things should be are almost without number. But remember that I said "verbal," because (as suggested earlier) you communicate even when you don't use words. Silence communicates a multitude of messages: rejection, anger, or merely acceptance—but much depends on how you grew up. If we took time to discuss things, many of them would be resolved, and our marriages would grow stronger as a result; but again we don't take the time.

Seventh, spend time together. We have heard that it's important to spend quality time, not quantity time, with our children. But that has not proven true. Good things take time, and five minutes of "quality time" just don't make up for the remaining 1,435 minutes left in each day. The same holds true for spouses. Five minutes a day aren't enough to build a great relationship. Far too many Christian couples end up in emotional divorce—living in separate worlds—with the wife usually overinvesting in the children and the husband overinvesting in his work, both of which are "acceptable" to the Christian community so long as the couple stays together legally. But God intended more—much more—for our marriages. Our marriages are to portray Christ's relationship with the church—and that is one of intimacy, growth, encouragement, understanding, and close union.

Eighth, mutual building up involves becoming a part of each other's world. So many couples remain in separate worlds for so long, that when they do slow down in later life, both partners discover they are living with a stranger—certainly not what God intended. Many couples tell me they put their marriages on hold during the child-rearing years. But if they do this, when they wake up one morning to an empty nest they will also wake up to an empty marriage relationship. This is not a picture of Christ's relationship with His church. He encouraged her to be all He intends for her. Wives need to take an interest in their husband's world, and vice versa. One of the most bonding times in my marriage was when I went to China with my husband as his scrub nurse. I learned the instruments on his instrument tray, and I was able to assist him during many hours of surgery. Wow! What an opportunity to watch him work, to see his compassion for people, to observe his dependence on our Lord. Those few weeks did more to draw us together as a couple than years could have done.

Stress is a family issue, not just an individual problem. Remember, you can't live in isolation. Who you are and how you behave affects every member in your family—your "context"—and who they are. And how they behave also affects you. You can't have a mate under stress without being affected.

We must learn how to communicate well, so the change that occurs will make our marriages become better examples of Christ's relationship to His church. So often this is hindered by our old sinful natures getting in the way. Our hurt feelings begin to dictate how we view our situations, and then we view things through a negative lens. Learning to focus on the positives in a relationship can often redirect anyone's course. As Paul encouraged us, "Finally, brothers, whatever is true, whatever is noble, whatever is right, whatever is pure, whatever is lovely, whatever is admirable—if anything is excellent or praiseworthy—think about such things" (Phil. 4:8).

Chapter Eleven

Helping Women
Take Responsibility

We live in a world without responsibility. Back in the Garden of Eden this was the mind-set presented by Satan to Eve. He suggested that there are no consequences for sin, that she need not feel responsible for her actions. Of course the world doesn't like the word *sin*, but the lack of responsibility is there nonetheless. Science is supporting this position with its present focus on genetics. Genes are being discovered right and left that determine certain conditions. For instance, genes have been pinpointed for a craving of sweets—a sweet gene! What a relief! I'm no longer responsible for my love of chocolates. I can't help myself. Genes have been tagged for alcoholism and for anger, and along with other things, scientists are looking for a gene that controls sexual preference.

Regardless of tendencies established by genetics, people are still responsible for the choices they make. I recently talked with a young woman who told me of her hatred for her mother because, in her words, "My mother knew that because there were so many alcoholics in our family, I would also become an alcoholic, and so I hate her." If a person has a genetic tendency for alcoholism (that is, an addictive tendency), she still has a choice to go down that road in the first place. Who forced her to take that first drink? The same is true with many other genetic tendencies: We have choices. The problem with the "no-choice" philosophy of genetic makeup is that people become victims. A victim by definition is "a person who suffers from a destructive or injurious action or agency."[1]

Often victims feel there is no way out, so they allow themselves to be acted on by ideas, by others, or by society in general.

How we personally view responsibility will impact the entire helping process. It is a central issue in all forms of interactions between people and how people view their behaviors. Since our understanding of responsibility is intertwined with the way we look at human nature, sin, and sanctification, we who seek to help women must have a clear understanding of responsibility.

We need to look at responsibility from several different contemporary perspectives and evaluate those viewpoints to see which are most consistent with the Scriptures. Most Christians have viewed responsibility primarily as right actions or right thinking and have failed to stress responsibility for our and others' hidden inner wishes and feelings and our sinful nature.

Responsibility can be defined as being "answerable or accountable, as for something within one's power, control, or management."[2] Above all, it involves accountability. We often want to place blame on someone or something else, and we don't take time to look at our own part in a problem. Remember, both Eve and Adam attempted to pass blame off of themselves—with Eve blaming Satan, and Adam ultimately blaming God.

I love it when couples come to my office with the attitude, "We are both at fault for our troubled marriage, and we will do anything it takes to get it back on track." But more often I hear, "She did this," or "He won't do that." A couple came to see me because they were facing separation. I asked both the husband and wife to tell me from each of their perspectives what the problem was. The husband immediately spoke, "It's all her fault because she wants to be the boss."

When I asked him if he was willing to take any responsibility for the part he played in creating their difficulties, he almost shouted, "Absolutely not! I have had nothing to do with it. She has destroyed our marriage. And this counseling will fail as well." I assured him that it probably would fail because he would sabotage the sessions, making sure they would not succeed. So I handed him my business card and said that I was going to let him take control of the situation by being the one to call for the next appointment. He immediately handed his wife the card, saying, "No, I want her to call because it's going to fail, and I'll have no part in it." I ended the session by telling them that I would inform my secretary to receive only an appointment made by the husband. He would have to take that step. He never called. Obviously he failed to assume any responsibility for problems in their marriage.

When we speak of responsibility, we are referring to where we locate the source or solution to a problem, not about who should be blamed in a guilt-inducing way. Having said this, we must also remember that we can't look at problems totally in isolation. Take, for example, an alcoholic. An alcoholic is certainly responsible for the alcoholism, but those in his or her immediate context usually do something to enable the alcoholism to continue, by making excuses, covering up, or constantly pleading for it to stop. The enabler gets stuck in a triangle between the alcoholic and the addiction. When one is stuck in the triangle, change does not easily occur. That is why Alcoholics Anonymous works so well—it is outside the context of the alcoholic.

I once watched a therapist work with a woman who was unconsciously enabling her husband's addiction by the things I just mentioned. The therapist had the woman go to her husband and say, "Honey, I want you to know that from now on I am not going to mention your drinking. I'm not going to make any more excuses for you, cover up for you, or nag you to quit, but I want you to do something for me and the kids. I know that your addiction will eventually kill you, and so I want you to take out a large insurance policy to provide for us after you're gone." Once this woman stepped outside the triangle, the husband was able to get help for his addiction.

WAYS OF VIEWING RESPONSIBILITY

There are several ways of looking at responsibility for problems that arise and how to deal with them.

One approach is to say that a problem exists because of the conscious, specific, willful sins of the individual. If we take this view, we might see a woman as responsible for her marriage problems because she refuses to be submissive. Or a man's depression may be attributed to his failure to carry out his responsibilities at work or to confess his sins. This view of

127

responsibility focuses largely on behavior and conscious actions and thoughts. Simply stated, a person has chosen to do the wrong thing and that is why he or she has problems. Certainly this view contains an important truth because our choices do strongly influence our lives, but it is limited because it focuses too narrowly on conscious behavior. It minimizes or denies the responsibility of others, and it neglects basic sinfulness that cannot easily be reduced to consciously willed thoughts or actions.

We are responsible for addressing and changing our problem behavior regardless of who was responsible for its origin. We need to understand for ourselves and when guiding others that no temptation is inherently stronger than our spiritual resources (1 Cor. 10:13).

Another view places all the responsibility for the development of problems in our partially unconscious sinful nature. This view is consistent with the Bible's stress that overt actions grow out of attitudes of the heart. Jesus said, "For out of the overflow of the heart the mouth speaks" (Matt. 12:34). This view looks at responsibility at a deeper level than one that locates the problem in specific acts or sins. There are many who believe that while good parenting is vital to sound psychological development, the ultimate source of problems lies in the child's inherent impulses. Anyone who has raised children knows that you certainly don't have to teach a child how to sin. The child comes to us with that capacity already in place. Only when we face our sin natures can we really begin to make fully responsible choices. God knows our thoughts even before they are spoken (Ps. 139:4).

We are responsible for maturing in a way that changes our inner sinful patterns that led to the problem in the first place. God's Word can get to the root of our sinful behavior: "For the word of God . . . judges the thoughts and attitudes of the heart" (Heb. 4:12).

Actually our problems exist because of a combination of our specific willful sins and our sin nature. We are responsible for turning from our sinful acts and addressing our sinful nature. God commands Christians to "be filled with the Holy Spirit" (Eph. 5:18). He never gives us a command to do something without the enablement to carry it out. If couples were truly filled with the Spirit, then His fruit, not the works of the sinful nature, could be produced in them. Galatians 5:16–17 specifically tells us to "live by the Spirit, and you will not gratify the desires of the sinful nature. For the sinful nature desires what is contrary to the Spirit, and the Spirit what is contrary to the sinful nature. They are in conflict with each other, so that you do not do what you want."

Some people, however, blame all their problems on others—parents, society, or life in general. In other words, "I am this way because I was abused." "It's somebody else's fault, not mine!" It is true that sinful ways are sometimes passed down from generation to generation. This began when Adam passed on his sinful nature to his children, for as Genesis 5:3 says, "He had a son in his own likeness, in his own image" (see also Rom. 5:12). We pass down to our children our sinful ways of coping with life. They watch us model our unconscious habits and become like us.

Yet we are all responsible for encouraging changes in the ways we sinfully deal with life. Christians are not helpless individuals controlled by Satan; we are redeemed children of God who have the power of the Holy Spirit within to respond in the right way. With the Lord's enabling, Christian leaders *can* model a godly lifestyle before others. We can show others what it means to be "imitators of God as dearly loved children" (Eph. 5:1).

We all need accountability. Some Christian women meet regularly with a group of other women to whom they are accountable. Knowing that we have to give account of our actions to another believer often encourages us to continue on the appropriate path. Questions such as these can prod us to deal with our problems: "Mary, are you finding victory over your problem this week?" "What can I do to help you succeed more?" "I'll call you during the week to see how you're progressing."

To get the best view of our problems, we need to see that they exist because of a combination of all of the above—our personal sinful choices, our sin natures, and the sinfulness of others. Everyone involved is responsible to deal with sin in his or her life. Paul wrote that "by dying to what once bound us, we have been released from the law so that we serve in the new way of the Spirit, and not in the old way of the written code" (Rom. 7:6). As the Holy Spirit fills us with His fruit, our relationships can become more like what God intended (Gal. 5:22; Eph. 5:18).

As I suggested earlier in this chapter, if we believe our problems stem from specific sins of a counselee, we are likely to say that his or her responsibility involves changing overt behavior in a relatively short period of time.[3] Although this is certainly part of responsibility, it does not include the full range of options. Even though changed behavior sometimes changes inner feelings and attitudes, the problem is not just at the behavioral level. Christ accused the Pharisees of being "whitewashed tombs, which look beautiful on the outside but on the inside are full of dead men's bones and everything unclean" (Matt. 23:27). And Paul acknowledged that growth was an ongoing process involving the continual renewing of the mind (Rom. 12:1–2; Phil. 3:12–14). Saying a person's problems stem from his or her specific sins overlooks the deeper, inner aspects of personality and the responsibility of others. And approaching problems in this way wrongly suggests that they can be solved by immediate or short-term behavior change. Since our sinful natures have a part in the development of our problems, we need to see that growth is a process involving insight into previously hidden sinful desires and hurts.

A comprehensive view of responsibility acknowledges that both our specific sinful choices and the sinfulness inherent in our fallen natures contribute to our problems. And it acknowledges that we are responsible even for our unconscious sins—not because we purposefully choose them but because they grow out of our fallen natures. Nor can we blame our environment or the people around us. Instead we must recognize that we are responsible individuals and must act accordingly.

Even though others may have sinned against us, we are responsible for taking steps to initiate change in our lives. During my doctoral studies I had the privilege of working with some women who had been greatly sinned against in their childhood. They had developed some very unhealthy strategies for coping with life. I was able to watch these women take responsibility for their adult lives and change many unhealthy practices, freeing themselves up by the power of the Holy Spirit to live Christ-centered, Christ-honoring lives. Fortunately they did not have to undertake that responsibility alone, since other women in the body of Christ assumed responsibility in helping them grow. By helping those women carry their burdens, they, as Paul put it, helped "fulfill the law of Christ" (Gal. 6:2).

This process of change will not occur overnight. If you feel it necessary, you might want to refer some women to a Christian counselor for professional assistance in this process.

We must help women take responsibility for changing things that keep them from being all they are capable of becoming in Christ.

Chapter Twelve

Ministering to
Women Who Hurt

*C*hristians often equate Stoicism with spirituality—that is, they think they are spiritual if they are seemingly indifferent to or unaffected by the tragedies of life. We are good at putting on fronts that cover our troubled hearts. Somehow we feel that if we don't show emotion, then the pain will disappear—but it doesn't. Our Lord showed us by example that emotions are expressions of our humanness. He also told us to minister to people who are hurting. But how can we know who they are if they have learned to be stoic, and they don't feel safe in our presence?

Ministering to those who grieve takes more than just a few days. If we are truly to minister, we must sense the depth of that valley, for grief devastates day after day after day. Losses come in various packages, but we all receive them—loss of loved ones or things, loss of unrealized dreams for ourselves or others, loss of jobs. Both men and women experience losses, and both grieve those losses, but often the grieving "looks" different for men and women. Without being too simplistic, I would like to make a general observation—women seem to have more freedom to grieve than men have. Men are expected to take care of everyone else in times of crisis and often are overlooked during their greatest times of personal need.

Grieving is the expression of our many thoughts and feelings regarding our loss. It is not a passive process; it is an active one. Grief is not a disease. Nor is there a quick-fix for the pain a grieving person is enduring.[1]

LOSS THROUGH DEATH

In a plane crash a woman lost her husband, their twenty-two-year-old son, their eighteen-year-old daughter, and their twenty-seven-year-old son-in-law. On the day of the great tragedy she wrote these jolting words in her diary: "Late afternoon—doorbell—Clayton and the awesome news of tragedy—(death, plus death, plus death, plus death = death). They rose—I fell! Cut loose to float in a timeless, unconscious yet conscious space beyond, but painfully here. I do remember, but I don't—faces and blanks—things and unthings—a merry-go-round of a horrid sort. God, please take care of Valerie—I can't."

Valerie, her daughter, married to her son-in-law who died with the rest of the family, was left back at home with her mother because she was pregnant. Nine days after the tragedy, the grieving woman continued in her journal:

Valerie is my arm to reality. My only love left. I need her desperately, but must not overcrowd. Much to be done—I am the center core of devastation that touches many. I must handle it right, but how? Where do I begin? Again, I know it is with Valerie. Organize, dismantle—move Karla out—move Valerie in! Through pain and tears, I do work. I must touch each item—I must make each decision—I must, I must. Upstairs, downstairs, boxes, stacks, piles, all is packed. It is as though an eraser wiped the slate clean—Karla was, but is no more. I have surely come to that dried up stream! They came to take Karla's car, and that was the tearing out of my heart. No more! I will give, but they must not take. My beautiful happy baby is now gone—only a small box of trinkets and pictures to remind me of 18 years of joy. My life so touched by her sparkling ray of sunshine that glittered always, her deep laughter echoes in my head. Surely the pain can get no worse. I love you, Karla, I love you, Baby! For what time do we have anything? The pores of my body are like headlights searching the dark for my throbbing loss. Suicide—prayer—tears—no sleep.[2]

How can we be used effectively in walking beside people, women specifically, who are hurting so deeply for whatever reason? One of the main problems we face is that many of us are uncomfortable with those who are grieving.

Shortly after my own husband was killed in a plane crash, I ran into a young female student at the post office. She was excited to see me and immediately asked, "Well, does it work?" I asked her to explain what she meant, and she replied, "You know, the Holy Spirit—does He make things all right?" Another friend had told me I had "the widow's glow"—whatever that meant. On another occasion, a colleague asked me how I was doing, and then quickly said, "Oh, you don't have to answer that because I can see it in your eyes; you're doing great!" I could go on and on with illustrations of well-meaning responses to a person's grieving process. So often these attempts at giving comfort fall flat and accomplish little.

I am convinced that it's all right to hurt. It's all right even to express our feelings of pain without feeling less spiritual. I am often comforted by reading the passage in John 11 telling of Lazarus's death, of our Lord standing at his tomb weeping. In order to get the full impact of this scene, we must remember who Jesus is—He is God in the flesh! He is omniscient! He knew that in a very short time He would raise Lazarus from the dead, but He still wept, expressing grief in His humanness. It's all right for us to express our humanness as well. And yet we often tend to deny our emotions. We feel uncomfortable in experiencing our emotions or observing them in others. If we are to help women find healing in their grief, we must understand the process of grief.

Grief has been compared to physical illness. Both take time for healing, and both include emotional and physical aspects. Bertha Simos, a social worker, compared physical illness and grief this way: "Both may be self-limiting or require intervention by others. And in both, recovery can range from a complete return to the pre-existing state of health and well-being, to partial recovery, to improved growth and creativity, or both can inflict permanent damage, progressive decline and even death."[3]

Grief is complex, but the same facts apply to mourning regardless of the kind of losses—whether death, divorce, job loss, losses experienced by victims of violence, abortion, and many others.

A person grieves in direct proportion to how much attachment there was between him or her and whatever was lost. People also grieve over a loss to the extent that unresolved issues existed between the two people involved.

Those who theorize about relationships have said that our attachments often relate to our need for security and safety. These basic needs develop early in life, are usually directed toward a few specific individuals, and tend to endure throughout a large part of life. Forming attachments with significant others is considered normal behavior not only for children, but for adults as well. A child's parents provide the secure base of operation from which to explore life. This relationship determines the child's capacity to make appropriate bonds of affection later in life. So what happens when a person's bonds of affection are broken?[4] Is a mourning process necessary? The immediate answer is yes.

When I was working as a chaplain in a local hospital, I walked into the room of a man who was crying. The nurses had told me they couldn't understand why he was crying because his surgery had been quite successful in removing his cancer. When I saw that his surgery had been the removal of his leg, I said to him, "It must be terribly hard for you to lose a part of yourself." Immediately he began to talk about his loss once he felt he had an understanding ear, and the emotional healing process began. The staff had attended to his physical needs but not his emotional ones.

Many Christians seem to deny that grieving is a process. They feel that any signs of grief would in some way evidence lack of faith in God's plan for their lives.

"TASKS" OF GRIEVING

Several writers discuss the steps involved in the mourning process, but I prefer J. William Worden's list of four. He calls them "tasks" because this implies that the person involved in the process has work to do. Grieving is not a passive process, regardless of the kind of loss.

The first task is to accept the reality of the loss.[5] For example, when someone dies, even if the death is expected, there is always a sense that it hasn't happened. In the case of death the first task of grieving is to come to the reality that the person is dead, that the person is gone and will not return. Part of the acceptance of reality is to come to the belief that re-

136

union is impossible, at least in this life. It is a natural response for the bereaved person to catch a glimpse of someone who reminds her of the one who is gone and then have to remind herself, "No, that isn't my friend [or spouse]. My friend [or spouse] is really dead."

Often a grieving person initially denies the loss. Denial can be practiced on several levels and can take various forms.[6] One common form of denial is to reject the fact of the loss. For weeks after my husband's death, when I would drive home at the end of the day, an urgent feeling of expectancy to see him would come over me the closer I got to my house. My heart didn't want to accept the reality of his death.

We women are so relational that a great loss affects our total being—who we are and how we view ourselves and view life in general. Parents who lose a child often keep the child's room as it was before the death. This is not unusual in the short term but becomes denial if it goes on for years. It is extremely difficult to dispose of the deceased person's personal items. I remember my father frantically searching for a favorite sweater of my mother's after her death, and nothing would comfort him until it was found. When time passed, and he had worked through his grief, he donated that sweater to the Salvation Army. Haddon Robinson, in his booklet *Grief*, describes a scene from *Gulliver's Travels*: "As Gulliver lay tied to the earth by the stakes and ropes of the Lilliputians, so the grief sufferer, too, is bound by a thousand emotional cords to the person who has been lost."[7]

Another way people seek to protect themselves from reality is to deny the meaning of the loss.[8] In this way the loss can be seen as less significant than it actually is. It is common to hear statements such as, "He wasn't a good father," "We weren't close," or "I don't miss him." Some people immediately get rid of everything belonging to the person, as if any artifacts would bring them face to face with the reality of the loss.

Another way people deny the full meaning of their loss is to practice "selective forgetting,"[9] in which a person blocks all reality of the loss from the mind, even to the point of not being able to recall the person's image. I find that people who have experienced painful divorces often attempt this. But we must remember that sometimes the intensity of grief is associated with unresolved issues, and in divorce there are usually many.

Some people deny that "death is irreversible."[10] Of course, we know that Jesus rose from the dead (1 Cor. 15:4); and on three occasions He chose to bring people back to life to show His glory. We also know that when our Lord returns, He will bring with Him those Christians who have died (1 Thess. 4:13–14). We know that He is able to do anything because He is sovereign. Abraham knew that God was able to raise Isaac from the dead (Gen. 22:5). With remembrances like these it is difficult for us to let go of the hope that God will do the same for us.

I was once asked to address a church congregation that was grieving the loss of several of their young people who were killed in a highway accident on the way to a church retreat. One man stood to his feet and asked me why God hadn't answered the church's prayers to bring those young people back to life? Of course, that's an unanswerable question for our finite minds. It's not a question of God's capability but of His will. We know He is omnipotent, omniscient, omnipresent, and sovereign over the universe. We also know that He does not make mistakes; He knows all the options for our lives and we know only a few. We know that His very nature is good, and that He does not change because of our circumstances. Accepting the fact of His sovereignty, however, doesn't mean we shouldn't grieve.

Accepting the reality of our loss takes time, since it involves not only an intellectual acceptance but also an emotional one. The grieving person may be intellectually aware of the finality of the loss long before the emotions allow full acceptance of the information as true. The distance from my brain to my heart is only about seventeen inches, but transferring what I know to be true in my head down to the reality of where I live can be one of the most difficult journeys imaginable. It is so easy to want to believe that our loved ones are just away on a trip and will return soon. "Belief and disbelief are intermittent while grappling with this task."[11] Traditional rituals such as funerals help many grieving people move toward acceptance. Unreality is particularly difficult in the case of sudden death, especially if the survivor does not see the body of the deceased. Again, it takes time to work through these things.

The second task is to work through the pain of grief.[12] Not everyone experiences the same intensity of pain or feels it in the same way, but it is impossible to lose someone you have been deeply attached to without experiencing some level of pain. Since most of us are uncomfortable with the feelings of the person grieving, we may give the subtle message, "You don't need to grieve, you are only feeling sorry for yourself." This interferes with the person's own defenses, leading to the denial of the need to grieve, expressed as, "I don't need to grieve." Often we imply that giving way to grief is labeled as morbid, unhealthy, or shortsighted. The way a person gets stuck in this task is to cut off feelings of grief, denying the pain that is present.[13]

Some people who do not understand the necessity of experiencing the pain of grief try to find a "geographic cure." They travel from place to place, trying to find some relief from their emotions, as opposed to experiencing the pain. I personally tried to get away from my loss by literally running. I found that the more I ran the more numbness I felt—both physically and emotionally. Although I am an avid advocate of exercise for keeping healthy, both physically and emotionally, I am also aware that too much of anything can be a sign of avoidance. There is no shortcut to working through the pain of loss.

The third task is to "adjust to an environment in which the deceased is missing."[14] Adjusting to a new environment means different things to different people, depending on what the relationship was with the person lost and the various roles that person played. For many widows it takes a considerable period of time to realize what it is like to live without their husbands. This realization often begins to appear around three months after the loss and involves coming to terms with living alone, raising children alone, facing an empty house, and managing finances alone. For women who define their identity through relationships and caring for others, bereavement means not only the loss of a significant other but also the sense of a loss of self.[15] Grief can lead to intense regression, in which the bereaved see themselves as helpless, inadequate, incapable, childlike, or personally bankrupt. However, over time these negative images usually give way to more positive ones, and the survivors are able to carry on their tasks and learn new ways of dealing with the world.

I have found in my counseling practice that one of the most helpful things is to be a model for others who have not come as far as I have in the healing process. Many grieving people have said that they gained hope by watching my life—to know that life can once again be full and enjoyable.

People can get stuck in this phase when they do not adapt to their loss. I have also seen individuals, especially women, living in the past, sometimes twenty years or more. Time seems to have stopped for them, as they view everything in light of their loss.

The fourth task is to "emotionally relocate the deceased and move on with life."[16] Make no mistake about it—we never lose memories of a significant relationship! While looking at my diplomas on the wall, a counselee said to me, "Just think, if your husband hadn't died, you'd never have all of these wonderful degrees." I replied that this was definitely "plan B" for my life, but with God's help "plan B" was working. When we have worked through the grieving tasks, we come out forever impacted by the loss, but the pain is no longer just beneath the surface—it is replaced with a different focus, different dreams, and different ways of relating to life.

Shuchter and Zisook comment on this fact: "A survivor's readiness to enter new relationships depends not on 'giving up' the dead spouse but on finding a suitable place for the spouse in the psychological life of the bereaved—a place that is important but that leaves room for others."[17] If you are helping individuals walk through their grief, it is important to help them find an appropriate place for the dead in their emotional lives— a place that will enable them to go on living effectively for the Lord in this world. Three months after my husband's death a young seminary student asked me, "Are you all over it yet?" I was able to answer that I would never be "over" the loss of my husband, but that eventually he would occupy a different place in my heart.

Since women and men process things differently, this certainly includes the way they tackle the tasks of grieving. Women can't separate things as easily as men can. We tend to handle losses as all-encompassing in our lives. People can get stuck in this fourth task by holding on to the past attachment rather than going on and forming new ones. For many people the fourth task is the most difficult one to accomplish, but it can occur. I remember a time when I was actually conscious of the fact that my pain was no longer just beneath the surface, the kind that crops up at the slightest incidence of remembrance. What a sense of God's grace that was for me! No longer was every waking moment filled with thoughts of my loss.

When is mourning finished? In the loss of a close relationship we should be suspicious of any full resolution that takes less than a year, and for many, two years is not too long. One sign of completed grief reaction is when the person is able to think of the deceased without overwhelming pain. There is always a sense of sadness when you think of someone you have loved and lost, but eventually it becomes a different kind of sadness—it lacks the wrenching quality it previously had.[18]

We can think of the loss without physical manifestations such as intense crying or feelings of tightness in the chest. Also mourning is finished when a person can reinvest his or her emotions back into life. Many people attempt to get on with life by reinvesting too early and so they don't reach a good resolution. This is more of an attempt to replace the loss, much as we attempt to replace a dead puppy or kitten with a live one to alleviate the hurt of a child. We start this method of coping early in life and grow up not knowing how to work through loss of any kind. An additional problem here is that the grief of loss doesn't go away by denying that it exists—it just accumulates. Dealing with past losses insufficiently adds to the next loss and the pain escalates.

Some people never seem to accomplish a completion to their grieving. I have seen fine Christians ten years down the road with unresolved grief. We as fellow Christians sometimes don't give them permission to grieve, and so the bereaved buy into this philosophy to their own detriment.

Grieving does not proceed in a linear fashion. Sometimes a person may make progress in overcoming grief only to find that later the earlier feelings of grief reappear. Some people believe it takes four full seasons of the year before grief begins to subside. The thought here is that we have to experience all the important events—holidays, anniversaries, birthdays, and special memories without the person being present. We have to begin with new memories, and that takes time.

"There is a sense in which mourning can be finished, when people regain an interest in life, feel more hopeful, experience gratification again, and adapt to new roles. There is also a sense in which mourning is never finished."[19] Sigmund Freud wrote the following words to a friend whose son had died: "We find a place for what we lose. Although we know that after such a loss the acute stage of mourning will subside, we also know that we shall remain inconsolable and will never find a substitute. No matter what may fill the gap, even if it be filled completely, it nevertheless remains something else."[20]

Romans 8:28 can be powerfully comforting to those who grieve: "And we know that God causes all things to work together for good to those who love God" (NASB). Some Bible versions omit the point in this verse that everything "works together." For example, the New International Version says "works for the good." The Greek verb *synergeō* means "to cooperate, to work together, to work with one another."[21] It implies that things do not work "in isolation." In other words, God takes both good and bad events and weaves them *together*. We often get the well-meaning advice from caring Christians that each isolated event in our lives exists independently for our good. But God is telling us that while we cannot always understand single isolated occurrences in our lives, He is somehow putting the good and bad together for our good and His glory. His very nature is good and does not change according to our circumstances. Yet we need to be careful we do not flippantly quote Romans 8:28 as if that will automatically make the grief go away.

CHARACTERISTICS OF NORMAL GRIEVING

In helping women (and men) work through their grieving process, we need to be aware of some common characteristics of normal grief (some call it "good" grief). We need to be aware of how grief presents itself in our feelings.

Shock often occurs in the case of sudden death. Actually the atmosphere that accompanies shock provides a numbing effect that temporarily surrounds the survivors, enabling them to have a somewhat calm appearance during the funeral activities. Shock probably occurs because there are so many feelings to deal with. If the person allowed them all to come into consciousness, those feelings would be overwhelming; so the person experiences numbness as a protection from emotional flood. This is a normal reaction.

A *sense of disbelief* often accompanies this initial shock, especially if the death was sudden. A woman can think to herself, "It didn't happen; there must be some mistake. I can't believe it happened. I don't want to believe it happened." In this initial time of shock and disbelief we often hear friends say, "Oh, she is holding up so well and accepting what's happened." But after the shock wears off, when reality begins to set in, the process of grieving begins.

One of the most common feelings found in a grieving person is *sadness,* which needs little explanation. Sadness becomes so much a part of a person's existence that she often feels guilty when moments of happiness appear.

Some type of *bodily distress*—headaches, stomach dysfunction, or fatigue—is common. Apathy or listlessness are sometimes experienced. Previously active people often have difficulty understanding the fatigue that grips them. Depending on how close the relationship was to the person lost, one's whole lifestyle can be suddenly changed—including eating, sleeping, and socializing habits. Many women have told me they had difficulty praying during times of great grief. But of course, God knows even our unspoken words. "Before a word is on my tongue you know it completely, O LORD" (Ps. 139:4).

It is also common for the bereaved to experience some form of *guilt,* displaying itself in the questions, "If only I had done this or that differently." One of the most comforting verses of Scripture I use to address this feeling is Psalm 139:16: "All the days ordained for me were written in your book before one of them came to be." We can and should pursue any number of medical solutions available to us, but the bottom line is that God is in control. It's as if He were saying to us, "I knew before I formed you that your loved one would die of cancer, or through a terrible accident, or have life snuffed out at such an early age, or would leave you through divorce, or be addicted to drugs. But I am the God who heals the brokenhearted."

Alan Wolfelt says, "Anger, hate, blame, terror, resentment, rage, and jealousy—all are explosive emotions that may be a volatile, yet natural, part of your grief journey."[22] But we need to note Paul's words in 1 Thessalonians 4:13: "We do not want you to be ignorant about those who fall asleep, or to grieve like the rest of men, who have no hope." We grieve, as our Lord modeled for us, but we are always to have Him in focus, knowing that He is sovereign and that He makes no mistakes!

Some people even feel emancipated after a death because of a difficult relationship they had with the deceased. Grieving people have often told me they feel guilty because of their sense of relief that the person has died. If a woman asks God to end her husband's suffering by death, she may well feel guilty afterward. Several years ago when I was speaking at a conference, a woman told me she wished her husband had been on the plane that crashed instead of my husband. That comment immediately told me she was in a situation that was extremely painful for her; and that the death of her husband would have meant freedom. But if her husband were killed in such an accident, her guilt would probably be overwhelming. A woman might not miss her husband's annoying habits that were constant sources of irritation, but if she believes this feeling demonstrated her lack of love, she may continue to feel guilty. As understanding listeners, we need to help such people see that this is a part of their mourning process.[23]

I once counseled with a woman of six small children whose husband suddenly dropped dead from a heart attack. She was angry with her husband for "taking the easy way out." *Anger* is often a common feeling because the person who died didn't take adequate precautions or follow a doctor's advice. Children often feel anger toward their dead or divorced parent for leaving because they can't fully comprehend the absence. A young boy once asked his mother, "If Daddy is up in heaven looking at me, why doesn't he come down and play with me?"

The emotion of anger is not wrong. Ephesians 4:26 acknowledges that we will have anger: "In your anger do not sin: Do not let the sun go down while you are still angry." How we deal with anger is what makes it right or wrong. Dealing with it means acknowledging that it exists and working through it. But so often we don't give others permission to feel the anger that's inside. So they sense that their angry feelings must be hidden or denied. Anger turned inward often manifests itself in depression, and that can become more difficult to deal with than the initial anger.

Hurting people often say they seem to sense confusion, to be unable to function as they did before the loss. Sometimes the most disturbing part of grief is the "sense of disorganization, confusion, searching, and yearning."[24] I found that in my loss I had great difficulty focusing on anything else other than my husband's death. I remember asking God to give me the ability to teach just one hour of Bible class without the overwhelming pain that touched my heart.

With the loss of any important person *anxiety* may appear. Two factors can make a grieving sufferer anxious. One is the feeling of being helpless and unable to exist without the person.[25] Anxiety can also stem from the fact that the death of someone close to us brings our own mortality into focus. Christians often live as though there were no tomorrow—as seen in the way we fail to take care of our bodies, the way we carelessly drive our cars, the way we spend our money unwisely, the way we make poor use of our time. But the death of a loved one has a way of yanking us back into the "here and now" and focusing our attention on what's really important in life. When we sense that a woman's anxiety has developed into a more intense and persistent situation, it is probably advisable to refer her to a Christian counselor.

Loneliness is usually felt by survivors, particularly those who have lost by death or divorce a spouse with whom they have had a close day-by-day relationship.[26] Since people often make bad decisions because of loneliness, it is advisable for the grieving person to postpone any major decisions of further change until the initial year of mourning has passed. After the first year a person may think more objectively. Unfortunately, many grieving women don't wait to "get rid of the loneliness," so they make quick decisions that turn out to be bad ones.

Major differences exist between grief and *depression*. In both, the classic symptoms of sleep disturbance, appetite disturbance, and intense sadness may occur. However, in grief there is not the loss of self-esteem commonly found in most cases of clinical depression. People who have lost someone do not regard themselves less because of such a loss; or if they do, it tends to be for only a brief time. And if the survivors of the deceased experience guilt, it is usually guilt associated with some specific aspect of the loss rather than a general, overall sense of culpability.[27] Freud distinguished between the two when he said, "In grief, the world looks poor and empty while in depression, the person feels poor and empty."[28]

HELPFUL INFORMATION
FOR GUIDING GRIEVING PERSONS

By knowing certain things, we can better predict how a woman might respond to a loss and thus be able to assist in her healing process.

First, we need to know something about the deceased person. We probably grieve differently for a grandparent who dies of natural causes than we do for a sibling killed in a car accident. Grieving the loss of a distant cousin differs from grief over the loss of a child, and our grief over the loss of a spouse is not the same as our grief over the loss of a parent. At my husband's funeral a friend told me she knew how I felt because she had lost a distant cousin in the past. She meant well and was trying to be comforting. But in no way could she have experienced the wrenching depth of the loss of my life mate. Many of my students have told me similar stories of well-intentioned people who don't know what to say. Even though our heads tell us that people are just trying to help, their words tend to fall insensitively on our hearts. As helpers we need to be full of empathy, which by definition is "the intellectual identification with or vicarious experiencing of the feelings, thoughts, or attitudes of another."[29] We need to try to put ourselves in their shoes.

Second, we need to know something of the attachment between the survivor and the deceased. The severity of grief often increases in proportion to the intensity of the love relationship. Parents grieve the loss of a child in ways different from that of grieving the loss of a spouse, but we can't say that one is more intense than the other. They are different. Often when a child dies, he or she continues to grow in the minds of the parents. I never knew my brother, Weldon, because he died when he was eight, six years before I was born; but as I grew up, each year my parents would inform me how old Weldon "would have been" that particular year. This doesn't seem to be the case with the death of a spouse. A spouse is almost caught in time—forever remembered at the particular age at death, never aging. So we should be very careful when trying to offer comforting words to those who grieve. We should avoid telling the grieving, "You don't know what real loss is until you lose a child."

Third, we need to know the method of death. How the person died will say something about how the survivor grieves. "Traditionally, deaths have been catalogued under the NASH categories: natural, accidental, suicidal, and homicidal."[30] Survivors of suicidal deaths have uniquely difficult times handling their grief. Again, well-meaning but thoughtless individuals have made such comments as, "If you had not been gone, he or she would not have committed suicide." The truth of the matter is that if a person is determined to take his or her life, that one will usually find a way. It is his or her decision. A number of studies suggest that survivors of sudden deaths, especially young survivors, have a more difficult time a year or two years later than people with advance warning. Young people often feel deserted as time goes by.

Fourth, we need to know the grieving person's history of losses. It is helpful to know how many previous losses there were, and how these were grieved. How old were they when these other losses occurred? Were their losses grieved adequately or are they bringing to the new loss a lack of resolution from a previous loss? Grief doesn't just go away without some type of resolution. It will reappear at some time and in some form.

Fifth, and of great importance, we need to know the level of spiritual strength of the grieving person. I am convinced that we don't learn anything in the midst of a crisis; we only react—we react based on what we take into the situation. If we have spent time knowing who our God is, and who we are in Him, then at times of loss we are able to engender the trust necessary to face the many unknowns. If we don't know Him adequately, then our trust will be too weak to praise Him in the midst of our pains.

Sometimes Ephesians 5:20, "always giving thanks to God the Father for everything," is misunderstood. We sometimes think it means we are to be happy because of adverse circumstances. But instead the verse suggests that our focus should be on praising God because He is in control of all things. As children of a sovereign God, we must be assured that nothing—absolutely nothing—comes into our lives that hasn't first been through His hands. He is in control, and He never makes mistakes. This verse doesn't mean we pretend we have no pain; it means we acknowledge and worship Him *in* our pain. Yes, Christians are surrounded by the grace of God and His comfort, and we sense His presence, but those facts don't remove the pain. We need to help the grieving sense the inner strength that comes from keeping their eyes on the Lord.

LOSS THROUGH DIVORCE

People who have experienced divorce—whether by their choice or the choice of their mates—grieve differently from those who have lost a loved one or close friend in death. Some psychologists say that losing a loved one in death brings the highest level of grief and divorce the second highest. The rationale behind this observation is that since death is final it carries more stress, whereas divorce carries the possibility of comfort through reconciliation or remarriage.

I have not found this to be accurate, for several reasons. First, with divorce there are often intense feelings of rejection. The person being left often feels rejected, unwanted, a failure, unattractive, unfulfilled, and tremendously guilty. The low self-esteem that accompanies divorce often exacerbates the grief feelings discussed earlier. Second, many Christians refuse to associate with divorcées as if the condition might possibly rub off on them. To associate with them is often seen as condoning the situation. Besides going through the tasks of mourning the loss of his or her spouse, a divorced person must also carry the stigma of being divorced.

We know that God hates divorce, as Malachi 2:16 states, but does this mean that He hates the divorced as well? As helping members of the body of Christ, we must walk alongside those who are hurting because of divorce. We must remember that if it were not for God's undeserved grace showered on us, we would be walking the same path. Our goal is to restore sisters and brothers in Christ to a close fellowship with "the God of all comfort" (2 Cor. 1:3).

LOSS THROUGH ABORTION

Abortion has become so habitual in our society that some women don't even consider it a loss. Over one and a half million babies have perished each year since the Supreme Court's decision in the *Roe v. Wade* case in 1973.[31] But the ramifications are far-reaching, and life-changing. As Christian leaders, we will be asked to guide women in the choices they make for their lives. We must have a firm biblical position as we lead.

The debate on abortion is not only between the world and Christians, but between Christians and other believers. How will you respond when a Christian woman comes to you with her question, "Why shouldn't I have the right to choose?" The issue is not whether a woman has the right to do what she chooses with her own body. Instead, the real issue is whether she has the right to take another human life. God has given her a freedom to choose between right and wrong. Her own body was created in the image of God and should be treated with respect and care. As a Christian woman her body is the temple of God (1 Cor. 3:17).

Several years ago one of my sons and I picketed a popular abortion clinic. Each of us was handed a poster-board sign to brandish as we marched up and down the walkway in front of the clinic. Mine said "Abortion Kills." I noticed a young woman standing to one side of the walkway, looking puzzled as she stared at my sign. So I laid it down and approached her. I asked her if she was waiting for someone, and she said she had driven her best friend to the clinic to get an abortion. Her confusion stemmed from the counsel of those at the clinic and my sign. "They told my friend that the 'mass' inside her uterus was just an extension of her own body, that she alone 'had the right' to choose what she did with it, and that she would be able to go out and 'party' that very night. What is she killing, since the 'mass' is not a human being?"

If the "mass" growing inside a woman's uterus is another life, then she does not have the right to destroy it. This life bears the image of God just as we all do. There is immeasurable evidence from science that life begins at the moment of conception. When the egg from a woman's body is united with the sperm from a male, it has everything genetically that constitutes a human being. It begins as one complete fertilized cell and develops into the eight hundred billion or more specialized cells that make up the human body. Because of chromosomal pairing, at the very moment of conception a little male or female starts on his or her journey of development. The genetic makeup is different from the mother's or father's because it is a unique individual. It quite possibly will have a different blood type, but that doesn't matter because the mother's blood never mixes with that of the growing child.

What makes a person human and not just another animal is that God created us in His image (Gen. 1:27), something he did not do with animals. Since God does not have a physical image, the term must be referring to men and women as spiritual, rational, and moral beings. As moral beings, we can distinguish between right and wrong, whereas animals behave instinctively.

The Bible provides an indication that life in the earliest stages is respected and valued by God. First, God personally fashions each one of us in our mother's uterus. Job acknowledged that God had molded him "like clay," clothed him "with skin and flesh" and "knit" him "together with bones and sinews" and gave him "life" (Job 10:9–12). David praised God for the same thing in Psalm 139:13–16.

Second, we know that even though God is the ultimate Creator of life, He gave the first man and woman the ability biologically to produce life that would inherit their natures. Genesis 5:3 says, "When Adam had lived 130 years, he had a son in his own likeness, in his own image." Because of the Fall, we all inherit the sinful nature of Adam, as David claimed in Psalm 51:5: "Surely I was sinful at birth, sinful from the time my mother conceived me." This shows that the fetus is a spiritual moral being made in the image of God (although marred by sin).

No Christian would deny that a baby is a human being made in the image of God, with the ability for spiritual, rational, and moral response. With these biblical passages before us, we must accept the fact that a fetus inherits those capacities at conception. In Exodus 20:13 God said, "You shall not murder." We do not have the right to take life God created. When asked the question, "Why shouldn't a woman have the right to choose?" we can answer that abortion is homicide because it terminates a genuine human life. God's revealed moral law in Holy Scripture, with its high view of sanctity of life, is an absolute; therefore to cut off human existence is always an evil, regardless of changing circumstances. We cannot be neutral because even our position of neutrality contributes to a mentality that allows the practice.[32]

LOSS THROUGH THE EMPTY NEST

Another type of loss many women experience is the "empty nest" when their children leave home. For many years mothers invest a tremendous amount of themselves in the lives of their husbands and children. Depending on how solid the marriage is and how much time was spent enhancing that relationship through the years, a woman will experience loss to a lesser or greater degree when the children leave. All of a sudden, she is faced with a different role to live, usually at a time when her husband is still actively involved in his work. We can help her redirect some of her energies into exercising her spiritual gifts, which were possibly put on hold during the child-rearing years. If she has support from her husband, this time of transition will run smoothly; if not, she will need more support from her Christian friends. I have often faced couples in my office who look at each other and say, in essence, "I don't know you." If couples wait for twenty to thirty years while they are investing in their children before they invest in each other, they may find that the scars are too deep to rekindle the relationship.

In our culture it is common for children to leave the nest twice—first for college and then for graduate school or marriage. Financially many adult sons and daughters can't support themselves, so they choose to live at home while pursuing a career. Relationships are different, or at least should be, during each of these stages of "leaving home." Some mothers are so attached to their children that they have difficulty allowing them to grow up and turning them loose. They continue to want to control their lives.

When children choose paths in life that are harmful to them, parents often grieve the loss of dreams they had for those children. Sometimes the father can focus more on his work, but the mother might need a listening ear, not a judgmental spirit. She might need someone who will listen to her pain and be available for prayer and support in some way. As Christians, we are quick to offer solutions, but often our quick fixes fall flat. I once overheard an older woman talking to a younger woman in the foyer of our church, giving this advice, "If you'd only prayed harder, your mother wouldn't have died of cancer."

No wonder when Christians are hurting for whatever reason, they tend to withdraw for fear of being hurt further. We need to practice the art of caring and active listening in which the person talking will feel heard. Pain needs an audience, not judgment. We need to direct those who are hurting to the One who can really understand. As Isaiah 40:28–29 says, "His understanding no one can fathom. He gives strength to the weary, and increases the power of the weak" (NIV).

All of us will know grief. Whenever we lose some person or possession or circumstance that has provided emotional security or satisfaction, we will experience grief, and we will need to live through the tasks of grieving. Our trust and the trust of those we help must be in God, as was Job's: "I know that you can do all things; no plan of yours can be thwarted" (Job 42:2). Prepare now to walk sensitively with those who hurt.

Chapter Thirteen

Ministering to
Single Women

*L*ate one evening in June 1987, I was seated in my den with about twenty-five young women, teaching the Book of Ecclesiastes. My lesson went something like this: The book has twelve chapters with three sections of four chapters in each. The first four chapters talk about the past—you can't live there because it's gone. The second four talk about the future—you can't go there because, outside of having assurance of your eternal destiny with Christ, the future is unpredictable. That leaves the present. You must be content with living here and trust the One who is in control of all things.

As I paused, a young woman responded with much emotion, "That's easy for you to say—you have a wonderful husband, three great kids, a big-screen TV, and a beautiful house. No wonder you're content with the present!" As I thought over her statement, I slowly replied, "If God took my husband tomorrow, I would hate it, but I would still trust Him and His leading." Three weeks later, I was standing in front of my husband's casket—hurled into the unknown territory of the "singles' world."

Jesus was single! He taught in Matthew 22:30 that marriage is a temporary situation of human experience, that marriage will not be our status when we reach the eternal state. Almost half of the adults in the United States are single. To minister effectively to single women in our churches, we must know something of their world. Some of us are still living with a "colonial America" mind-set. When we see a young single woman, how many of us think, "I wonder why she isn't married," immediately assuming "something's wrong"?

In colonial America there was great pressure to be married for economic and religious reasons. It was not practical to be single because we as a nation were trying to populate and shape this new land. When a woman found herself widowed, the town leaders would plan her remarriage almost before her husband's funeral was over. There were fewer women than men, and so it was relatively easy to find a husband. The average young pioneer girl was married by about age thirteen.[1] Today's American scene is vastly different.

According to the U.S. Bureau of the Census in 1995 there were 46,045,000 single women, as compared with 39,953,000 single men.[2] Not surprisingly, then, most of our churches have more single women than men—different from the ratio in colonial days. George Barna's research shows that today's church is one of three places, along with work and school, to meet other singles. Ten years ago singles relied most heavily on friends, bars, and clubs, and on parties and other social gatherings.[3]

With more single adults coming to church, what are we doing to meet their needs? Are we adequately reaching out to them? I have often heard singles make statements like these: "We feel left out because the church stresses families." "We feel incomplete because people look at us as if we were half of what we should be." "Most of the sermons we hear are directed to husbands, wives, and families." So how can we effectively minister to a growing population of singles, especially women who do not fit the image of women even twenty years ago? In past years young women who were not married by a certain age were called "old maids" or "spinsters," terms that fortunately have dropped by the wayside, but the stigmas have not. Our culture has always looked on singles as incomplete. But is this image changing for our present generation?

Marriage is not the Christian's highest goal in life; glorifying God is. How then can we as leaders encourage singles to be all that they can be in Christ? Paul discussed the question of singleness in 1 Corinthians 7. He taught that celibacy is good, that it can leave one vulnerable to temptation, and that it is a gift from God.

PRIMARY CONCERNS
FOR MINISTERING TO SINGLE WOMEN

To minister successfully to single women, what should be our primary concerns?

First, single women need role models. Yet when we try to come up with names of prominent single women who are Christians we have to step back in time and recall women like Henrietta Mears and Amy Carmichael. But what about today? Do we have to be single ourselves in order to be role models for single women, or can we focus on godly lifestyles rather than marital status for singles to imitate? I believe that what single women want today is acceptance and encouragement for who they are and where they are in life. I doubt that many of them feel they can relate only to other single women. I was a single woman (widowed) for ten years before I chose to remarry, and as a single woman, I was often treated as "half a person." Many times I received comments from men like "Lucy, you need to be married." They meant well, but what kind of a message does that convey to a woman who is trying to be all God intended her to be?

Second, since most single women are in the work force, we must minister to them where they are. This will mean going to them, meeting them for lunch, meeting them on their terms, adjusting our schedules to fit theirs. Gone are the days of "women's circles" that met during the day and included most of the women in the church. An increasing number of churches are finding it helpful to schedule a weekend getaway retreat for singles once or twice a year. A Saturday-noon luncheon meeting or a monthly weeknight women's fellowship makes it easier for employed women to attend.

Third, we must oppose two stereotypes. One has to do with the idea that every adult should get married (discussed in this chapter), and the other pertains to working women (discussed in the next chapter).

In March 1996, 43 percent of our population over fifteen years of age were unmarried (never married, widowed, or divorced).[4] Although the singles population in our nation comprises these three distinct groups, those who have never been married are primarily responsible for the explosion of the singles market in America.[5] Those who have never been married make up 60 percent of all single adults. In fact, the proportion of never-married adults increased by nearly 40 percent between 1970 and 1990. By comparison, the proportion of adults who were divorced at the time of the 1990 census was no different from the 1970 census. The proportion of adults who had been widowed had increased substantially, but in absolute numbers this group remained the smallest among the three subgroups of singles.[6]

INCREASING NUMBER OF NEVER-MARRIED SINGLES

Why is there such a sizable increase in the number of people who have never married? Reasons suggested are the growing economic independence of women, skepticism about marriage because of the high divorce rate, the increase in longevity, more reliable birth control, the social acceptance of cohabitation without the commitment of marriage, and the emphasis on career achievement.[7] Also many singles are living with their parents because their jobs can't support their living on their own. This ever-increasing number of never-married adults abandoning their independence to move in with their parents is creating a new dimension that will affect our ministries. These singles tend to move back home when they are in their middle or late twenties. Sometimes it occurs right after college, while the singles are working on graduate studies or working to save money for future independence.

For some, emotional or personal difficulties or failed relationships have caused them to remain single against their own wishes. Returning to the nest is comforting and reaffirming. While singles who move in with their parents represent a small proportion of the total population (15 percent of all adults eighteen or older), this lifestyle preference is growing quickly. In 1970, 47 percent of single adults lived with their parents; by 1980, it was virtually unchanged (48 percent). But by 1988, it had risen to 54 percent.[8] The recession of the early nineties helped that figure climb even further, to an estimated 58 percent in 1992.[9] The decision of these "late nesters" to remain in their parents' homes for an extended period points out the tendency today of many young people to delay their growing up. The median age of the never-been-married segment is twenty-one. Since maturity and life experiences shape character and values, perhaps lack of maturity helps explain differences between the never-marrieds, the marrieds, and the divorced.[10] This will certainly influence how we minister to women who are adults but who still live with their parents.

To add to this mix, many are remaining single because of their changing lifestyles. How can we reach these women when their moral standards are vastly different from our own? Can we reach them with God's love without turning them away from the church?

A few years ago Carolyn Koons and Michael Anthony conducted a national survey of adult singles. About 80 percent of the questionnaires were distributed through church groups and the remaining 20 percent were given out in singles conferences, Sunday school classes, and retreats, for a total of 1,343 responses from 459 males and 884 females.[11] This research showed that although 39 percent of the single women were virgins, 27 percent had as many as four or more previous sexual partners, and 5 percent had as many as twenty partners. About 22 percent of the women surveyed had lived together with someone of the opposite sex.[12] Barna's survey of those who had never been married revealed that 63 percent felt that "everything in life is negotiable, and 48 percent felt that freedom meant being able to do whatever you want to do."[13] No longer can we assume that the Christian single women we are ministering to are a sexually inactive group.

Many of the singles are choosing to marry at a later age than in years past. Recently I did premarital counseling with two couples. All four of the individuals were forty years old and never before married. Age will certainly affect how we focus our ministry to these women. What are their interests? What are their goals? Do they plan to have a family? How can we help them feel a part of the body of Christ in a church environment so geared toward children?

As we enter the turn of the century with such different values in our culture, how can we be relevant to them, while remaining true to God's Word? These women may be the group most likely to feel the confusion caused by our inconsistent cultural values about marriage. On the one hand, they have heard parents, authority figures, and peers proclaim the value of marriage. On the other hand, they have seen how hypocritical behavior and the pressures that marriage place on people can easily destroy the bonds of matrimony. They know too that certain facets of our culture condone divorce and alternative lifestyles when marriage proves difficult or inconvenient.[14]

The never-married group tends to be younger than most adults and to have a lower annual income. Men are more likely than women to belong to the never-married category. In fact, among all women forty-five or older, just under 5 percent have never been married.[15] This means that a large number of single women are divorced or widowed. This suggests we need to think through our views on divorce. How can we work effectively with women who perhaps hold different views?

Finances have always been a key concern of families, but the number of singles with relatively low incomes is on the rise. Making ends meet is much more difficult for a single adult than for those who are part of a married-couple household. This is partly attributable to the fact that many of those who have never been married are young adults just getting established in a career.

The presence of dual-income households among married couples also makes the monetary comparison considerably more lopsided. I have overheard young singles in evening services, geared especially for singles, talking about enjoying the service because they didn't have to compete with the "dress code" of the morning-service crowd. What kind of image are we presenting to singles who are fearful about attending church because they don't have appropriate clothing? How can we make them feel accepted and comfortable, so that they will hear the message of Christ's redeeming sacrifice?

CHANGING VALUES

Many never-been-married adults hold values that set them apart from other groups. For instance, nine out of ten of them say family is important, but it is no more important to them than having good health. In fact, the never-marrieds are the only group to rate anything else as important as family. They are also more likely than married adults to describe money, a comfortable life, good career, and their time as highly important. Furthermore, this group is less likely to cite the Bible as being important in their lives.[16]

Singles who have never married also tend to hold more liberal views on current issues. For instance, they are less likely to believe that abortion is morally wrong, to contend that today's music has a negative influence on people's lives, to describe themselves as conservative, and to say that if the traditional family unit falls apart American society will collapse. By the same token, they are more likely than currently married adults to believe that the moral and ethical standards of Americans are as high as ever, to define freedom as meaning a person can do anything he or she wants to do, to say that it is unlikely for a man and woman to have a deep, lasting friendship that does not turn into a sexual relationship, and to suggest that everything in life is negotiable.[17]

I recently attended a Josh McDowell youth rally on a Christian college campus, during which young people were asked questions about right and wrong. I was surprised when one of their responses was that abortion wasn't always a right-or-wrong issue. We are living in an age of relative truth; many young people are not coming into adulthood with the sense of absolute truth we had. How will we reach these young women when they come to us for answers? By the time we have contact with them, they will have accumulated much emotional baggage in their lives, which we will have to address. We must be extremely grounded in God's Word because He alone has answers that will free this generation from the bondage of such dysfunction.

Since fewer never-marrieds describe themselves as religious, what will be our common ground? Compared to married adults, who say religion is among the more important elements in their lives, the never-marrieds see religion as only a moderately important influence in their lives. This is because they lack genuine Christian role models to show that Christ's way is the only way that brings meaningful life—the one thing for which they are so desperately searching.

Many singles in the church I attend have admitted to me that they attend church in order to meet other Christian singles, not to grow spiritually. The present group of never-married singles is less likely than currently or previously married people to believe that the Bible's teachings are totally accurate; that Jesus Christ rose from the dead and is alive today; that they have a responsibility to share their religious beliefs with other people; and that there is a God who hears people's prayers and has the power to answer them.[18] Singles today possess a cautiousness about people and relationships that explains, in part, why they are remaining single until later in life. Many are skeptical about marriage, believing that anyone getting married these days should expect to eventually get divorced. And this is no wonder, with Christian marriages ending in divorce almost as often as non-Christian marriages.

This fact is closely related to their view that they really can't trust anyone other than family and close friends. This might help explain why they are three times more likely than married adults to say they are lonely. This problem can be one of the best avenues of entry into young women's lives. Offering genuine friendships will give us a platform on which to share the love and power of Christ. But without this time commitment our testimonies may fall on deaf ears.

Many singles marry for the wrong reasons. Instead of searching for a permanent, loving relationship and the opportunity to raise children, today's never-married adults are more interested in long-term companionship—again searching to fill their lonely lives. The research conducted by Koons and Anthony shows that the top four disadvantages of singleness are loneliness, financial insecurities, becoming self-centered, and restrictions on sex life.[19] With so many singles having grown up in homes where they witnessed turmoil in marital conflict and divorce, they are extremely distrustful of marriage. They still believe in the concept and look forward to having their own families, but instead of boldly proclaiming that they are looking for the right person with whom they can spend the rest of their lives, they often settle for someone with whom they can establish a close, warm, satisfying, long-term friendship. In such a relationship love is desirable but not necessarily expected. Sadly, millions of never-married adults believe that finding a lifelong love relationship is unlikely.[20] Although they want partners who treasure enduring relationships, never-marrieds dismiss these expectations as impractical. I have heard young women say, "We don't want to get our hopes up."

The majority of older married adults look down on the never-marrieds' willingness to settle for mere friendship as the basis for selecting a spouse. But have their marriages been role models for the younger hopefuls? Have these older couples been willing to walk beside younger couples to encourage and guide them? For the most part, I think not. For the majority of singles who want to get married, this is neither a choice nor a compromise; it is contemporary reality, the only viable option in a marriage-hostile culture. Life, in their eyes, is a series of trade-offs, and settling for close companionship is better than remaining lonely.

Many single adults in America now believe that as long as you "love" or "care for" another person, sexual intimacy is a natural and permissible part of the relationship. Many adults who have yet to experience marriage have no hesitation about experiencing premarital sexual intimacy. The problem I find with this, apart from the fact that it's against all biblical principles addressing the issue, is that people who so desperately want intimacy in relationships go for the intimate act of sex, only to find that without true intimacy between partners, this act becomes empty. When couples become sexually active, they usually stop interacting in ways that could develop real intimacy, and they become consumed with the physical. Sex does not hold a marriage together. In fact, I find more often than not, in troubled marriages the sexual part of the relationship disappears first. But kept in its proper perspective, sex enhances a strong intimate relationship between two married partners.

From watching today's movies and television programs, you would expect that most people marry to find sexual intimacy. The data points out, however, that surprisingly few people who have never been married list sex as a motivation for marriage. This may well be due to the fact that the majority of people who get married these days have already been sexually active.

The figures are alarming. A majority of people have had sex outside of marriage by the time they are nineteen years old. That proportion has been rising steadily, despite sex education in the public schools, the well-publicized spread of sexually transmitted diseases, and a growing awareness of the fatal consequences of AIDS. Nor is sexual involvement limited to a single adventure to satisfy curiosity or reduce peer pressure. Three out of ten high school seniors have had four or more sexual partners. Among people getting married for the first time this year, it is estimated that only one out of every four (28 percent) will be virgins. And if the recent averages remain constant, of those who marry for the first time, almost two out of three newlyweds (62 percent) will have had sex with someone other than his or her spouse prior to the marriage.[21]

Many couples today have walked away from God's mandates for marriage. When God created man and woman and initiated marriage, He said, "For this cause a man shall leave his father and his mother, and shall cleave to his wife; and they shall become one flesh" (Gen. 2:24, NASB). Yet most of today's adults view marriage simply as a means of personal fulfillment. They feel that if a marriage promises to provide relational comfort and support, then it is an attractive option. Otherwise, they perceive marriage as a liability.

Apart from the moral harm caused by rampant sexual involvement, the health hazards are substantial. Focus on the Family's videotape, *Sex, Lies, and Videotapes,* presents a tremendously clear picture for our young people today. The video focuses on the lies young people are fed today by our society. The video also teaches that there is no such thing as "safe sex," just as there is no safe sin! When a person chooses to live in direct contradiction to the laws of God, there is no place to hide. David made this profound observation concerning God: "Where can I go from your Spirit? Where can I flee from your presence? If I go up to the heavens, you are there; if I make my bed in the depths, you are there. If I rise on the wings of the dawn, if I settle on the far side of the sea, even there your hand will guide me, your right hand will hold me fast" (Ps. 139:7–10).

More than one million unintended teenage pregnancies occur each year, half of which are ended by abortion. How can we reach these young women for Christ? Many young girls today tell me they purposefully get pregnant in order to have someone who will love them unconditionally. How can we prepare these young women for motherhood, when they are but children themselves? The task of ministry appears overwhelming against such odds.

Today many Christian families condone abortions for their pregnant teens. Sadly, more than three million teens contract sexually transmitted diseases each year. Barna quotes one young woman concerning her sexual activity: "I probably sleep with one or two guys a week. I'm careful because of AIDS and other diseases, but the quality of men I date would not put me at risk. Anyway, I'm not an immoral woman just because I have sex with a lot of people. It's the way we live today. None of us are desperate about marriage."[22] Where do we begin addressing this modern culture?

Young adults whose parents failed to model skills for negotiating conflict, compromising, and effective communication are more likely to show similar limitations in their relationships. The church may well remain the only institution forcefully promoting sexual abstinence. Although James Dobson says that many outside the Christian faith are now agreeing that the sexual revolution was an unmitigated disaster, they don't have any answers. Adults will continue to pay lip service to the need for caution, advocating so-called safe sex, but that will be merely a facade for sex-on-demand with precautions taken to guard against AIDS and other sexually transmitted diseases.

As Christians, how can we defend God's requirement that people refrain from sexual intimacy before marriage? In a society in which morals have been diluted to mean each individual's personal preferences, believers must stand up for God's truth and articulate His position in a logical, unemotional manner. We have to be careful to avoid judgmental posturing.

Yes, sin is sin, and many young women have made sinful, wrong choices. Yet we must show compassion for young people who grow up these days in a moral vacuum and face the hurt of broken families and confusing choices. The church has a major responsibility—and opportunity—to restate the case for the traditional family, committed personal relationships, and responsible sexual behavior. If we can do this in a loving manner, others may be persuaded to abandon cohabitation and premarital sex. Our opportunity for ministry is tremendous!

We need to teach young women under our leadership to recognize that God's rules are intended to spare them from the consequences of sinful behavior and the pain of broken relationships. When we walk away from the truth, we are following the path of succumbing to the temptation of Satan. He first questioned God's Word, by asking Eve, "Did God really say?" (Gen. 3:1).

That same question is asked over and over today when we question

God's mandates for marriage, abstinence from sex before marriage, abortions, and many other things by asking, "Has God really commanded us to abstain? He must be holding us back from enjoyment, and after all, shouldn't we be able to make our own decisions?"

Twenty years ago when I was teaching a sixth-grade girls' Sunday school class, the young girls asked, "How far can a couple go before marriage without sinning?" From the minds of innocent children came questions that society has posed for years.

The problem with pushing the limits is that one begins to question the One who set the limits in the first place. When the limits become ambiguous, they are usually dropped because the Maker of limits is put in question—in this case, God.

How can Christian leaders advise young women about the options of marriage versus singleness? Luci Swindoll, unmarried sister of Charles Swindoll, believes that some women should choose singleness. In her book *Wide My World, Narrow My Bed,* she says that when a woman knows her own temperament she can better decide whether to marry or remain single.[23] To discover one's temperament, she suggests asking certain questions: When I am alone, can I be content? Am I a self-starter? When things go wrong, can I laugh at my dilemma, or do I need someone else to pull me up? Is the majority of my time spent in constructive growth or in stagnation? How much do I lean on other people? In crisis situations do I usually panic?[24]

Luci Swindoll suggests that one way a young woman can know herself better is to ask why in various situations. "Why did I behave in that manner?" "Why did I laugh at that when it was at someone else's expense?" "Why don't I find joy in what I'm doing?" "Why am I lonely?"[25]

Perhaps one of the greatest ways church leaders can help never-marrieds is to encourage them to find contentment regardless of whatever condition they are in at a given time. As Paul explained in Philippians 4:11, 13: "I am not saying this because I am in need, for I have learned to be content whatever the circumstances. . . . I can do everything through him who gives me strength." This is our task as leaders—to model before our women a contentment that can come only from the Lord. We must teach our women to embrace their singleness, developing themselves to the fullest of their potential in Christ, believing that God's highest goal for them is to glorify Him—while waiting on His timing to place them in relationships of His choosing.

WHAT CAN BE DONE?

In summary, church leaders need to do the following:

- Provide activities for singles in which they can develop healthy friendships.
- Plan conferences and retreats for singles in which they have opportunity to deepen friendships and to interact with issues of concern to them.
- Schedule some women's meetings in the evenings or Saturdays so that working singles can attend.
- Put never-marrieds in touch with mature women and mature married couples who can model Christian standards.
- Set up a "Heart-to-Heart" program in which younger singles are assigned individually to older women for prayer, fellowship, and discipling.
- Show compassion to hurting singles.
- Provide counseling services for women who sense the need for help.
- Teach biblical principles of morality, marriage, sex, singleness, divorce.
- Teach what the Bible says about how to deal with one's loneliness, frustrations, worries, anger.
- Emphasize what the Bible says about contentment and patience.
- Offer practical help to women who are looking for employment and housing.
- Offer to help women with repairs in their apartments or on their cars.
- Enlist never-marrieds to serve in various church ministries, such as the nursery, the church library, Sunday school, boys and girls clubs, camping, and music.

"If the church does not effectively minister to its singles in the next decade, [those singles] will turn to secular programs that cannot answer their spiritual needs."[26]

Chapter Fourteen

Ministering to
Women Who Work at Home

*H*ave you ever filled out an application where your choices of occupation were either "Housewife" or "Place of Work?" I never felt like either box fit me. I wasn't married to a house, and I certainly worked hard from dawn until bedtime and sometimes during the night if the children were sick. I didn't receive a paycheck for a "nine-to-five" job, and I didn't know my Social Security number because I never used it. I consider it a privilege that I was able to stay at home and manage our household and raise our three wonderful children, but this privilege is enjoyed by fewer and fewer women because of our demanding economy. It often takes the income of both spouses to maintain households today, and I'm not talking about having a luxurious style of life. Later I will talk about single mothers who have to juggle both worlds—that of homemaker and businesswoman. The demands on their lives are tremendous because their income usually places them at the lower end of the economic scale.

THE GULF BETWEEN

The needs of women who choose to work in the home and those who work away from the home differ greatly. Actually, the categories are more diversified than these two would imply, for women who work at home can have as their primary focus of endeavor the managing of the household and taking care of the children, or they can also run a home business (a fast-growing option). Women who work outside the home also can be divided into two groups: those who choose a career outside the home as their primary focus, and those who find it mandatory to work outside the home to carry part of the financial burdens of the family. Single or married women can fit into any of these groups. Since many women must juggle their roles between work at home and outside the home, these distinctions are no longer clear-cut. Levels of dissatisfaction vary, depending on how stretched the woman feels and how satisfied she is with her outside career. Whether by personal choice or mandated, many women who work outside the home receive the disapproval of women in the church who judge their choices as wrong. This chapter addresses the concerns of women who choose to stay in the home (and are able to do so).

In past years I worked for a Christian organization called Creative Leadership Ministries, a nonprofit leadership-training organization led by Randy Frazee and Bill Donahue.[1] A study course they designed for women who stayed at home was called *The Creative Homemaker*.[2] The first objective of this organization is "to more effectively deal with issues facing homemakers and be able to give and receive support and encouragement wherever needed." The second objective is "to develop skills necessary to strive for excellence in homemaking so they may glorify God." And the third is "to see a vision for the responsibilities and relationships to which God has called them, especially in the areas of marriage, parenting, home management and personal life."[3] This program has expanded in recent years to include curricula for mothers of teens, mothers of adult children, and single moms.

FOCUS ON MARRIAGE

I was once asked to address a group composed of young mothers with six or more children in each household. The consensus of the group was that each wife had put her marriage, as she described it, "on hold" until the children were out of the nest. They said that it was impossible to work on marriage at the same time as parenting. However, if a woman's marriage is put on hold for the child-rearing years, there will be no marriage at the end. The husband and wife might stay together because of their Christian commitment and their mutual involvement with the children, but what would have occurred would be an emotional divorce—unfortunately, a condition that's accepted in Christian circles.

As long as a couple stays together, they're biblical in our eyes, but are they in God's eyes? "For this reason a man will leave his father and mother and be united to his wife, and they will become one flesh. The man and his wife were both naked, and they felt no shame" (Gen. 2:24–25). God focuses on the importance of marriage, not children. When God said, "It is not good for the man to be alone. I will make a helper suitable for him" (2:18), He wasn't telling the man that He was going to provide someone for his children and a housekeeper to take care of the things he didn't have time to do. He was saying that He was providing a soul mate—a suitable counterpart who would be a companion physically, emotionally, psychologically, socially, and spiritually. The "one-flesh" image involves all of these—not just physical companionship.

A number of older couples have sat in my office and told me that they had long since become strangers to their mates. One broken woman sitting next to her husband looked at him and said, "We've been married for thirty years, but I don't really know this man."

Good marriage relationships take work—constant work. It's almost like housework—it's never done! Once you think you've covered one area, it comes around again. In our society it is so easy for a typical family to look like this: The husband is married to his work, and the wife is married to her house (that's probably where we got the awful term *housewife*) and heavily involved with the children. After all, these small little creatures can be molded into filling great emotional voids in a woman's heart—to the children's detriment, I might add.

FOCUS ON PARENTING

Children need to be allowed to be children, parents need to be parents, and spouses need to be spouses. The difficulty comes because a couple actually has two very important roles: the spousal role and the parental role. We so easily enmesh the two that we lose sight of our greatest teaching tool for our children—that of modeling, first, what a couple is like when both partners deeply love their God and each other, and second, what authority is like in the hands of loving parents.

Too often these roles are confusing to the children. The spouses call each other "Mommy" and "Daddy," conveying to their children that everyone is on the same level. Good parenting also takes time. I have shared with mothers of school-aged children that each morning after my children left for school, as I was straightening up their rooms, I would kneel beside each bed and pray specifically for that child's individual needs. Whenever they left our home, even in their college years, I continued to pray at their bedside each day. I patterned this after Job's lifestyle described in Job 1:5: "Early in the morning he would sacrifice a burnt offering for each of them, thinking, 'Perhaps my children have sinned and cursed God in their hearts.' This was Job's regular custom."

FOCUS ON PERSONAL GROWTH

One of the most difficult things homemakers continue to talk about with me is the way the church and community compare them with businesswomen. Mothers have told me that they wouldn't think of shopping at the grocery store around the time businesswomen tend to shop. The picture homemakers have of the working woman is someone who looks like she has it all together—nails, hair, dress, jewelry, weight, and so forth. To the harried mom, the businesswoman appears composed, content, and never frazzled. At least, that's what our culture tries to portray.

Each morning on my way to work, I pass a large billboard with the picture of an artist's rendition of a "housewife": unironed housedress with food-stained apron, hair still up in curlers, holding a small child in one arm while holding a mixing bowl in the other, one child sitting in the middle of the floor playing with stuff pulled out of the trash can, another spilling cereal on the couch in front of the television, a dog tracking mud across the carpet, pictures crooked on the wall, laundry piled high on the washer, and an equal amount of unfolded clean clothes in the basket. The artist clearly portrayed a dismal situation, the view many people have of "homemaking."

And then there's Betty Friedan, pioneer of the feminist movement, who came along and "told" homemakers how they felt—and it was always a feeling of dissatisfaction and longing for something "better." Yet that same Betty Friedan (now almost eighty years old) has just received a one-million-dollar grant from the Ford Foundation to study flexible work structures that are more supportive of family and community.[4]

AREAS OF CONCERN

I have also seen the other side of this coin in Christian circles where women who stay at home criticize those who don't. They judge mothers who have to juggle their roles between home and work in order to keep food on the table or to help their husbands make it through graduate school. Some of these working wives have told me that occasionally they have been accosted for their dual roles—being judged that they are "unbiblical." One young working mom shared with me that when she attended a wives' fellowship, another mom told her that she was out of God's will by working and not staying home.

We Christians are quick to judge others. Does playing God make us feel superior or more spiritual? As leaders, we need to instill in other women a gentle, loving spirit—one that will encourage rather than tear down, and offer assistance rather than judge.

Another area of concern today is home-schooling. Some of the women we will be working with have chosen to home-school. This is a difficult topic to discuss in any group because there are such strong opinions on both sides. On several occasions I have been asked to meet with church groups to mediate discussions on this topic. Sometimes when mothers feel burdened to home-school their children, they jump into the program with such fervency that they can see no other perspective. The feelings of self-sacrifice sometimes surface to the point that some moms feel "super-spiritual." In their opinion, they are giving up a part of themselves that other moms aren't willing to give up. This superior attitude spills over into the church, and factions are created, wrong things said, wounds are created, and splits occur.

Several years ago I conducted a seminar for a church that was having difficulty with some very vocal "home-schooling moms." After one of my sessions, a young mom shared with me some problems in her marriage. She went into detail to describe her marriage, her routine with her three children, and her lifestyle in general. Her children had scored above their grade level in every class they took. As I began to ask more questions about her marriage, I realized that she was investing by far the majority of herself in her children. The more troubled her marriage became, the more she poured herself into the one area where she could excel—because it could be graphed on grade levels.

When she paused to ask suggestions for her marriage, I said, "Well, this is Sunday, so tomorrow morning, if I were you, I'd put my three children in the car and drive them to the nearest school and enroll them in appropriate classes for their ages." She was shocked at my suggestion and said, "That's impossible, they're doing so well at home!" I replied, "But in the long run, what kind of lesson will you be teaching them when your marriage falls apart?" She walked away because the price was too much to pay in order to save her marriage.

I am certainly *not* saying that home-schooling is wrong! And fortunately many, if not most, home-schooling mothers do not have marital problems. We are living in a very hostile world, and our growing children need protection—but so do our marriages. And to feel that we are more spiritual than others because we are making such sacrifices places us in the category of the Pharisees, who felt themselves superior to others because of their pious lifestyle.

Balance is the key. After all, each of us needs balance in our Christian lives. Our marriages, by God's design, are to show Christ's relationship to His church, and if we do not have enough strength to devote adequate time and energy—both physical and emotional—to our marriages, adjustment needs to be made elsewhere. It has been wisely said that the best lesson you can teach your children is to love your mate.

I am a schoolteacher and have been for many years. I know what it takes—what kind of investment it requires in time and energy. If we could put that kind of energy into our marriages, what a lesson that would be for a dying world that seems to have lost all sense of value, priorities, self-worth, commitment, and order.

SINGLE MOMS

In 1993 alone there were 1,196,600 births to unmarried women.[5] Most women in this group will face different stresses because of limited finances forcing them into the workplace, which will usually involve day care for the children and limited involvement with them because of lack of time. We will discuss this group more in our next chapter on women in the work force, but fortunately some single moms have the opportunity to stay at home. I am aware of some older parents who provide financial assistance for their adult daughters so they can stay at home with their children and not have to be employed. Other single moms are able to stay at home because of insurance or divorce settlements. For whatever reason, we need to see the specific needs surrounding this group of women. Sometimes the overwhelming responsibility of making all decisions, of having no spousal support or encouragement, and the overall aloneness that accompanies single motherhood creates needs different from those in other groups.

One problem that needs to be addressed here is the tendency of the single mother to bring the children up into her emotional world, making them "emotional spouses." I interviewed a woman who had been a single mom for five and a half years. During this time she had made her small daughter her "best friend" and confided in her as she would a peer. Some children can rise to these occasions and develop very deceiving appearances of maturity. Often parents of this kind of children will playfully say, "She's ten, going on twenty-five." But a ten-year-old child can't really process adult thoughts and interactions well. She needs to be ten.

In the interview the mother told me that her daughter felt more like an adult than a child, and that the daughter wanted to control situations. One evening when the mom was sitting on the couch with her date, her young daughter came in and said, "You've been with my mommy long enough for today, so it's time for you to go home." The real difficulty began to show up when the mom married this man, because she had allowed her daughter to sleep in her bed for the past five years. The "little adult" felt terribly displaced and needed counseling to adjust to the new situation. With counseling, some things were resolved, but they could have been avoided to some extent if that single mother had been able to have some interaction in her church with some helpful women for support.

It's difficult for a person like a single mother to keep a proper perspective when having to make so many decisions alone. Here again, in the Christian community we are so protective of our lives, not allowing others to enter, possibly for fear of being judged. Perhaps a group of women with similar life situations could be drawn together into a group for encouragement. Or perhaps pairing these women up with older women who have worked through some of these issues would be helpful.

I have also worked with single moms who chose to have children for the wrong reasons. There is a trend today among teens to want a child to give them their rite of passage into womanhood. Some teens are so lonely that they are looking for someone to love them completely, and they grab onto the idea of a child being able to love in this way. They are sadly confused when they give birth to a totally helpless, demanding infant who needs love and care, rather than being able to give it. Somehow our churches need to become more involved in the lives of their people—getting them help through education, but also through mentoring, modeling, and caring. Some of these young women we're discussing are forced to live with their own parents because of finances and lack of skills to live life on their own. For them to be searching so desperately for someone to love them tells us a lot about their family environment, so perhaps we also need to back up and work with parents, teaching them how to love their children.

ASSUMPTIONS TO EMBRACE

Somewhere the cycle is getting broken, or young women's lives wouldn't be so empty and unfulfilled. How can we as leaders get together and plan organized programs in our churches that meet the needs of our women today? Or do we continue in programs of the past that have long since lost their effectiveness? If we don't continue to grow and stay aware of the issues, we won't be able to minister effectively to those whom God has placed under our leadership.

We cannot impart what we don't possess. "These commandments that I give you today are to be upon your hearts. Impress them on your children. Talk about them when you sit at home and when you walk along the road, when you lie down and when you get up" (Deut. 6:6–7). If the truths of God's Word have not gripped our own hearts, how can we expect to excite the women God has placed in our path with the relevancy of God's Word for them? It can't be done because what we are speaks so loudly that they will not be able to hear what we say. For our ministries to be effective, our lives must model before the women of today something that is worth copying.

Chapter Fifteen

Ministering to
Women Who Work outside the Home

*F*orty-three percent of married women who are mothers in our evangelical churches work outside the home.[1] This doesn't even include the number of single, unmarried women we've already discussed.

Special tensions, needs, and dynamics define each category of working women. According to our culture's picture of fulfillment in life, women cannot possibly find fulfillment in the home. For years women have heard this message from school, media, and the feminist voice. When women first left the home, many tried to juggle home responsibilities as well as work responsibilities and found a lot of frustration with the added requirements. For the Christian woman another tension emerged—criticism from fellow Christians, hearing that "a woman's place is in the home." As stated before, some women pursue a career by choice, while others seek work out of necessity to supplement family income. Once in the work force, many women have become disillusioned because of the tremendous pull between home and the world of work.

CHANGING TRENDS IN THE WORK FORCE

Whether we like it or not, we are living in a fast-changing society. We are getting away from tradition in almost every sector of our lives—home, society, and church. As Christians we are constantly being challenged to assess what is of utmost importance to us, what our individual needs are, how we are to respond to this rapidly changing society, and where our stand on biblical principles places us in all of the above areas. In our society it is sometimes difficult to juggle all the balls that have been thrown to us. The traditional home life consisting of a father who is the sole breadwinner, the mother who is totally dedicated to raising and nurturing the children and providing a pleasant environment for her husband to come home to—with hot meals, warm support, and appreciation for what he is doing for the family—is rapidly disappearing.

To a great extent economics have dictated that this picture be altered. Men often could not bring home enough money to meet all the growing needs of their families, but also some women developed a deep longing in their hearts to find a fulfillment of their dreams which stretched beyond the home. To some extent, dissatisfaction with being at home has come from many sources—partly from our society which says that at-home women are not reaching their potential, but also from husbands not honoring the roles of their wives, treating many of the traditional chores as menial and insignificant. In addition, women began to discover that their spiritual gifts were not being fully utilized. The more we look at Scripture and history, the more we see how versatile women were in past centuries, and how many hats they wore in society, government, church, and home.

For a given period of time women were forced to enter the work force because the men were engaged in war, but when the men returned home and went to work, many women didn't want to quit their jobs. Society shouted that the workplace outside the home was the place to find significance. "There is no doubt about it—the march of women into the workplace disrupted the family unit. With no support from companies or government, parents faced a simple but overwhelming question, 'Who is going to care for the kids?'"[2] Day-care centers that sprang up everywhere were not well-planned or equipped, so they were poorly prepared to take over the responsibilities of the family.

One thing is certain today—women are a critical mass in the work force. Of the 1996 work force 58,501,000 were women and 68,207,000 were men.[3] In other words, 46 percent of the workers were women. At the beginning of the twenty-first century 50 percent of the work force will be female, and more than 80 percent of women between the ages of twenty-five and fifty-four will be employed. The majority of women with infants (53 percent) now work; this is up from 38 percent in 1980.[4] Naisbitt and Aburdene said that for the twenty years between 1970 and 1990, women in the United States "have taken two thirds of the millions of new jobs created in the information era and will continue to do so well into the millennium."[5]

If the family is once again to be the core of our lives, it needs help—from the church and from society. How can we as church leaders help women who are juggling so many balls in the air—personal relationships with God, marriages, children, work, and home management? That old "beautifully painted picture of the 1960s" is beginning to fade. Having the best of both worlds sometimes means enjoyment of neither and frustration in both. If, in fact, Americans are refocusing on the family, what does that family look like today?

Patricia Aburdene and John Naisbitt have noted two changes in the typical American family: Families are smaller, and single parents head up more of them. In 1990 there were 10 million single parents, up more than 40 percent since 1980 (about 8.5 million were women, and 1.5 million were men). Women now head 29 percent of the households in the United States.[6] In 1970, 85 percent of households were composed of married couples with children under eighteen. By 1996, however, that percentage fell to 68 percent, because so many new single-parent households were formed.[7] Can we perhaps be of help to the single moms by reaching out to their children? These mothers must be overwhelmed in today's society. When I talk with mothers who are part of a two-parent household, they constantly say that being a mother to several children is definitely a "full-time" job. Where does that place the single moms who have to juggle both home and work?

Over the past ten years there has been a gradual shift in thinking. Rather than accumulating more money, couples are beginning to rethink their values toward relationships. This is a shift in our society from the consumerism vision of the good life to a realization that we need more time, not more money. A survey conducted by the Family Research Council in Washington, D.C., found that 78 percent of adults would prefer to work flexible hours, even if it meant slower career advancement, so they could spend more time with their families.[8] The director of the Institute for American Values in New York said, "There's a shift from being achievement-oriented to finding your sense of identity and fulfillment in the family."[9]

Leisure time—not money—is becoming the status symbol of the 1990s. The market research firm Yankelovich Clancy Shulman found that 28 percent of working women in 1990 wanted to quit their jobs to put more energy into being mothers and homemakers—nearly double the 1981 number.[10] This will give us a tremendous opportunity to get involved in their lives. Are our churches ready to help them in this transition?

OPTIONS FOR WOMEN IN THE WORK FORCE

Today mothers have a number of options available to them. First, a growing number of mothers are choosing to employ "nannies" for their children. The International Nanny Association (INA), a nonprofit organization based in Austin, Texas, estimates there are 75,000 experienced nannies nationwide. This is becoming a middle-class phenomenon. At the California Nanny College, in Sacramento, students take six months of classes in child development, infant and toddler health and safety, nutrition, and CPR certification, and a supervised internship. Each year about two hundred students graduate from this college.[11]

This system gives working mothers opportunity to have their children cared for in their own home rather than in day-care centers. But this plan can be greatly abused. For example, I personally see the nanny who takes care of the five children living next door to me more than I see their mother, who does not have a job. We must ask, "Are these nannies being used in place of day care, so that the mothers can work, or are they being used so that the mothers won't have to be tied down to raising their children? How can we encourage mothers to spend important time with their growing children?" Once those developmental years are gone, they can never be retrieved.

Another option some women are pursuing is a "home business." Either full-time or part-time home-based businesses increased to 38.4 million in 1991, up 12 percent from 1990. Of these, 12 million were self-employed home workers. Another 10.5 million were moonlighters or people who had several part-time jobs they carried out at home. The number of self-employed women working full-time at home tripled between 1985 and 1991, from 378,000 to 1.1 million.[12] This seems to be the trend for the next century and perhaps this will open doors of opportunity for us to minister to these women.

A third form of "home work" is telecommuting, in which a company-employed person works part-time or full-time at home during normal business hours. This new form of work at home grew by 38 percent, to 5.5 million, between 1990 and 1991. Many companies, including Sears, Pacific Bell, New York Life Insurance Company, John Hancock Insurance Company, J. C. Penney, and IBM, employ telecommuters who work two or more days at home.[13] Today 36 percent of the labor force works at home. By the year 2000, the portion could be well over 50 percent.[14]

How can our churches support women at work and encourage them spiritually? How can we develop innovative ways of reaching them for Christ? How can we help these women maintain balance in their busy lives?

In 1996 the Bureau of Labor Statistics of the U.S. Department of Labor listed six major categories of occupations of employed women. Women working in managerial and professional fields comprised 34.1 percent; technical sales and administrative support, 41.3 percent; service occupations, 12.8 percent; operators, fabricators, laborers, 8.9 percent; precision production, craft, and repair, 2.4 percent; and farming, forestry, fishing, 0.5 percent.[15]

CAREERS BEST SUITED FOR WOMEN

According to national analysts, ten careers are presently rated best for women. The first choice is working at a job that takes into consideration a woman's needs, talents, and desires for creative self-expression—a "dream job" tailor-made just for her.

The second choice is that of CEO or entrepreneur. Analysts suggest that women can take an entrepreneurial approach and start their own businesses. The Small Business Administration (SBA) predicts that women will own nearly 40 percent of small businesses by 2000. The year 1992 was the "crossover year" when women-owned businesses employed more people than the top five hundred businesses in the United States. A great example of an extremely successful small business belongs to a woman named Jean Griswold, founder and CEO of Special Care, a Philadelphia-based provider of home care to the elderly, handicapped, and children, with seventeen franchises in eight states. Griswold, confined to a wheelchair because of multiple sclerosis, is the wife of a minister who saw firsthand that elderly people need companions. Visiting nurses can stay only a few hours, but Special Care's more than three thousand nurses' aides help with baths, shopping, and companionship, providing around-the-clock care.[16]

I have a friend whose son sent her a piece of torn sailboat sail from camp and asked her if she could do anything with the material. My creative friend made him a pair of shorts out of the sail and sent them back to him. Within a few days, he had thirty-five requests from fellow-counselors for similar shorts, so from that simple beginning emerged a full-blown sports line, made from sail fabric, which was initially constructed in her home. Entire cheerleading squads began to order shorts and tops made in their school colors, and with the addition of a personalized logo, the line was patented and marketed in stores.

A third career choice is healthcare. Any look at the boom industries of the 1990s must begin with healthcare—an $800-billion-a-year business that will soon reach $1 trillion a year. From technician to physician, from unskilled worker to Ph.D. researcher, healthcare offers many opportunities. There were 8.4 million healthcare workers in 1990. In that year alone medical employment grew 7.7 percent—the largest for any major job category. The Bureau of Labor Statistics says six of the ten fastest-growing occupations from 1990 to 2005 will be in healthcare: home health aides, personal and home-care aides, physical therapists, medical assistants, radiological technicians, and medical secretaries.[17]

Longevity of life is increasing the need for nurses today. The United States alone needs 767,000 more nurses by the year 2005. By that time the number of registered nurses will reach 2.5 million, up from 1.7 million in 1990, an amazing jump of 44 percent in only fifteen years. The National League of Nurses reports that most newly licensed nurses—80 percent—

describe themselves as "satisfied" with their jobs. The nursing shortage boosted average salaries for staff nurses to $34,500 in 1991. The American Association of Colleges of Nursing says that nursing professors earn in the mid-$60,000s, but a nursing professor with a doctorate at a top private college can earn more than $100,000. Nursing directors average $62,300.[18]

With incomes like that, it is no wonder nursing is ranked the eighth-best-paying profession for women, according to the Bureau of Labor Statistics.[19] In 1991 some women nurses earned more money than nonentrepreneurial female physicians.

Job satisfaction among nurses has grown since hospitals restructured their tasks. Primary-care nurses are responsible for twenty-four-hour planning for a patient, just as physicians are. Working with the physicians, the nurses follow patients from admission to discharge. At Boston's Beth Israel Hospital, the nursing vice president and nurse in chief have equal rank with the hospital's chief of medicine. These facts are astounding and present an option for some women to consider. Many wives put their husbands through seminary by working in nursing. Often these women can choose their hours of work to revolve around family.

The fourth available option is the field of finance. According to surveys finance is one of the most suitable kinds of employment for women. More than half of the accountants in the United States are women. A *Business Week* survey of male and female MBAs from the top twenty business schools showed the narrowest wage gap was in finance—there women earned only 3.3 percent less than men.[20]

A fifth choice is to return to some of the traditional jobs of past years that have recently gained new respect. In the past a career woman could choose to be a nurse, secretary, or a teacher—and that was all. But when millions of women broke into business and the professions, the demand for competent people in traditional female jobs increased—as did wages and status. Nursing has already proven to fit such a description. In the area of teaching, the U.S. Department of Education says that our nation will need new public-school teachers at the rate of two hundred thousand a year, and by the year 2000 our schools will need nearly two million new teachers. And since one-third of all present tenured professors will retire by 2000, the need for more college teachers will greatly increase. The average U.S. teacher's salary in the 1990–1991 school year was $32,880. Starting salaries averaged $21,542, according to the American Federation of Teachers. In 1992, U.S. high school principals averaged $61,768 a year.[21]

The U.S. will need 250,000 new secretaries by 2005. In addition, we now need 158,000 medical and 133,000 legal secretaries. For the young woman who does not want to attend college but is willing to go to a one- or two-year training course, being a secretary could have great appeal. In New York City a top secretary earns $75,000. In the past, being a secretary was an occupation with little prestige. No wonder 62 percent of secretaries surveyed in 1991 wanted a different job title, and 52 percent preferred "administrative assistant," according to Professional Secretaries International.[22]

The sixth possibility is working in "high tech" firms or in some field of science. According to the Bureau of Labor Statistics 1991 figures, two of the best-paying job categories for women are computer science and engineering. Women do not hold the top jobs, but they are earning a respectable income in high technology. By the year 2005 our nation will need 366,000 new systems analysts and computer scientists, about 79 percent more than in 1990. In addition we will need more than 300,000 computer programmers.[23] Of the fast-growing careers this is probably the best-paying option.

A seventh vocational choice is related to food services. Millions of women put dinner on the table every night, but until recently the world's top chefs were male. Before 1970 the Culinary Institute of America, in Hyde Park, New York, did not admit women. Today women make up about 20 percent of its students.[24] A fast-growing branch of this area is catering. Many women can have approved kitchen facilities away from their homes (because certified kitchens cannot be in living facilities) and can operate the business portion out of their homes to cater weddings and parties. This arrangement gives them flexibility in their family schedules.

An eighth option is the professions of law and medicine. Women now earn 40 percent of law degrees and one third of M.D. degrees. Women make up 50 percent of new primary-care physicians, in specialties like family practice. The American Medical Association includes over one hundred thousand female physicians. Women are enjoying these two fields because earnings continue to be relatively high and healthcare is growing rapidly. Specialties that have emerged within the medical field are particularly attractive to women—especially adult women's medicine.[25]

Ninth, some women are entering the traditionally "male-dominated" occupations of firefighters, airline pilots and navigators, law-enforcement officers, sports reporters and broadcasters, construction workers, and politicians. For example, the National Women's Political Caucus said that in 1997 eighty-one women held statewide elected executive office posts— 25 percent of the total. In that year forty-three states had women mayors of cities with populations of more than 30,000; California led the country with fifty-four. Also Congress included a record number of nine women senators and fifty women representatives—11.5 percent of the elected members. In the President's Cabinet in 1997 four positions were held by women: Attorney General, Health and Human Services Secretary, Secretary of State, and Secretary of Labor.[26]

A tenth choice is in the arts and media,[27] a huge arena in which to serve God. Christian artists are using these avenues to proclaim the gospel throughout the world.

GUIDELINES TO CONSIDER

As Christians we must always undergird all our desires with the Word of God. Often we come into a situation with our preconceived ideas of what is right for us and for others as well. If others don't fit within our acceptable lifestyle, we tend to separate ourselves from them, criticizing their choices. The body of Christ is made up of a greatly diversified group of individuals—with differing needs and responsibilities. We are quick to judge others, much more than we are willing to judge ourselves. Whether a woman should be employed outside the home is a major question for many Christian families. Families must decide what is important for them and how they can best go about achieving those goals.

We also need to consider that it's easy to get caught up in the consumerism of our American culture. About one-third of the nation's population describe themselves as either heavily or moderately in financial debt, one-third report being slightly in debt, and only one-third report no financial debts (excluding home mortgages) at all.[27] This rise in indebtedness is due mainly to credit cards. Between 1990 and 1996, credit-card debt doubled.[28] In our mentoring of women, we need to help them refocus on what should be a Christian's priorities in life. One of the most popular class periods in the Premarital Counseling seminary course I teach is when I invite a guest lecturer trained in finance to speak to the class. The majority of young couples starting out today have little or no clue about how to establish a budget and stick to it, about the pitfalls of credit-card debts, or the discipline of delaying purchases until money is available. So the financial adviser addresses these issues. He sets up private consultations with individual couples at no charge to help them begin to understand good stewardship. Because money issues are major sources of stress in families, we must help our women know how to make wise choices.

Women who are juggling both home management and outside work are working an average of fifteen hours more per week than men. Women who have chosen full-time careers outside the home are constantly measuring themselves against corporate men who enjoy the support of "at-home wives."[29]

Research has determined that women leaders are better at balancing than their male counterparts. Women do not identify exclusively with their careers, as most men traditionally have done. Businesswomen more consistently take time out for recreation, and because of this trait, churches have a tremendous opportunity to minister to them. Any kind of program concerned about meeting the needs of working women must be adaptable to their work schedule. We can't expect them to be available for the regular hours traditionally designated for women's ministries in our churches, and yet they need to have opportunities for spiritual growth.

SEEKING OUT AVENUES FOR MINISTRY

In past years I have taught once-a-week classes from 7:00 to 7:50 A.M. for businesswomen in the church I attend. They were based on the Creative Leadership Ministries leadership-training program, created by Randy Frazee and Bill Donahue. The program starts with each woman creating a personal "Life Vision," which includes character development, marriage, children, church, work, personal life, location, other relationships and responsibilities, and time and money.[30] Time and money are always two of the more difficult things for which to establish a vision—and to follow. The women are encouraged to determine their giving practices, time management, savings, children's education, protection, budgets, debts, vacations, and hobbies. All these things must be thought through and prioritized. After creating a life vision for each of these areas, the women begin intensive training in Bible survey, how to study the Bible, and how to communicate the Bible, all designed to equip them to be more effective defenders of the faith in the marketplace.

Once I was invited to watch a panel of business people question several women and men who had completed the entire series, and I was greatly impressed with the poise they had in answering questions thrown at them by their business associates. I was especially impressed with a surgeon who attended the session in his green scrub suit because he had just finished surgery. He had in his pocket a small group of laminated cards he had made for himself with key Bible verses and doctrines in outline. He would review them at stoplights and other available times.

Using creative means to reach businesswomen in our churches will enable them to grow spiritually and become more effective witnesses in the workplace. After all, Paul was so well-versed in the views of the philosophers of his day that he seized the opportunity to address their desire for knowledge and to present the truth of God's Word to them (Acts 17:16–34). We can help equip women to be confident in God's Word so that they will also be able to seize opportunities in this age of tolerance to present Christ to others.

Too often we overlook businesswomen because of the scarcity of time available in their schedules or our personal impression of their assumed lack of interest. Sometimes their perceived aloofness comes as protection against what they sense as rejection from other Christians of what they do. Married or single, a woman of God can accomplish much at home and in the marketplace.

Chapter Sixteen

Ministering to
Women of Different Cultures

*J*ust as we should view male and female as different without labeling one "inferior" and the other "superior," so we should view cultural differences the same way. In the past thirty years the American "melting pot" has been turned upside down and its contents poured out to create the pluralistic society we see today.[1] The United States Bureau of Census has projected that by the year 2000, 12.9 percent of our population will be African American, 11.1 percent Hispanic, 4.5 percent Asian/Pacific Islander, and 0.9 percent American Indian/Eskimo/Aleut.[2] Of course within each of these categories there is much diversity—foreign-born immigrants and their American-born children, English- and non-English-speaking groups, varying social statuses, differences in educational levels, and different positions held in the lands of origin.

To minister effectively we must do a number of things. First, we must recognize that prejudice is wrong and seek to overcome it with the Lord's help. Prejudice is thinking negatively of others without sufficient justification. It is the process of "stereotyping, by which certain characteristics, either positive or negative, are ascribed to all members of a group."[3] Prejudice often arises because of the differing cultured contexts in which we were raised. Bearing the name of Christ, Christians need to oppose any form of racism or prejudice.

Second, Christian ministry calls for increasing our cultural sensitivity,[4] that is, our own awareness of cultural differences, and our seeking to raise the cultural sensitivity of those to whom we are ministering.[5]

Third, we must learn to present God's truths to a world filled with ethnic diversity. The gospel is "not the expression of one ethnic group or tradition, but rather the proclamation [of good news] for all humanity."[6]

When I was a seminary student, a "day of evangelism" was scheduled each year. Classes were dismissed, students went by pairs into the community, knocking on doors and sharing the gospel. One year my partner was a young man filled with a passion to share the gospel. So when we knocked on the first door, I stood back and let him take the lead. A young Hispanic woman came to the door, with a baby in her arms and two other small children holding on to her skirt. In her broken English, she invited us into her apartment. My partner started witnessing to her in words that seemed to confuse the young mother. I had taken two of her children to one side and was playing with them, when the young mother turned away from my partner and sat on the floor with me. The Lord allowed me to share the gospel with her and to win her to Christ.

When my partner and I left her apartment, his first question to me was, "How in the world were you able to reach her so quickly?" I explained that as a mother, I knew of her preoccupation with three children, and as a teacher of small children in Sunday school, I knew I would have to communicate in the simplest of terms in order to be understood. In a multicultural society, we must learn to explain our faith in terms that will truly communicate.

Reuben H. Brooks presents six facts about cross-cultural ministry we should incorporate in our Christian world-view: "(1) The Bible shows no ethnically pure 'correct' culture. (2) As in the Bible, so today we should accept people from every culture and ethnic group as our neighbors and treat them with mutual respect and dignity. (3) The Old Testament Scripture is replete with examples of a transcultural gospel. (4) The New Testament does not show one culture to be the correct one and all others wrong. (5) The true message of Christianity is a person, Jesus Christ. (6) To cross into other cultures is the expected norm for God's people, not the exception."[7]

FIVE ETHNIC GROUPS

To understand women's needs, we must be familiar with their unique cultures. And even though we must also avoid stereotyping, each woman has an "ethnic heritage that causes her to identify with certain value orientations and behavioral styles that may not be a part of the shared theological or national American culture."[8] In light of this, let's examine some distinctive characteristics of major ethnic groups in the United States.

Women of African Origin

Unlike all other immigrants, the ancestors of most people of African descent came to the Americas in great fear.[9] Today African Americans make up about 12 percent of Americans—about 34 million.[10] Several shared experiences set them apart from other groups: (a) their African legacy, rich in culture, custom, and achievement; (b) their history of slavery; and (c) racism and discrimination.[11] In spite of these difficulties (or perhaps because of them), African Americans have a strong sense of spirituality. African American churches are important social institutions for black individuals.[12] The three largest black denominations are Methodist, Baptist, and Pentecostal.[13] Since approximately one-third of all African American families are in poverty,[14] we must address this fact in our ministries. Because of these hardships, many in the black community have established networks of "family," which assume responsibility for the economic and emotional well-being of those less fortunate. Actually the concept of the extended family can be traced back to family life in West Africa, and we do them a disservice by forcing them into our "traditional" concept of family.

Many black inner-city adolescent girls have become mothers without having married. In 1997 about two-thirds of all childbirths to African Americans involved an unmarried female.[15] In my counseling practice I have found that the main reason young teens (black or white) give for having children outside of marriage is the need to feel loved. One young teen said to me, "I want someone who will love me completely, without strings attached." Can't we find ways to reach out to these lonely young women to show them Christ's love? His love extends beyond cultures, but often that love isn't felt because we fail to be used by Him as His agents.

Women of Hispanic Origin

In 1997, Hispanics (as labeled by the government), numbered 29,156,000,[16] in contrast to 16,940,000 five years before[17]—the fastest-growing ethnic group in America. Most United States Hispanics are below the age of thirty.

This group is extremely diversified. Many are in the low-income category, but there is a growing middle-class group of Mexican-American professionals. They are sometimes criticized for having little contact with the overall problems of Mexican Americans as a minority group; they have been more involved in the corporate world than in social causes.

Many of the cultural values of this ethnic group are traditional, with the family playing a highly valued role in their lives. Like the African American family, the Hispanic family is characterized by the strong presence of the extended family, which shares in responsibilities of caretaking and discipline. These boundaries of child support also extend to individuals with whom the parents have established close bonds as a result of relationships of trust.[18] Their family structure is usually hierarchical in nature, with the father as the authority and the mother in the submissive role. Young girls are brought up with clearly defined sex roles. The traditional idea of *machismo* is the strong, revered male, who is protective of the submissive and virtuous woman, the dedicated caregiver of their children.[19] My daughter has a Mexican-American woman working for her in her home, and the young woman frequently comments how wonderful it is to watch the mutual respect my daughter and her husband have for each other. Modeling the love of Christ goes much further than lectures ever could. Are we willing to allow others to watch our lives, so that we can show them Christ?

Whereas American Caucasians value achievement, Hispanic people value personalism, a form of individualism that values inner qualities in people.[20] What an opportunity to show Hispanic women the value Christ places on them as individuals!

Women of Asian Origin

The Asian-American category consists of several groups: Chinese, Filipino, Japanese, Asian Indian, Korean, Vietnamese, Laotians, and Cambodians (named in order of population numbers). Whereas Hispanics speak the common language of Spanish (or Portuguese), among Asian-American groups at least thirty-two primary languages are spoken. Language is one of the major areas of tension in their families between the older generation with their native language and the younger generation demanding to speak English. Many Asian churches have two separate services—one for the native language and one for the English-speaking youth.

As a group, Asian Americans have the highest average family income in the United States, but of the subgroups, the Vietnamese, Laotians, and Cambodians are among the poorest. Religiously, they are just as diversified. Among Chinese Americans, the most popular religions are Buddhism, ancestor worship, and Christianity. Over 70 percent of Korean Americans are Protestant Christians and attend church regularly. Filipinos are predominantly Roman Catholic. Japanese Americans follow Shintoism, Buddhism, and Christianity. Vietnamese practice Buddhism or Catholicism. The religions of both Cambodians and Laotians are strongly influenced by the Brahmanism of the Hindus, as well as by Buddhism. With the strong influence of Communism in many of their countries, many immigrants may not practice any religion at all.[21]

An effective ministry to people in these groups will require knowing the individuals to whom you will be carrying the gospel and something of their backgrounds. To know about them shows that you care. For example, many of the older generations were exposed to the traumas of war. Many Cambodian women lost their husbands during the bloody Pol Pot regime and had to become heads of their households in America.[22] Their children, growing up in America, cannot identify with their deep sorrows, but we can introduce them to the "Father of compassion and the God of all comfort" (2 Cor. 1:3).

When we are working with Asian women, we need to know that their families have much control over them, even in adulthood. A number of Asian women have shared with me that even in this country, if funds are limited, their brothers were given preferential treatment and sent to college first. Only if money was left over were they allowed to go to college. After all, the girls are supposed to marry and to bear sons. Shame and dishonor are to be avoided at all costs, and compliance to family rules is essential. It is difficult for Asian women to discuss family problems with outsiders, so you will have to support them gently and pray that God will open doors for you to be of help.

Many Asian women I have worked with keep the majority of their emotions inside—a trait they learned from early childhood. I mentioned in an earlier chapter that several years ago my husband and I visited China. He taught Chinese surgeons how to perform a number of surgical procedures. On one occasion we were watching a doctor remove a large coin from a small child's trachea (windpipe). We both watched in amazement as the doctor placed the child on the operating table, had the mother lay across her son to hold him steady, inserted a bronchoscope down his trachea, and removed the coin with forceps—without any anesthetic! Not a whimper came from the small boy. And when the procedure was finished, the mother asked her son, "What do you say to the doctor?" The child replied, *"Xiè xiè"* (pronounced "Shi-Shi," "Thank you"). We were told that children were taught at a very early age to hold their emotions inside.

Women of Native-American Origin

This group of more than 2.3 million people[23] is called by many names— "Original Americans," "Native People," "American Indians," "Amerindians," and "Native Americans"—some of which are extremely offensive to them. The term "Indian" originated in a mistaken association with the "Indians" of India, and the majority of people in this group prefer a name with "Native" attached because it recognizes the antiquity and geographical priority of our country's first inhabitants.[24] When the early Spanish explorers first came to this land, there were at least "two thousand cultures and more societies which practiced a multiplicity of customs and lifestyles, held an enormous variety of values and beliefs, spoke numerous languages, and did not conceive of themselves as a single people."[25]

How do we reach out to the Native-American women who cross our paths? We must be aware of the tremendously difficult oppression their people have experienced through the years. Even as late as the 1960s, the federal government developed a termination/relocation plan, taking many Indians from their homes and families and relocating them to urban centers.[26] We can't even begin to imagine the rippling effects of this action—but suicide, violence, school dropouts, teen pregnancies, and unemployment have increased. There is some similarity between the African American and Native-American families, in which family roles are determined by relationships, not just by blood. Once a young girl marries into a Native-American family, there are no distinctions between natural and inducted family members—they are blended, not joined, through marriage.

Native Americans value the natural world, believing that "God, humanity, and self are all connected. Having the right relationship with nature gives the right relationship with God, which gives the right relationship with the self."[27] Value is also placed on cooperation and conformity instead of competition. Related to this concept is the great respect Native Americans have for their elderly, a fact also true of Asians. Another attribute American Indians value is generosity, in contrast to wealth that most Americans pursue. Their lifestyle is much more people-oriented than that of the dominant culture. Their focus is more on group activity than on individual achievement. They're attempting to enjoy today rather than plan for tomorrow.

Our fast-moving, achievement-oriented culture isn't known for its listening ability, but this is a quality highly valued by the Native American culture. We need to learn the art of listening; this skill will be especially well received by Native-American women.

Women of Non-Hispanic White Origin

Eighty-two percent of the total U.S. population classify themselves as non-Hispanic whites.[28] This majority culture usually sets the standards—whether in fashion, politics, education, or lifestyle. The "ideal" is usually portrayed by the upper middle-class white—the right cars, clothes, weight, makeup, leisure sports, schools, and neighborhoods. All other cultures are expected to strive for this "norm." Our young girls are sometimes expected to emulate the "Barbie doll" mind-set, and by the time they reach adulthood, they often have difficulty focusing on the reality of a non-airbrushed fantasy. How can we be most effective in addressing the important issues in life for these women? How can we teach them the right priorities when they're surrounded by such a materialistic society?

CONCLUSION

If we can slow down and give more of our time, interest, and love to women of various cultural backgrounds, they will sense that we understand them a little, and they will be more open to hearing about our Jesus.

But we must be extremely careful that in becoming "all things to all people" (1 Cor. 9:22), we do not compromise the Word of God in any way. Paul's commitment to the gospel was unwavering, yet he blended with people of various cultures so as to not offend them and thus hopefully to win some of them to Christ.

Chapter Seventeen

Women in Missions

A married couple told me that when they are in the heat of an argument, they lose sight of who's right and who's wrong—each just wants to win, no matter the cost. Is this what's happening in some of our churches today? I wonder if the focus of our debates over women in ministry is sometimes on winning battles rather than on being obedient to the Word of God. All over the world women are serving God in different capacities—in mission organizations, church planting, Bible translation, teaching in colleges and seminaries, and serving in numerous church roles from pastor to secretarial assistants. Some of these positions have been questioned. Some say women should have no leadership capacity in the church, and at the other end of the spectrum some argue that women can and should serve as senior pastors.

This chapter focuses on women's roles in missions both here in the United States and abroad.

What about the role of single women in present-day missions? From North America alone, for the past thirty years single women have made up over 60 percent of the total missionary force.[1]

In 1826 the first woman missionary, Miss Cynthia Farr, was appointed by an American agency to serve overseas. Her appointment as an "assistant missionary" came in response to an urgent request made by the Marathi Mission of India for a single woman to minister with them.[2]

J. Hudson Taylor, founder and longtime director of the China Inland

Mission, now the Overseas Missionary Fellowship, recruited many unordained laypersons, including large numbers of single women, to serve in China. In fact, in the first CIM group that sailed for China, Hudson and Maria Taylor and their four children were accompanied by sixteen missionaries—six men and ten women. They joined four men and one woman who were already in China.[3]

Taylor was criticized for sending unmarried women into the interior (a testimony to the courage of these women).[4] But he also expected married women to do their share of mission work. By 1882, less than twenty years after CIM was founded, this mission had fifty-six wives and ninety-five single women as missionaries.[5] The work of Lottie Moon (1840–1912) as a single female missionary in China became legendary. The missions journal of the Southern Baptist Convention hailed Moon at her death as the "best man among our missionaries."[6]

Fredrik Franson was founder of the mission that later became known as The Evangelical Alliance Mission (TEAM). A contemporary of Hudson Taylor, Franson wrote a paper, "Prophesying Daughters," in which he said, "The fields of labor are large, and when we realize that nearly two-thirds of all converted people in the world are women, then the question of women's work in evangelization is of great importance. In China each day 30,000 people go into eternity without having heard the gospel. There is no prohibition in the Bible against women's public work, and we face the circumstance that the devil has been able to exclude nearly two-thirds of the number of Christians from participation in the Lord's service through evangelization. The loss for God's cause is so great that it can hardly be described."[7] He did not approve, however, of women "preaching."

Franson recruited a volunteer named Malla Moe, who had immigrated to Chicago from Norway, to go to South Africa, where she served for fifty-six years. She filled many roles, including being an evangelist, church planter, preacher, and bishop. She was not ordained and was never referred to as a bishop, but she functioned as one, assigning pastors to the churches she founded and overseeing their continued growth and development. Franson said, "It is amazing how one can get such a false idea as that not all God's children should use all their powers in all ways to save the lost world. There are, so to speak, many people in the water about to drown. A few men are trying to save them, and that is considered well and good. But look, over there a few women have untied a boat also to be of help in the rescue, and immediately a few men cry out; standing there idly looking on and therefore having plenty of time to cry out: 'No, no, women must not help, rather let the people drown.' What stupidity!"[8]

A. B. Simpson, a Presbyterian minister, founded the Christian and Missionary Alliance in 1887. He said that if women furthered the primary mission of the church to reach lost souls for Christ, then he enthusiastically endorsed their ministry to achieve that objective.[9] He was criticized for his open policy for women in ministry, but he was quick to defend his position. After a series of meetings in Atlanta he responded to attacks by saying the matter was an issue "which God has already settled, not only in His Word, but in His providence, by the seal which He is placing in this very day, in every part of the world, upon the public work of consecrated Christian women."[10]

Today the church acknowledges that thousands of women, both married and single, have effectively served overseas, giving their lives in faithful love to Christ and the building of His church. Fortunately, women missionaries in general are no longer considered "assistants" but are regarded as full-time workers. The wide variety of roles filled by women in missions reflects the versatility, adaptability, and competency with which they serve.[11]

This topic wouldn't be complete without mentioning the life of Agnes Gonxha Bojaxhiu, fondly known as "Mother Teresa," Roman Catholic nun and Nobel Prize winner. Most of her work was done among the destitute and dying in India, where in 1948 she founded her religious congregation—the "Missionaries of Charity." She cared for the sick and dying of all religious faiths and remained the head of this congregation until 1997, at which time it had become a worldwide organization of more than five thousand women and men. In 1971 Mother Teresa opened a home for the destitute in New York's Harlem. In 1985 she received the U.S. Presidential Medal of Freedom, the nation's highest civilian award. She died on September 5, 1997. Here was a woman deeply committed to helping the helpless, a woman whose service to others stands as an example of remarkable dedication and diligence.

Although a few tasks in missions are carried on predominantly by men, women are now involved in more avenues than formerly. However, some barriers exist in certain countries, often because of cultural factors. For instance, in Islamic lands female missionaries are usually limited to a ministry among females. Also physical strength sometimes presents a natural obstacle, although many women have proven their amazing endurance in rugged, demanding circumstances. Travel and overnight housing can present difficult problems to a single woman serving in a male-oriented culture. Many of these women are perhaps well-trained in the area of teaching, Christian education, or youth evangelism, but may find themselves serving as secretaries, bookkeepers, or hostesses in a mission center.[12] Natural limitations such as these must not be confused with restrictions imposed by a mission agency. In general, restrictions on women's roles are being lifted, and today a wide range of ministries is available to women in missions.

AREAS OF SERVICE

Many areas of ministry are open to women in missions.

- *Education.* Women have contributed tremendously to the training and development of Christians around the world. Women are involved in many kinds of educational work, such as elementary and secondary schools, colleges, Bible schools, seminaries, and missionary children's schools, and women's Bible studies. In addition, women are effective in teaching women and children in Sunday school classes and children in vacation Bible schools, weekly clubs, and camps. Curriculum development is another area where many women are effective.

- *Health services.* Many highly trained women are serving overseas as doctors, nurses, dentists, midwives, clinicians, researchers, laboratory technicians, and dietitians. Women have founded hospitals, leprosariums, clinics, mobile health centers, and first-aid stations. Some nurses also teach health classes.

- *General missionary work.* In some countries, only women can reach women, just as in Paul's day. Many women have been used of God to lead many unsaved women and children to Christ and to disciple them. Also women can serve as "housemothers" in schools for missionaries' children. Many missionaries depend on dedicated women to serve as spiritual mothers to their children, as well as providing an example of appropriate Christian behavior. Serving as hostesses, women provide warm hospitality for fellow missionaries and guests. Women who are secretaries, bookkeepers, office workers, and computer operators are indispensable to missions. One missionary wife in Japan conducts evangelistic cooking classes.

- *Literature.* The women of Wycliffe Bible Translators have been used extensively for many years as linguists, translators, and teachers in literacy programs. Others are writers, photographers, artists, and bookstore managers.
- *Radio ministry.* Women serve as scriptwriters, announcers, program planners, station managers, and shortwave radio operators.
- *Music.* Some women are especially gifted in teaching music, organizing musical groups, composing, conducting, and singing.
- *Audiovisual work.* Women missionaries have contributed to the development of both visual materials for use in evangelism and teaching, including tape recordings, slide presentations, flannelgraph lessons, and overhead transparencies. Gospel Recordings, Inc., was founded by Joy Ridderhof, who had a vision for reaching the otherwise unreached by means of phonograph records. By 1960 over two million records in more than two thousand languages had been distributed. As a result, many, many people have heard the gospel message from these simple phonograph records.
- *Counseling.* This relatively new field has created demands for the services of Christian psychologists, psychiatrists, and lay counselors. Life on the mission field can be greatly assisted by sound biblical counsel. Many hurting women, both Christians and non-Christians, need the listening ear of a biblically trained counselor-missionary.
- *Relief work.* Women are successfully involved in the management of relief projects in some countries, including the handling of funds and the directing of distribution programs.
- *Administrative assignments.* Some women have appointments in administrative positions, serving on field executive committees and in other administrative roles.[13]

Seminary Women Graduates in Ministry

Women who graduate from evangelical seminaries are filling a great variety of ministry positions all over the world. In 1990 I sent a letter to every female graduate of Dallas Seminary, asking several questions about the kind of ministries in which they are engaged. I received responses from women graduates in eight foreign countries (Austria, Egypt, England, Hong Kong, Indonesia, Kenya, Malaysia, Spain) and seven states.

I discovered that our female graduates overseas and in the States are serving the Lord in many ways: in evangelism, discipling, counseling, teaching, mentoring, coordinating. In addition women graduates in the States serve in small-group ministries, premarital counseling, coordinating of children's work, directing children's church, leading women's missionary fellowships, and youth work. Many of these graduates emphasized the need for women to be trained in how to win people to Christ, how to build friendships, how to counsel, how to develop and lead small groups, how to administer, how to manage conflict, and how to mentor others.

Clearly, women overseas (and here in the United States as well) have numerous opportunities for serving Christ.

Part Four

Establishing a
Women's Ministery

Chapter Eighteen

Developing a Women's Ministry
in Your Church

WOMEN IN A HECTIC SOCIETY

Many young women in churches today feel far away from home. In our culture we are transient people, moving from state to state, leaving relatives and friends far behind. It is not uncommon to find people changing jobs and careers frequently, which often dictates the area of the country they must choose.

Jay Kesler writes about a woman whose situation illustrates a common problem in our moving culture: "When my husband and I got married eight months ago, we moved far away from family and friends. I never imagined how lonely and depressing this could be. My husband's medical work keeps him away most of the time, and I don't know anyone I can really talk to. I write many letters to my old friends, but they don't usually write back."[1]

In past generations this was seldom true in our country. There were often large family networks living on adjoining or nearby lands. Women had a large network of support, instruction, companionship, and encouragement. Men often worked off the land, providing for or swapping for anything that was needed by their families. The young women had numerous role models for practical training, as well as spiritual training. Life was difficult but also simpler than in our present society.[2]

One of the main problems with the mass shift to city life and constant moving is the lack of stability. This lack doesn't just come from not having roots; it also stems from not having proper role models for even the simplest things in life. Where does a young mother go today for her many questions concerning child rearing, or being a godly wife, or dealing with the stresses that overwhelm her world? Of course, she can read books, but she can't interact with the authors. She can't say, "Explain to me how this worked in your life." Another problem with books is knowing how to choose books that have good advice and to reject those that don't. Books will never replace people!

Another problem is that young couples today try to draw all their emotional support from each other, since the extended families are so far removed, and this puts more stress on their relationship. No two people can supply everything that each other needs. People need people—people whom they can depend on for maturing them in their faith, for encouragement, for advice, for support, and for accountability.

Where can we find such people? Our churches are the answer, but this requires strong commitment and perhaps some drastic changes in our thinking. Gone are the days when the simple women's circle meeting met the needs of most women in our churches. We have been sadly lacking in discipleship programs. Since discipleship by definition is teaching and leading another person in the ways of Christ, this type of ministry is needed more today than ever before because the foundations with which many women come into adulthood are not as strong as in past years. Broken homes, job demands, frequent moves, lack of strong church ties—all these play a factor in this scenario.

When I was a child, every night I sat with my father for an hour, listening to him read the Bible and talk of its truths. I remember sitting through the Bible reading, waiting to get to the "fun stuff"—made-up stories full of adventure and excitement about a character named "Death Valley Scottie." The adventure stories have faded away, but the truths of God's Word never have. Many young people I see today are from broken homes, came to know Christ through a college ministry, and then show up in our churches. They are missing the base of strong Bible training in their homes. Therefore a discipleship program in our churches is desperately needed.

Several years ago I discipled four younger women in my home. We met each week for two years, engaged in a basic Bible study called "Equipping the Saints." As we memorized Scripture, ate some meals together, and participated in various kinds of entertainment, we developed a strong bond of friendship. They were able to see my life in both good and difficult times, and I was able to watch them grow in their dependence on the Lord. The mutual encouragement was very exciting—we all grew. These types of situations are not one-sided. As testimonials have shown, all participants benefit. We need to expand ministries of this type to a larger sphere of women in our churches.

DISCIPLING MINISTRIES

Start with Prayer

If we want to implement some type of spiritual-growth ministry for women, where do we begin? Establishing any kind of program in your church should be bathed in prayer. Oftentimes our ministries fail because we fail to pray. We get ideas, and then we hurriedly try to implement them in our own strength and wonder why they don't work. Our faith is often in our own abilities rather than God's. Simply stated, "When I try, I fail; when I trust, He succeeds."

Prayer changes us! We often forget that God is able—a word repeated over and over in Scripture. He was able to save Shadrach, Meshach, and Abednego from a blazing furnace (Dan. 3:17). He was able to save Daniel from the lions' mouths (6:20–22). He was able to give a child to ninety-year-old Sarah (Gen. 21:1–2). He is able to give us all we need (2 Cor. 9:8). He is able to save completely those who come to Him through Jesus (Heb. 7:25). He is "able to do immeasurably more than all we ask or imagine" (Eph. 3:20). He is able to . . . You fill in the blank.

It is an exercise in futility to pray if we don't have faith that God is able to answer. Bill Hybels comments this way on faith in our praying: "Faith comes from looking at God, not at mountains. Whatever it takes for you to own the doctrine of the all-powerful nature of God, do it. Until you own it, you will be a fainthearted pray-er. You'll make a few wishes on your knees, but you won't be able to persevere in prayer until you know in your heart that God is able."[3]

Develop a Purpose Statement

After waiting on God in prayer, then begin to pursue a ministry in your church that will bring women together for a mutual growing process. Writing a purpose statement will help the women know the purpose and direction of your organization. A purpose statement should represent a well-balanced program of "fellowship, nurture, equipping, and evangelism."[4] There must be a balance between building our women up in the faith and meeting their needs for encouragement, socialization, and outreach.

Know Who Is in Your Church

Unlike Roman Catholic churches, in which parishioners attend the church in the diocese where they live, many people in evangelical churches travel some distances to find "the right pastor," "the right singles' group," or "the right women's group." Churches attract people for different reasons. For example, my son and daughter-in-law attend a church of three thousand members that has almost no older adults. Setting up a program for widows would not be the first priority for their women's ministry.

Most churches do, however, have widows, divorcées, single moms, and women who work in and outside the home. Therefore we need to devise a workable plan to bring the needs of the various groups together in a way that will be beneficial for all. If your church has a good mix of younger and older women, certain programs would work well for them. Younger women who are in the busiest times of their lives with spouses, children, homes, and jobs often cry "Help." And older women, who have entered a different phase of their lives with children gone from home and whose husbands are sometimes still involved with jobs, often feel stagnant. Both kinds of women—and others—need to see that participating in a women's ministry can be fulfilling.

Determine the Needs of Women in Your Church

How do you determine the needs of your church women? To begin with, it is helpful to invite all the women in your church to a luncheon or dessert meeting. At the meeting ask each woman to make a list of facts about herself—address, interests, hobbies, available time, age of children, marital status, job experience. This input will help your church leaders best determine where to start. After all, your programs should be people-focused, not program-focused.[5] Briscoe, McIntyre, and Seversen ask a number of questions that are helpful in this regard: Whom are we trying to reach? Who is actually being reached? Who is absent? Why? How has our audience changed? What are their greatest needs? What are our current barriers to ministry and how can they be removed? What are our greatest strengths and weaknesses? In what areas do we need to change?[6]

Develop Relevant Programs for Your Women

Churches across the country have come up with many different programs to meet the needs of their women. One such program, mentioned in an earlier chapter, is called a "Heart to Heart" ministry.[7] The purpose of this ministry is to develop supportive friendships between older and younger women. Titus 2:3–5 indicates that mature, godly women are to teach and disciple younger women.

Regardless of what our culture says, women think like women. They have gone through many of the same experiences and feel the same emotions. Sometimes godly counsel from older women can keep potential problems in young women's lives from developing.[8] Some unhealthy situations that develop among Christian workers might possibly be avoided if women spent more time helping other women work through their difficulties.[9]

For years I have counseled with women who were in my Bible classes, sometimes spending two hours at a time in my home listening to their hurts and discouragements. I have often wondered how many couples spend this much undivided time listening intently to one another without distractions. For women to be able to fill this role in the lives of younger women, they need to be women after God's own heart, which requires that they know the Scriptures and are able to model its truths to others.

The "experience, empathy, maturity, and spirituality of these women create an enormously powerful reservoir of untapped, God-given strength from which the church can benefit and should utilize. Women need it. Scripture commands it. The 'Heart to Heart' ministry attempts to tap this reservoir."[10] When establishing this type of ministry, Vickie Kraft suggests several guidelines. They need to "make a one-year commitment to the relationship; make contact once a week and meet at least once a month; pray for one another; and do things together."[11]

As I visit churches across our country, I have found that this type of ministry works. The Heart to Heart ministry is primarily a ministry of encouragement; it is not necessarily a discipleship program.[12] I have even seen this program work in churches with predominantly young congregations where the age differences are no more than five or ten years. Every woman has something to offer—the woman who has children out of grade school can help those whose children are still in school. In any church we can find women who have gone through experiences just ahead of someone else.

Other innovative ministries have been developed in recent years to reach a broader spectrum of women's needs. Jill Briscoe started a group at Elmbrook Church in Waukesha, Wisconsin, called "Morning Break," which drew together women of different interests, experiences, and age-groups who had a common desire to learn what God was saying to them through His Word.[13] "Moms and More" grew out of a "Morning Break" elective. "It did not just happen—it began with a need, was watered by desire, and took root when willing women took a risk."[14] Next came the "Evening Edition" group which included working women who couldn't attend the "Morning Break" time. Later this church responded to requests from widows and developed a group called "The Widow's Might." We need to take note that each of these programs developed out of specific needs within this local body of women. Programs flourish when they meet needs; they die when they don't.

What Should We Teach Our Women?

First, we must help women develop a strong interest in Bible study. For a woman to be rightly related to God, her husband, children, and others,

210

she must get into the Word. The greatest "self-help" resource in the world is Scripture. God's Word lived out in the lives of women creates powerful models for the body of Christ.

Second, many younger women can benefit from instruction and counsel on homemaking. When I taught basic parenting-skills classes in my church, the questions young mothers asked always amazed me. The questions were so basic and yet the answers were so essential for running a household. Information that may seem simple may have been missed along the way by some younger women. It's like cookbooks. The first time I as a young bride tried to make a chicken casserole, every recipe I found said to cut up a "stewed chicken," and add the rest of the ingredients. The problem with these instructions was that the book didn't tell me how to "stew" chicken. It was assumed that the cook would know how, but I didn't. Similarly many young women today don't know some of the basic skills necessary to accomplish simple tasks in their homes.

Third, we can teach women about priorities. Sometimes older women have learned the hard way about setting priorities, and they are now able to assist younger women in learning early how to establish them: God first, husband second, children next, and other activities last. If we have been able to establish these priorities in our own lives, we can pass on the know-how to others. Years of experience have taught me that if this priority list is kept in focus, many sidesteps of disaster can be avoided.

We must help women establish a right relationship with God. If we encourage them to spend time during the quiet times of their lives getting to know Him, then in the panicky times they will sense His presence and be able to respond in His strength. But if their relationship with the Lord isn't strong, then their responses won't be either.

Also we must help women cultivate proper relationships with their husbands. Busy wives must put their husbands high on their priority lists. Marital conflict will occur. Since it's difficult for young wives to drag their parents into these conflicts, help can possibly come from an older woman in the church. She can listen with a little more freedom than one's own mother might be able to do. Older women can teach younger women practical ways of how they solved particular conflicts; little things that have worked for them can be passed on.

Older women can also help encourage young mothers in their child rearing. Children are certainly a time-consuming addition to any family. Women who have raised children and are now empty-nesters, or whose children are older than those of younger mothers, can be extremely helpful. Talking about what's normal, what to expect, helping them keep a balanced perspective—all these can help younger mothers be more relaxed. An older mom in the church can be a tremendous resource for the frightened mother who's just starting out. What's more, young mothers need guidance in knowing how to train and instruct their children in the ways of the Lord.

Setting priorities involves boundaries as well. If a woman doesn't have good boundaries in her life, she won't be able to stay with her priorities. Galatians 6:2 reminds us to "carry each other's burdens." The Greek word for "burden" is *baros,* which implies a "heavy" burden.[15] These burdens are like boulders; they can crush us. We need help with the boulders— those times of crisis and tragedy in our lives. Many women do not have enough strength, resources, or knowledge to carry their "boulders" alone, and they need help. By helping others with burdens they can't carry themselves, we show the sacrificial love of Christ.

On the other hand, Galatians 6:5 adds that "each one should carry his own load." The Greek word translated "load" differs from the word for "burden." *Phortion* is a load that a person is expected to carry on his or her own. It was used of a man's pack or a soldier's kit.[16] Each one of us has responsibilities, our own "load," we need to carry. Sometimes women confuse the burdens and the loads. They act as if their boulders are daily loads, and so they refuse help. Or they act as if their daily loads are boulders they shouldn't have to carry.

Psychologists point out that the best way to encourage change in a person is not by lecturing; it's by guiding the person to experience the difference for herself. For example, it would be almost worthless to tell a couple that they need to communicate better. That's obvious, or they wouldn't be seeking help. Good counselors will have the couple communicate in front of them, guiding, asking for clarification, stopping often to get feedback from the other partner, rewording phrases for each that would be helpful, and so forth. It's sometimes helpful to say, "Have you tried this?" Or, "Can you reword your statement to be a little less confrontive and still get across what you want to say?" Or, "Do you feel like you're being heard?"

It is up to us as Christian women leaders to guide younger women into a closer walk with our Savior. We can encourage them by sharing ways He has worked in our own lives. Whether you are coming together for fellowship, nurturing, or Bible study, women can strengthen women in these changing times. Learn the needs of your women, and then develop programs to meet those needs.

Chapter Nineteen

Teaching Women about Leadership

*I*n 1935 Konrad Lorenz, a Nobel Prize-winning ethologist, was recognized for his studies in animal behavior. He showed that there is a short period of time early in the lives of goslings and ducklings in which they begin slavishly to follow the first moving object they see—their mother, a human being, a rubber ball, whatever. The object becomes "Mother Goose" to the birds, so that thereafter they prefer it to all others and in fact will follow no other.

Similarly many people today follow anyone with a loud voice or a cause. And that cause doesn't even have to be a good one. The leader need only give people enough promises to dupe them into a false sense of security. The leader's credentials are unimportant. Integrity is not necessary.

After all, how a person leads, it is argued, has nothing to do with one's private life. For example, you might be an avid animal activist waving banners in front of a mink-coated woman on Saturday and personally go in for an abortion on Monday. It makes no difference. You're a noble person to some because you care about "defenseless" little minks. What a person does in private is his or her concern, not the concern of anyone else. In an article for the *New York Times*, Gloria Steinem argued that the "allegations of a sexual dalliance between the President and a 21-year-old intern were nothing to get worked up about."[1]

But God's view of leadership is vastly different. He tells us over and over how important a person's life is—both public and private. In fact,

He lays down strict guidelines for those who want to lead. Leadership carries with it a high price tag. The question for us is, "Are we willing to pay the price?"

NECESSITIES OF LEADERSHIP

A woman in a leadership position must possess certain strengths and characteristics in order to go before other women to show the way. Deuteronomy 6:5–7 commands, "Love the LORD your God with all your heart and with all your soul and with all your strength. These commandments that I give you today are to be upon your hearts. Impress them on your children. Talk about them when you sit at home and when you walk along the road, when you lie down and when you get up." God's Word must first be on our own hearts before we can impart His truths to others. We cannot impart what we do not possess! First and foremost, a leader must show the way. What is important to us as leaders will become important to those who follow.

Followers

To be leaders, we must have followers. How do we get others to follow us? Even Jesus had to prove Himself before others followed Him. True leadership is mostly about a relationship between a leader and his or her followers.[2] We must build a relationship with those we intend to lead.

Three statements can be affirmed about true leadership: (a) Leadership requires love. (b) The best leaders are servants. (c) You lead by giving to others.[3] "Servant leadership begins with the heart—with our attitude, with our motives."[4] God is concerned with what we are doing, but He is also concerned with why we are doing it.[5] The strongest power in leadership is love. "This type of love refers to a mind-set, an act of the will. It is not the exercise of emotions."[6] Christ commands us to "love one another. By this all men will know that you are my disciples, if you love one another" (John 13:34–35).

216

Vision

We must have a vision for women in order to lead them. I have found through the years that we need to guide them and encourage them to fulfill their highest calling on this earth—to glorify God. In order to accomplish this, we need to give them tools that will energize their Christian walk. They will need a deeper knowledge of our Lord (Phil. 3:10), a deeper love for God (Deut. 6:5), a passion for God's Word (Ps. 119:11), a greater love for others (Phil. 2:3), a desire to win lost souls to Christ (1 Cor. 9:22), and contentment (Phil. 4:11). Christ's vision for us is that we might "have life, and have it to the full" (John 10:10), and so it should be for those we are called to lead.

OLD TESTAMENT LEADERS

The Bible includes ample material on the qualifications, duties, and limitations of spiritual leaders. We need to clarify our perception of requirements for spiritual leadership, so that we can apply them to our individual ministries when working with women. Truly biblical spiritual leaders are scarce today because we have not taken time to clarify what spiritual leadership should "look like." We can learn about true leadership by observing some people whom God placed in leading roles.

Moses

Initially Moses attempted to take on leadership in his own strength, and he acted hastily in killing an Egyptian who was beating a Hebrew. When Moses learned that someone had seen him, he ran into the desert and ended up in Midian. Even though he was an adopted son of Pharaoh's daughter, destined for leadership, he failed miserably in his own efforts. He ended up leading sheep in the backside of the desert (Exod. 2:11–3:1).[7] Perhaps many of us too have attempted to lead in our own strength.

I painfully remember a time when I was asked to be a counselor after the showing of the Billy Graham film, *The Restless Ones*, in California in the 1960s. Scripture memory had always come easily for me, and so I went to the showing of the film without ever getting on my knees for guidance. As the Lord would direct, the first group assigned to me consisted of three young men with long hair, black leather jackets, and cigarette packages rolled up in the sleeves of their T-shirts. The scenario went something like this: The guys would ask a question about God, and I would answer by quoting a verse of Scripture, and they would ask me to show them the verse, and I would turn to where I thought it was, but it wouldn't be there. They would ask another question, and the same thing would happen again and again and again—each time I failed to find the quoted verse of Scripture. At that time, some thirty years ago now, God imprinted on my heart the words, "I can do everything through him who gives me strength" (Phil. 4:13), and without him I can do nothing (John 15:5).

When God called Moses to lead His people out of Egypt, he learned the importance of placing his confidence in the sufficiency of God. When Moses asked, "Who am I that I should go?" (Exod. 3:11), God's answer was, in essence, "It doesn't matter who you are. What matters is who I am." He told Moses, "I will be with you," and "I am who I am." What a comfort to know that our strength comes from God and not ourselves. He never calls us to do anything for which He doesn't give us the enablement.

In appraising Moses' spiritual character, God said, "He is faithful in all my house" (Num. 12:7). There is nothing more important for God's servants than faithfulness. How faithful are we in our ministries?

Consistency was another significant trait of Moses. Also he was meek and patient with those whom he led. God and Moses communicated "face to face" (Num. 12:8; Deut. 34:10), that is, personally and as friends. Do we spend adequate time with the Lord? Leading others effectively requires our fellowshiping with the Lord. From a small book of poetic thoughts come these words: "A cup of sweet savor, no matter how quickly jarred, can only spill forth sweet savor." What are we filled with—ourselves or our Lord? What is pouring out of our lives—God's truths or the world's wisdom?

Moses' leadership was greatly enhanced by his intercessory praying. This, in fact, was his most significant work. For example, when Israel sinned, Moses pleaded with God for the people: "Please forgive their sin— but if not, then blot me out of the book you have written" (Exod. 32:32).

Are we involved this much with those we lead? Or are we constantly criticizing their actions and feeling spiritually superior?

With great privileges of leadership come high standards.[8] When Moses struck the rock in the wilderness a second time, God confronted him about his disobedience, saying it was actually a lack of trust. "Because you did not trust in me enough to honor me as holy in the sight of the Israelites, you will not bring this community into the land I give them" (Num. 20:12).

We might wonder why God could not overlook at least one mistake. But the point was that the flowing water must be attributed to God's power, not Moses' efforts. By his disobedience Moses was calling attention to his own authority, rather than trusting God's directive.[9] Those who lead God's people must obey Him in every aspect of their lives.

As a leader Moses didn't try to do everything himself. He surrounded himself with capable individuals who could lead as well. "He chose capable men from all Israel and made them leaders of the people, officials over thousands, hundreds, fifties and tens" (Exod. 18:25). As a leader he trained the priests who would minister to the people, and he wrote the manual for them to follow, which is the Book of Leviticus. In addition he oversaw the building of the tabernacle and the arrangements for the nation's worship (Exodus 35–40).

Abigail

This beautiful, gracious, godly wife of wicked Nabal was willing to take responsibility for her husband's evil actions. When she found out that Nabal had totally rejected David's kindness to Nabal's shepherds, she said, "Let the blame be on me alone" (1 Sam. 25:24). We usually don't like to take the blame for what we do—let alone for what we don't do. Here was an opportunity to get rid of her rotten husband. But instead of letting David take care of this wicked man, she pleaded with David for her husband's life. She used her wisdom to convince the king not to bother with shedding Nabal's blood and be guilty of wrongdoing. By doing this she was leaving the situation in God's hands. This godly woman evidenced tremendous qualities of leadership: humility, wisdom, and trust in the sovereignty of God.

The Elders

The elders were to adjudicate conflicts, helping Moses carry the burdens of the people (Num. 11:17). With this responsibility, they would need to know God's Word well. Their qualifications were described in Exodus 18:21: "capable men . . . who fear God, trustworthy men who hate dishonest gain." We could compare this with the qualifications of the seven men chosen in the early church; they were to be "full of the Spirit and wisdom" (Acts 6:3). And elders are to be "above reproach, the husband of but one wife, temperate, self-controlled, respectable, hospitable, able to teach . . . not a lover of money. He must manage his own family well and see that his children obey him" (1 Tim. 3:2–4).

A spiritually mature, God-fearing person is one who truly trusts the Lord and seeks to obey His commands. To lead others, we must strive toward spiritual maturity.

The Priests

Old Testament priests had essentially three tasks. First, they were to teach the Law. "For the lips of a priest ought to preserve knowledge, and from his mouth men should seek instruction—because he is the messenger of the Lord Almighty" (Mal. 2:7). Second, they were to burn incense in worship of the Lord (Exod. 30:7–9). Similarly our prayers are to be raised to the Lord like incense. David prayed, "May my prayer be set before you like incense; may the lifting up of my hands be like the evening sacrifice" (Ps. 141:2). Also Revelation 5:8 tells us that the prayers of the saints are like incense to God. Prayer was one of the main functions of the priests. They were intercessors. Third, they were to offer sacrifices for the people, as corporate leaders of worship and service.[10]

Called by God, these leaders were to be holy, faithful, sober, and have exemplary marriages.

The Prophets

The prophets were called by God to speak His Word with divine authority (Deut. 18:18–22). They preached and applied the Word, and predicted the future as proof that their message was authentic.

They predicted coming blessings and God's impending judgments on sin. The prophets often exhorted the people to turn from sin and to follow the Lord.

The prophets had no authority inherent in themselves. Their message carried authority because they were God's anointed messengers.[11] This is evident in the fact that the phrase "Thus says the LORD" appears 3,800 times in the Old Testament.[12] God put His words in the prophets' mouths (18:18). As God's leaders we, too, must be channels for God's Word to the world.

Kings

As national leaders in God's theocracy over Israel, the kings were supposed to be chosen by God (Hos. 8:4), who enabled them to rule. They were to be obedient to the Lord and to lead the people in righteous living by wise decisions and exemplary conduct. Today's Christian leaders, whether men or women, are to recognize that God enables them to lead, that they are to make wise, godly decisions, and that they are to lead exemplary lives.

Scribes and Teachers

Israel's scribes and teachers lived from the time of Ezra to the second century after Christ. They were neither a religious sect nor a political party, but a professional group. "Lawyer," "scribe," and "teacher (of the Law)" are synonymous terms in the New Testament. They interpreted and taught the Old Testament Law and delivered judgments on cases brought to them. They also applied the Law to daily life. In Jesus' time most of the scribes were Pharisees (although not all Pharisees had the theological expertise required of scribes).[13] New laws determined by the scribes became binding on the people; the laws were "prescribed by the scribes." Their authority was considered as binding as that of the prophets.

However, their traditions and interpretations had often gone beyond the Scriptures. Therefore Jesus was critical of these Jewish teachers. He warned the people, "Watch out for the teachers of the Law" (Mark 12:38). Also He said, "The teachers of the law and the Pharisees sit in Moses' seat.

So you must obey them and do everything they tell you. But do *not* do what they *do*, for they do not practice what they preach" (Matt. 23:2–3, italics added). His point was that true authority rests in the Word of God, not the teachers. Any teaching that did not point to Jesus as the Messiah was false.

Elders and Judges

While scribes and teachers took the place of prophets and priests, elders took the role of spiritual leaders. In the synagogues special seats for elders were provided on the *bēma* ("raised platform"). The Jewish supreme court, consisting of seventy members from both the Pharisaical and Sadducean parties, was known as the Sanhedrin and was presided over by the high priest. Sanhedrin members had to be men of wisdom and mature age, with extensive knowledge of languages and customs. High moral qualifications were also required.

Priests

Many of the priests in Jesus' day achieved their positions through political corruption or bribery. They were not appointed because of their learning, piety, or moral character. The priests at that time had tremendous power and yet in many cases were incapable, unlearned, or even unbelievers. Nevertheless they were supposed to offer sacrifices, to serve as judges on the Sanhedrin, to teach the Law, and to model holiness.

NEW TESTAMENT QUALITIES OF LEADERSHIP

Divine Calling

The disciples were called by Jesus to leave everything and follow Him. If we believe God has called us to lead, then we, too, must be willing to sacrifice what it takes to glorify Him in pursuing that call.

Servanthood

Christ often emphasized that leadership calls for a servantlike attitude. "Whoever wants to become great among you must be your servant, and whoever wants to be first must be your slave—just as the Son of Man did not come to be served, but to serve, and to give his life as a ransom for many" (Matt. 20:26–28). "The greatest among you should be like the youngest, and the one who rules like the one who serves" (Luke 22:26). Leadership is serving, not lording it over others (1 Pet. 5:3).

Prayer

The Lord commanded us to pray (Matt. 6:9–15), and He prayed for us (John 17). Paul urged us to "pray continually, give thanks in all circumstances" (1 Thess. 5:17–18). In our fast-moving society, in which we feel that to be effective for God we must always be "doing" something, we feel that prayer wastes time.

I was once in a church group that met to discuss some troubling events. One member said, "I suppose the only thing left to do is pray about it." Another chimed in, "Is it down to that?" Prayer is doing something—it's calling on the very power of God. Prayer changes us, for it helps us focus on the source of our strength, and it helps us get our eyes off ourselves and on our Lord. To lead others effectively we must maintain a consistent and fervent prayer life.

Faith

When the disciples were with Jesus in a boat, a vicious storm arose on the Sea of Galilee. As the storm intensified, they became more frightened and they awakened Jesus. When He calmed the storm, He asked them why they were afraid: "Do you still have no faith?" (Mark 4:40). The Lord often tests the faith of leaders; so we must learn to choose His way, not our own.

Sacrificial Love

Paul told the Philippian Christians to have the same attitude Christ had when He emptied Himself, taking the form of a bond-servant, humbling Himself in sacrifice for us (Phil. 2:5–8). That is, we, like Him, are to be humble and to give ourselves sacrificially to others. A sacrifice is the "surrender of something prized or desirable for the sake of something considered as having a higher or more pressing claim."[14]

This kind of love is a forgiving love—one that considers others first.

Holiness

Christian leaders are to be exemplary in holiness. That is, they are to be set apart to God and from sin, to be sanctified from all impurity (1 Thess. 4:3). Yet many Christians, even leaders, seem no different from the unsaved. To accomplish anything for His glory, we must bear spiritual fruit by abiding in fellowship with Christ (John 15:4–5). Believers are to be examples in speech, life, love, faith and purity (1 Tim. 4:12), by bearing "the fruit of the Spirit" (Gal. 5:22–23), which in turn is possible only as we are "filled with the Spirit" (Eph. 5:18).

Committed to Evangelizing

Perhaps the most familiar passage on evangelism is Jesus' Great Commission to "go and make disciples of all nations, baptizing them in the name of the Father and of the Son and of the Holy Spirit, and teaching them to obey everything I have commanded you" (Matt. 28:19–20). With this command, Christ gave us the provision by which to carry it out, namely, the power of the Holy Spirit (Acts 1:4–5). God's leaders are to be burdened for the lost (2 Cor. 5:14), to "do the work of an evangelist" (2 Tim. 4:5).

Committed to Teaching

When Jesus commanded His followers to "make disciples" (Matt. 28:19), He was calling for them to extend the work He had been doing with them.[15] As Paul wrote, we are to teach others so that they in turn can teach yet others (2 Tim. 2:2). Teaching was a significant part of Jesus' ministry and of the ministry of Paul and others.[16]

Summary

To serve the Lord most effectively as His leaders, we need these eight qualities: divine calling, a servant's heart, faithful prayer, confident faith, sacrificial love, holiness, commitment to evangelizing, and a commitment to teaching. These all focus on spiritual maturity and sound character. Women in leadership must embrace these credentials. Others will want to see our "fruit" before they will follow.

THE UNIQUENESS OF CHRISTIAN LEADERSHIP

William Lawrence discusses several qualities that make Christian leadership unique.[17] First, it is distinctive in its position. No Christian leader can be "number one." He or she must know that Christ is the Leader and is in control. As Christ said, "You call me 'Teacher' and 'Lord,' and rightly so, for that is what I am" (John 13:13). The main characteristic of a Christian leader must be yieldedness to Christ as *the* Leader! Second, Christian leadership is distinctive because it calls for Christian character, as discussed in the preceding section. Leadership requires following Christ.

Third, Christian leadership is unique in that the source of our spiritual power is the Holy Spirit. We dare not work in our own strength, because counterfeit leadership leads in the wrong direction. We are only vessels through whom He works.[18]

Fourth, Christian leadership is distinctive in its ambition. Leaders are anxious not for self-glory; instead they have the "drive and desire necessary to carry the burdens and responsibilities of leadership."[19] In Mark 10:35–45 Jesus "redefined ambition and turned it into service for others."[20] Paul was telling us about this kind of ambition when he encouraged us to "run in such a way as to get the prize" (1 Cor. 9:24).

Fifth, our leadership is distinctive in its motivation. We are motivated by love and concern, not power and position. The Greek word *proistēmi,* "to lead, " in Romans 12:8 means "to care for, give help."[21] Leadership is the developed gift of giving direction to others out of care and concern for them and their needs.

Sixth, this leadership is distinctive in its authority. Our authority stems not from ourselves but from the Lord (Matt. 28:18). We should be humble when we realize that we have leadership ability only because God gave it. Apart from Christ, we can do nothing of eternal value (John 15:5). We did nothing to earn our leadership abilities, so we have no cause for boasting.

THE DEMANDS OF LEADERSHIP

Leadership demands that we take responsibility. Kenneth Gangel says that leadership calls for the "willingness to make decisions and to stand by them, even when they are not pleasant."[22]

Leadership also demands that we take an interest in and have an understanding of people. "A biblical view of leadership will always find us exercising great concern for the needs and interests of our co-workers."[23]

Leadership also demands dependability. Can others count on us? Gangel says that being a leader is often a "thankless task because it seems never ending."[24]

Courage and patience are also demands of leadership. Often we are tempted to become impatient with coworkers because they don't do things exactly as we would, or with followers because they are following so far behind. Being in leadership is not always popular, and sometimes it is a lonely place; but if God has called you to lead, it is *the* place for you to be.

Being a leader also calls for our being creative. "A creative person has the ability to bring into existence something unusual. It might be a teaching method; it might be a promotional idea; it might be a decoration for a party. But it is always something which comes out of the development of an imaginative mind."[25]

Leadership also calls for competence. Churches sometimes settle for willingness on the part of leaders without giving attention to whether they are capable of carrying out their responsibilities.[26]

Finally, leadership calls for sacrifice. As spiritual leaders we must invest time and energy in discipling (as Jesus did) those who will someday lead in our place. As we lead others, we must remember that no one is indispensable in the Lord's work. We are only vessels He uses.

Chapter Twenty

Developing a Philosophy
of Women's Ministry

I knocked on the door and waited with great anticipation. It was my first opportunity as a hospice chaplain.[1] I had been training for weeks, standing by the director's side and watching him minister to people who had chosen to live out the remaining days of their lives in their own homes. This was my first time alone, and I wasn't familiar with the poorest neighborhoods of Dallas. It was away from my comfort zone, but I was anxious to be used.

An elderly woman opened the door and invited me in. As I entered the sparsely decorated living room I wasn't prepared for what I saw. Seated in a wheelchair was an elderly man who almost didn't look human. The majority of his facial bones had been eaten away by cancer, only one ear remained, and one leg had been amputated. I quickly asked God to remove from my face what had to be an expression of surprise, horror, and revulsion all mixed together. That first meeting began a friendship of prayer and growing together with that couple until the Lord took him home.

One day when I was visiting Henry and his dear faithful wife (his grown children had long sense deserted him because of his appearance), I asked if there was anything they needed done. Sue hesitatingly said that she would love for Henry's fingernails to be cut, but they were too thick and hard for her. It took me two hours to do it because I had to hold his hands so gently because of his constant pain. When I finished, Henry held up his hands, stared at them, and said, "Now I look like a man again!" Years have passed since Henry's funeral, but I can still see the joyful smile on that dear man's face.

What is our concept of service? Is it remaining in our comfort zones, or is it being willing to go anywhere our Lord leads? If we are willing, He will take us places where we'll have to depend on Him totally. We each need a philosophy for living life—which is our personal ministry, so that near the end of our own life we can say with Paul, "I have fought the good fight, I have finished the race, I have kept the faith" (2 Tim. 4:7). But corporately in the body of Christ we need to develop a philosophy for how we will serve others—women in particular.

By a "philosophy of ministry" I mean the principles that guide us in seeking to accomplish our goals. This means evaluating the ways we do things, our reasons for doing them, and whether our group is going in the right direction. Are we doing things a certain way just because that's the way they've always been done? Are we trying to address the needs of our women, or are we assuming everything without any investigation? Any program, no matter how wonderful, needs to be adapted to your special situation—to the women in your particular church. The following are some basic concepts necessary for developing a workable philosophy of women's ministry.

INVOLVING OTHERS TO CARRY THE LOAD

"Moses took his seat to serve as judge for the people, and they stood around him from morning till evening" (Exod. 18:13). Many of us can identify with Moses because we were probably brought up with the concept, "If you want anything done well, do it yourself." That's all right until you find yourself leading and guiding and doing everything in your particular program as if you are the only one. Of course, if you *are* "the only one," then you need to work on your own personal philosophy of life. But if there is a group of women to lead, then you can develop and train a few of them to take some of the responsibility. Sometimes we treat women as we did our children. It was usually easier to do things ourselves because they got done faster and better; but then, our children learned to expect us to do everything. People learn by doing, so we need to train other women to help carry the load.

BEING A SERVANT

"Ministry" is the "service, functions, or profession of a minister of religion; the body or class of ministers of religion; clergy."[2] Even though this describes a popular usage, it greatly distorts biblical truth. According to the Bible, ministry is not the activity of a spiritual elite or the work of a professional class. Rather it is the "lifestyle, responsibility, and privilege of every believer."[3] A ministry that fails to recognize this fact is not truly biblical. On the other hand, we must still recognize that God has gifted individuals differently to serve the body of Christ.

The New Testament uses several words for ministry. For example, every believer is a "slave" (Greek, *doulos*) of the Lord Jesus. People in the ancient world felt only abhorrence and disrespect for slaves, because personal freedom was a prized possession.[4] A slave owed his master exclusive and absolute obedience (Matt. 8:9). But we as believers should rejoice in the privilege of being the Lord's slaves, following His own example of humble servitude (John 13:4–9). Paul urged us to "serve one another in love" (Gal. 5:13).

The concept of service also appears in the term *diakonos*, "a helper or assistant." Appearing often in the New Testament, this word is used in a general sense for loving service and the performance of menial activities, such as waiting on tables or caring for household needs. Since this type of service involved dependence, submission, and restrictions of freedom, the Greeks regarded it as a degrading and dishonorable position. But the New Testament uses this word to introduce a radically new attitude toward ministry because it pictures the lifestyle of a follower of Christ Jesus.[5]

To a Greek the highest goal for an individual was the development of one's own personality. What a profile of our own modern-day culture! A culture focused on self-actualization and self-fulfillment will have little interest in servanthood. In Judaism, service, if it was performed at all, was an act of social obligation toward someone considered more worthy. A superior would not stoop to become a servant! That is why our Lord's example of washing the disciples' feet was such a tremendous contrast to their idea of leadership.

Ministry is not an activity limited to an elite class; it is brothers and sisters in Christ caring for each other. A *diakonos* is one who by choice and position has come under the authority of Jesus Christ and therefore serves others in love and gratitude.

Christ modeled for us the basic ingredients for a meaningful philosophy of ministry. Gary Inrig discusses five principles of servanthood that Christ taught His disciples.[6]

The Ambition of a Servant

When the disciples argued about which of them would be the greatest, Jesus took a little child, who had no status in that culture, and had him stand beside Him. "Then He said to them, 'Whoever welcomes this little child in my name welcomes me; and whoever welcomes me welcomes the one who sent me. For he who is least among you all—he is the greatest'" (Luke 9:48). By example He encouraged His disciples to reach out and welcome those who are needy.

Our culture often puts on a front of humility and servanthood, but actually there is much seeking after recognition. Christ didn't rebuke the disciples' desire for greatness; He redefined the concept. God's approval, not men's applause, is the only adequate standard of evaluation.[7] Christ said, "Whoever serves me must follow me; and where I am, my servant also will be" (John 12:26). How we serve others is the measure of greatness. If we're really following where Christ is leading, it may be into the lowest place; but if He's in front, then that's where we need to be.

The Choices of a Servant

The mother of James and John went to the Lord and asked Him to seat her two sons in positions of prominence in His kingdom, a request that angered the others, who shared a similar preoccupation with rank and greatness. Jesus replied, "You know that the rulers of the Gentiles lord it over them, and their high officials exercise authority over them. Not so with you. Instead, whoever wants to become great among you must be your servant, and whoever wants to be first must be your slave—just as the Son of Man did not come to be served, but to serve, and to give his life as a ransom for many" (Matt. 20:25–28).

Jesus taught them three things about service.[8] First, greatness in His kingdom is not patterned after gentile rule and domination. We are not to pattern ourselves after the world, in which people say "Me first!" Second, ministry and spiritual greatness involve doing the work of a servant (*diakonos*) and taking the role of a slave (*doulos*). The Lord was not merely saying that service is a way to greatness—service *is* greatness. Third, Christ Himself is the model of service. His purpose in His incarnation was not to have people serve Him, but to serve them. He willingly chose a position of service.

The Relationships of a Servant

The disciples apparently entered the Upper Room still arguing about greatness. Behind their selfish argument were two assumptions of the ancient world: the right of authority and the privilege of age. Those in authority took titles such as "the august one" (Augustus), "benefactor" (Ptolemy III and Ptolemy VIII), and "he who deserves adoration" (Augustus and Tiberias, as indicated by inscriptions on coins found at Caesarea Philippi). The privilege of rank was to be served by all lesser men. The privilege of age was to be waited on by those who were younger. In Matthew 23:8–12, Christ warned against clamoring for titles and creating distinctions among the people.

I have seen so much dissension within the Christian community over titles—hurt feelings, misunderstandings, confusion. It's hard to imagine the hours spent deliberating over just the "right title" for a church position. Some women have left churches because they were not given the title they thought they should have. For whose glory are we serving? Our Lord set aside His "titles," as Philippians 2:6–7 says: "Who, being in very nature God, did not consider equality with God something to be grasped, but made himself nothing, taking the very nature of a servant, being made in human likeness." We must remember Christ's words, "The greatest among you will be your servant. For whoever exalts himself will be humbled, and whoever humbles himself will be exalted" (Matt. 23:11–12). This humbling is a choice—"whoever humbles himself."

The Paradox of Service

As the time of Jesus' death drew near, He said, "The hour has come for the Son of Man to be glorified. I tell you the truth, unless a kernel of wheat falls to the ground and dies, it remains only a single seed. But if it dies, it produces many seeds. The man who loves his life will lose it, while the man who hates his life in this world will keep it for eternal life" (John 12:23–25). That was the paradox of Christ's life. He could not save the seed, which was His life, and still see more seeds.

If I try to hold on to my life, living selfishly, I will waste and lose it. By comparison, to serve is to walk away from self-love as a life pattern. The paradox is that when a servant follows her Lord in suffering, she will share with Him in glory. As Jesus said, "My Father will honor the one who serves me" (12:26).

So ministry is self-giving and sacrificial, involving "death" and "hating one's life," as a servant keeps following her Lord. But service is the secret of life, for it produces fruitfulness, a productive life, and praise from God.[9]

The Reward of Service

Luke 12:37 shows us a neglected truth about service: "It will be good for those servants whose master finds them watching when he comes. . . . He will dress himself to serve, will have them recline at the table and will come and wait on them." God will reward our service for Him. We need to serve, and we do not deserve praise for doing our duty. "Would he thank the servant because he did what he was told to do? So you also, when you have done everything you were told to do, should say, 'We are unworthy servants; we have only done our duty'" (17:9–10). Even the finest service establishes no claim on God since believers are at best unprofitable servants. But God is gracious, and He has promised to reward us for serving Him.

SHARING GOD'S WORD

We are mere vessels to be used by God to convey His message of salvation. As Paul wrote from prison, "I became a servant of this gospel by the gift of God's grace given me through the working of his power" (Eph. 3:7). God has entrusted to us the same message He gave to Paul: "that Christ died for our sins according to the Scriptures, that he was buried, that he was raised on the third day according to the Scriptures" (1 Cor. 15:3-4). We must share the gospel, seeking to win unsaved women and men to Christ.

A good servant is one who is controlled by the truth of God's message and wants to share it with others. We are not to promote ourselves or to try to impress people with our wisdom. "For we do not preach ourselves, but Jesus Christ as Lord, and ourselves as your servants for Jesus' sake" (2 Cor. 4:5). It is His message, His authority, His enablement—so He should receive the praise.

EQUIPPING OTHERS TO MINISTER

Paul said, "I have become its [the church's] servant by the commission God gave me to present to you the word of God in its fullness" (Col. 1:25). The apostle had an overwhelming desire to lead every believer to maturity in Christ by proclaiming Christ and pouring himself into the lives of fellow believers.[10] True ministry is people-centered. That's why we must not develop our programs without understanding the needs of the women in our groups. Never attempt to fit the women into a program, but rather create the program to fit the women.

As servant-leaders we are to "prepare God's people for works of service, so that the body of Christ may be built up until we all reach unity in the faith and in the knowledge of the Son of God and become mature, attaining to the whole measure of the fullness of Christ" (Eph. 4:12–13). Ministry is not carried out by a select few for the benefit of others, nor is it merely an occupation. Every member of the body of Christ is to be involved in service. Nor is the ministry limited to certain tasks, such as preaching, counseling, and administering. Ministry is all that believers do for each other in obedience to the Lord.[11]

BEING EMPOWERED BY THE HOLY SPIRIT

Just as the Holy Spirit was the source of the disciples' spiritual power (Acts 1:4–5), so He is ours. Our ministry does not depend on human resources or enablement; the flesh cannot carry out a spiritual ministry. "Our competence comes from God," Paul affirmed (2 Cor. 3:5). "We have this treasure in jars of clay to show that this all-surpassing power is from God and not from us" (4:7). The indwelling and enabling of the Holy Spirit is essential for ministry and provides the basis for our confidence: "Such confidence as this is ours through Christ before God" (3:4). W. H. Griffith Thomas wrote, "In all Christian work, there are three elements absolutely indispensable: the Spirit of God as the power, the Word of God as the message, and the servant of God as the instrument. The Spirit of God uses the message by means of the servant."[12]

MODELING CHRISTLIKENESS

Women's-ministry leaders must set the example of Christlikeness for other women to follow. Others will constantly look to us as role models. And so we should encourage them to follow our example. As Paul said, "Whatever you have learned or received or heard from me, or seen in me—put it into practice" (Phil. 4:9). He was saying, in essence, "Look at my life, and I'll show you Christ." Can we say that to the women we are leading? "Watch me closely, and do what I do." More often than not, we are saying, "Do what I say, not what I do." As women follow in our footsteps, will those steps lead them to a closer walk with our Lord? Or will they lead to the way of the world?

UTILIZING SPIRITUAL GIFTS

All ministry is based on spiritual gifts. The fact that Christ, the Head of the church, has given believers spiritual gifts through His indwelling Spirit is of crucial importance to our philosophy of ministry. Those gifts are to enable us to serve each other. "Each one should use whatever gift he has received to serve others, faithfully administering God's grace in its various forms" (1 Pet. 4:10).

Every believer is divinely gifted, and certain people are called by the Lord to function as enablers and equippers.[13] The body of Christ "grows and builds itself up in love, as each part does its work" (Eph. 4:16). We must work together and not stand passively by as observers.[14]

CARING FOR OTHERS' NEEDS

Service is "work done for another either voluntarily or compulsory (as a slave), the benefit of which will accrue to the one for whom it has been done."[15] The New Testament tells us of many individuals who served in practical ways, lovingly caring for the needs of others. Paul named many servants of God who assisted him, without whose help his ministry could never have had the impact it did. He called them "fellow workers in Christ Jesus" (Rom. 16:3).

We must not forget that we are to minister to the whole person.[16] James illustrated this with a hypothetical situation: "Suppose a brother or sister is without clothes and daily food. If one of you says to him, 'Go, I wish you well; keep warm and well fed,' but does nothing about his physical needs, what good is it? In the same way, faith by itself, if it is not accompanied by action, is dead" (James 2:15–17). We often feel that a Bible verse thrown at someone in need will suffice. Of course, God's Word is powerful (Heb. 4:12), but we must also address a person's daily needs. If a woman doesn't have enough food to feed her children, how can she know the love of God? We must minister to women's needs in order to impact them for Christ. Teaching them one hour a week is usually not enough to help them grow in the way they should. We must tend that growth with care and concern.

These eight factors are basic to a meaningful ministry to women: involve others, be a servant, share God's Word, equip others to minister, be empowered by the Holy Spirit, model Christlikeness, utilize spiritual gifts, and care for others' needs.

Endnotes

CHAPTER 1
WHY MINISTER TO WOMEN?

1. Borgna Brunner, ed., *1998 Information Please Almanac* (Boston: Houghton Mifflin, 1997), 819, 821–22.
2. Helen Fisher, "A Primitive Prescription for Equality," *U. S. News and World Report*, 8 August 1988, 57.
3. Many men have more distance from their emotions and a greater capacity to detach themselves from immediate reactions, whereas women respond to situations more immediately and spontaneously, and find it more difficult to distance themselves from the way they feel.
4. Merrill McLoughlin, "Mind: Different Ways of Thinking, From Math to Morals," *U. S. News and World Report*, 8 August 1988, 54.
5. Ibid.
6. Ibid., 55.
7. Merrill McLoughlin, "Attitude," *U. S. News and World Report*, 8 August 1988, 56.
8. Fisher, "A Primitive Prescription for Equality," 57.
9. McLoughlin, "Attitude," 53.
10. Sharon Begley, "Grey Matters," *Newsweek*, 27 March 1995, 48.
11. Daniel Levinson, quoted in Diane E. Papalia and Sally Wendkos Olds, *Human Development* (Boston: McGraw-Hill, 1998), 439.
12. Ibid., 439–40.

CHAPTER 2
ARE CHURCHES IN TOUCH WITH WOMEN'S NEEDS?

1. George Barna, *The Future of the American Family* (Chicago: Moody, 1993), 189.
2. Ibid., 188.
3. Church Data Service, database, 1983.
4. Dolores Curran, *Traits of a Healthy Family* (New York: Ballantine, 1983).
5. Church Data Service, database, 1983.
6. Ibid.
7. Ibid.
8. Ibid.
9. Patricia Aburdene and John Naisbitt, *Megatrends for Women* (New York: Villard, 1992), 108.
10. Ibid., 108–9.

CHAPTER 3
WHAT HAS HAPPENED TO THE TRADITIONAL FAMILY?

1. Barna, *The Future of the American Family*, 19.
2. Ibid.
3. Ibid., 25.
4. Ibid., 26.
5. Ibid.
6. Ibid., 31.
7. Ibid., 25–38.
8. Ibid., 37.
9. Ibid.
10. George Barna, *Absolute Confusion* (Ventura, Calif.: Regal, 1993), 32.
11. Barna, *The Future of the American Family*, 82.
12. For more on the family in America see Kenneth O. Gangel, *Ministering to Today's Adults,* Swindoll Leadership Library (Nashville: Word, 1999).

CHAPTER 4
THE CONSEQUENCES OF THE FALL ON MEN AND WOMEN

1. Allen P. Ross, *Creation and Blessing* (Grand Rapids: Baker, 1988), 134.

2. Stuart Berg Flexner et al., eds., *Random House Unabridged Dictionary* (New York: Random House, 1983), 469.

3. Ross, *Creation and Blessing*, 133.

4. Ibid., 134.

5. Ibid., 135.

6. Ibid.

7. Ibid., 136.

8. Ibid., 137.

9. Martin Luther, *Luther's Commentary on Genesis* (Grand Rapids: Zondervan, 1958), 1:68.

10. Andreas J. Köstenberger, Thomas R. Schreiner, and H. Scott Baldwin, eds., *Women in the Church: A Fresh Analysis of 1 Timothy 2:9–15* (Grand Rapids: Baker, 1995), 153.

11. *The American Heritage Dictionary*, 2d ed. (Boston: Houghton Mifflin, 1985), 1126.

12. Ross, *Creation and Blessing*, 146.

13. Ibid.

14. Umberto Cassuto, *From Adam to Noah,* vol. 1 of *A Commentary on the Book of Genesis,* 3d ed. (Jerusalem: Magnes, 1978), 165.

15. Ross, *Creation and Blessing*, 147.

16. Allen P. Ross, "Genesis," in *The Bible Knowledge Commentary, Old Testament,* ed. John F. Walvoord and Roy B. Zuck (Wheaton, Ill.: Victor, 1985), 33.

CHAPTER 5
WHAT IS THE ROLE OF WOMEN
ACCORDING TO THE NEW TESTAMENT?

1. Mary J. Evans, *Woman in the Bible* (Downers Grove, Ill.: InterVarsity, 1983), 66–67.

2. Berkeley Mickelsen and Alvera Mickelsen, "Does Male Dominance Tarnish Our Translations?" *Christianity Today,* 5 October 1979, 23–29.

3. Margaret Howe, *Women and Church Leadership* (Grand Rapids: Zondervan, 1982), 60.

4. Letha Dawson Scanzoni and Nancy A. Hardesty, *All We're Meant to Be: Biblical Feminism for Today,* 3d ed. (Grand Rapids: Eerdmans, 1992), 30.

5. Ibid., 31.

6. Ibid., 100.

7. F. F. Bruce, *Paul: Apostle of the Heart Set Free* (Grand Rapids: Eerdmans, 1983), 420, n. 45.

8. James B. Hurley, *Man and Woman in Biblical Perspective* (Grand Rapids: Zondervan, 1981), 164.

9. Walter Bauer, William F. Arndt, and F. Wilbur Gingrich, *A Greek-English Lexicon of the New Testament and Other Early Christian Literature,* 2d ed., rev. F. Wilbur Gingrich and Frederick W. Danker (Chicago: University of Chicago Press, 1979); Joseph H. Thayer, *Greek-English Lexicon of the New Testament* (Grand Rapids: Zondervan, 1956); Hermann Cremer, *Biblico-Theological Lexicon of New Testament Greek,* trans. William Urwick (1886; reprint, Naperville, Ill.: Allenson, n.d.); and James Hope Moulton and George Milligan, *The Vocabulary of the Greek Testament Illustrated from the Papyri and Other Non-Literary Sources* (Grand Rapids: Eerdmans, 1930).

10. Hurley, *Man and Woman in Biblical Perspective,* 164.

11. Stephen Bedale, "The Meaning of *kephalē* in the Pauline Epistles," *Journal of Theological Studies* 5 (1954): 211–15.

12. Wayne Grudem, "Does *Kephalē* ('Head') Mean 'Source' or 'Authority over' in Greek Literature? A Survey of 2,336 Examples," *Trinity Journal,* n.s., 6 (1985): 41.

13. Bauer, Arndt, and Gingrich, *A Greek-English Lexicon of the New Testament and Other Early Christian Literature,* 430.

14. Grudem, "Does *Kephalē* ('Head') Mean 'Source' or 'Authority over' in Greek Literature?" 48–49.

15. Ibid., 59.

16. David K. Lowery, "1 Corinthians," in *The Bible Knowledge Commen-*

tary, New Testament, ed. John F. Walvoord and Roy B. Zuck (Wheaton, Ill.: Victor, 1985), 529.

17. John MacArthur, *The MacArthur New Testament Commentary: 1 Corinthians* (Chicago: Moody, 1984), 260–61.

18. James A. Hurley, "Did Paul Require Veils or the Silence of Women? A Consideration of I Cor. 11:2–16 and I Cor. 14:33b–36," *Westminster Theological Journal* 35 (1973): 213.

19. Lowery, "1 Corinthians," 541.

20. Craig S. Keener, *The IVP Bible Background Commentary: New Testament* (Downers Grove, Ill.: InterVarsity, 1993), 611.

21. Philip Barton Payne, "Οὐδέ in 1 Timothy 2:12" (paper presented at the Evangelical Theological Society Annual Meeting, 21 November 1986), 1.

22. Ibid., 2–4.

23. Ibid., 4. For a different interpretation see Thomas S. Schreiner, "Head Coverings, Prophecies and the Trinity in 1 Corinthians 11:2–16," in *Recovering Biblical Manhood and Womanhood,* ed. John Piper and Wayne Grudem (Wheaton, Ill.: Crossway, 1991), 124.

24. Stephen B. Clark, *Man and Woman in Christ* (Ann Arbor, Mich.: Servant, 1980), 305.

25. Ibid.

26. Susan T. Foh, "The Head of the Woman Is the Man," in *Women in Ministry,* ed. Bonnidell Clouse and Robert G. Clouse (Downers Grove, Ill.: InterVarsity, 1989), 81.

27. Ibid., 96.

28. Ross, "The Ministry of Women" (unpublished paper, 1989), 20.

29. Ann L. Bowman, "Women in Ministry: An Exegetical Study of 1 Timothy 2:11–15," *Bibliotheca Sacra* 149 (April–June 1992): 203.

30. Douglas J. Moo, "1 Timothy 2:11–15: Meaning and Significance," *Trinity Journal* n.s. 1 (Spring 1980): 73.

31. Ibid. See also Bowman, "Women in Ministry: An Exegetical Study of 1 Timothy 2:11–15," 206–12.

32. J. I. Rodale, *The Synonym Finder* (Emmaus, Pa.: Rodale, 1978), 1184.

33. John Stott, *Involvement: Social and Sexual Relationships in the Modern World* (Old Tappan, N.J.: Revell, 1978), 1:127–56.

34. Ibid.

35. Ross, "Women in the Bible," class notes, Trinity Episcopal School for Ministry, Ambridge, Pennsylvania, 1992.

36. Ibid.

37. Theodore H. Epp, *Living Abundantly: Studies in Ephesians* (Lincoln, Nebr.: Back to the Bible Broadcast, 1973), 2:96.

38. Ross, "The Ministry of Women."

39. Ibid.

40. Harold W. Hoehner, "Ephesians," in *The Bible Knowledge Commentary, New Testament,* 641.

41. Ross, "The Ministry of Women."

42. R. Kent Hughes, *Colossians and Philemon: The Supremacy of Christ* (Westchester, Ill.: Crossway, 1989), 117.

43. Stott, *Involvement: Social and Sexual Relationships in the Modern World,* 2:140.

44. Ross, "The Ministry of Women," 23.

CHAPTER 6
ARE SOME PRACTICES FOR WOMEN
LIMITED TO BIBLE TIMES?

1. Ruth A. Tucker and Walter L. Liefeld, *Daughters of the Church: Women and Ministry from New Testament Times to the Present* (Grand Rapids: Zondervan, 1987), 465.

2. J. D. Douglas, ed., *The Illustrated Bible Dictionary* (Wheaton, Ill.: Tyndale, 1986), 2:1121.

3. Clark, *Man and Woman in Christ,* 654.

4. Richard N. Ostling, "The Second Reformation," *Time,* 23 November 1992, 56.

5. Ibid., 53.

6. Ibid., 56.

7. Derk Kinnane Roelofsma, "Women Making New Trip to Altar," *Insight,* 6 April 1987, 11.

8. Ibid.

9. Ibid.

10. Ibid.

11. Ostling, "The Second Reformation," 57.

12. Susan T. Foh, *Women and the Word of God* (Nutley, N.J.: Presbyterian and Reformed, 1980), 238.

13. Gretchen G. Hull, in *Women, Authority and the Bible*, ed. Alvera Mickelsen (Downers Grove, Ill.: InterVarsity, 1986), 24.

14. Clayton Bell, "Women in the Work of the Church" (unpublished paper, n.d.).

15. John Piper and Wayne Grudem, "An Overview of Central Concerns: Questions and Answers," in *Recovering Biblical Manhood and Womanhood*, 72.

16. Ibid.

17. Thomas R. Schreiner, "The Valuable Ministries of Women in the Context of Male Leadership: A Survey of Old and New Testament Examples and Teaching," in *Recovering Biblical Manhood and Womanhood*, 211–15.

18. Bell, "Women in the Work of the Church."

19. Lowery, "1 Corinthians," 530. Pictures of shawls are given in Hugo Blümmer, *The Home Life of Ancient Greeks* (New York: Cooper Square, 1966), 44–46.

20. Ibid., 529.

21. Tucker and Liefeld, *Daughters of the Church*, 79.

22. Thomas Schreiner, "Head Coverings, Prophecies and the Trinity in 1 Corinthians 11:2–16," in *Recovering Biblical Manhood and Womanhood*, 126.

23. Lowery, "1 Corinthians," 529.

24. See Roy B. Zuck, *Basic Bible Interpretation* (Wheaton, Ill.: Victor, 1991), 94–97.

25. Lowery, "1 Corinthians," 530.

26. Piper and Grudem, *Recovering Biblical Manhood and Womanhood*, 76.

27. Schreiner, "The Valuable Ministries of Women in the Context of Male Leadership," 233.

28. Ibid.

29. Ross, "Women in the Bible."

CHAPTER 7
WOMEN IN THE NEW TESTAMENT
AND IN CHURCH HISTORY

1. Ross, "Women in the Bible."
2. Ibid.
3. Ibid.
4. Ibid.
5. Ibid.
6. Ibid.
7. Ibid.
8. The word *Magnificat* comes from the first word in the Latin translation of this passage.
9. Luter and McReynolds, *Women as Christ's Disciples*, 55.
10. *The Illustrated Bible Dictionary*, 2:960.
11. Luter, Boyd, and Kathy McReynolds, *Women as Christ's Disciples*, (Grand Rapids: Baker Books, 1997),67.
12. Ibid., 99.
13. Tucker and Liefeld, *Daughters of the Church*, 71–72.
14. Ross, "Women in the Bible."
15. Ibid.
16. *The Illustrated Bible Dictionary*, 2:924.
17. Luter and McReynolds, *Women as Christ's Disciples*, 117.
18. Ibid., 125.
19. Ibid., 124.
20. Ross, "Women in the Bible."
21. Ibid.
22. Ibid.
23. Ibid.
24. Karen Torjesen, "The Early Controversies over Female Leadership," *Christian History* 7 (1978): 20–24.
25. Ross, "Women in the Bible."
26. George Arthur Buttrick, ed., *The Interpreter's Dictionary of the Bible*, (Nashville: Abingdon, 1984), 2:1027.
27. Ross, "Women in the Bible."
28. Ibid.

29. Ibid.

30. Tertullian, *To His Wife*, 1.1, quoted in Tucker and Liefeld, *Daughters of the Church*, 104.

31. Tucker and Liefeld, *Daughters of the Church*, 132.

32. Ann K. Warren, "Five Religious Options for Medieval Women," *Christian History* 17 (1988): 12–13.

33. Ibid.

34. Ibid., 14–15.

35. Ibid., 15.

36. Ross, "Women in the Bible."

CHAPTER 8
IS FEMINISM BIBLICAL?

1. A. Duane Litfin, "Theological Issues in Contemporary Feminism," in *Walvoord: A Tribute*, ed. Donald K. Campbell (Chicago: Moody, 1982), 336.

2. The *Danvers Statement*, composed in 1987 in Danvers, Massachusetts, by the Council on Biblical Manhood and Womanhood, presents ten affirmations concerning biblical teachings on men and women.

3. Susan Foh refers to this group as "Christian feminists" (*Women and the Word of God*, 2).

4. Litfin, "Theological Issues in Contemporary Feminism," 336.

5. Rosemary Radford Ruether, *Women and Redemption* (Minneapolis: Fortress, 1998), 7.

6. Ibid.

7. Ibid., 8.

8. The EWC passed resolutions supporting passage of the Equal Rights Amendment, the ordination of women, inclusive language in Bible translations and Christian education materials, and an end to discrimination against women in Christian institutions.

9. Foh calls women in this group "Biblical feminists" (*Women and the Word of God*, 5).

10. The resignation was in protest against EWC's affirmation of civil rights for gay men and lesbians.

11. Paul K. Jewett, *Man as Male and Female* (Grand Rapids: Eerdmans, 1975), 142.

12. Scanzoni and Hardesty, *All We're Meant to Be,* 103.

13. Herbert J. and Fern Harrington Miles, *Husband Wife Equality* (Old Tappan, N.J.: Revell, 1978).

14. Virginia Ramey Mollenkott, "A Challenge to Male Interpretation: Women and the Bible," *Sojourners 5* (February 1976): 22.

15. Ruether, *Women and Redemption*, 30.

16. Scanzoni and Hardesty, *All We're Meant to Be,* 17.

17. Mollenkott, "A Challenge to Male Interpretation: Women and the Bible," 30.

18. Ibid.

19. Jane Dempsey Douglass and James F. Kay, eds., *Women, Gender, and Christian Community* (Louisville: Westminster Knox, 1997), 3.

20. A. Duane Litfin, "Evangelical Feminism: Why Traditionalists Reject It," *Bibliotheca Sacra* 543 (July–September 1979): 136.

21. Mary A. Kassian, *The Feminist Gospel: The Movement to Unite Feminism with the Gospel* (Wheaton, Ill.: Crossway, 1992), 225.

22. Betty Friedan, *The Feminine Mystique* (New York: Norton, 1963).

23. Mary Daly, *The Church and the Second Sex* (Boston: Beacon, 1968).

24. Tertullian, *On Prayer,* chapter 20: "Of Women's Dress," in *The Ante-Nicene Fathers,* ed. Alexander Roberts and James Donaldson (Grand Rapids: Eerdmans, 1976), 3:687.

25. Litfin, "Theological Issues in Contemporary Feminism," 334.

26. Kassian, *The Feminist Gospel*, 226.

27. Litfin, "Theological Issues in Contemporary Feminism," 336.

28. Ibid., 337.

29. Virginia Mollenkott, *Sensuous Spirituality: Out from Fundamentalism* (New York: Crossroad, 1992), 26–27.

30. Daly, *The Church and the Second Sex* , xii.

31. Jewett, *Man as Male and Female*, 119.

32. David M. Scholer, "1 Timothy 2:9–15 and the Place of Women in the Church's Ministry," in *Women, Authority and the Bible*, 200.

33. Stanley Grenz, *Women in the Church: A Biblical Theology of Women in Ministry* (Downers Grove, Ill.: InterVarsity, 1995), 117.

34. Evans, *Women in the Bible*, 42.

35. Litfin, "Theological Issues in Contemporary Feminism," 342.

36. Ruether, *Women and Redemption*, 275.

37. Daly, *The Church and the Second Sex*, xii.

38. Dempsey and Kay, *Women, Gender, and Christian Community*, 4.

39. Litfin, "Theological Issues in Contemporary Feminism," 343.

40. Ibid., 344.

41. Jewett, *Man as Male and Female*, 143.

42. Jenny Yates Hammett, *Woman's Transformations: A Psychological Theology* (New York: Mellen, 1982), 21.

43. Litfin, "Theological Issues in Contemporary Feminism," 345.

44. Naomi Goldenberg, *Changing of the Gods: Feminism and the End of Traditional Religions* (Boston: Beacon, 1979), 9.

45. Mollenkott, *Sensuous Spirituality*, 17.

46. Ruether, *Women and Redemption*, 275.

47. Jewett, *Man as Male and Female*, 114.

48. Francis A. Schaeffer, *A Christian Manifesto* (Westchester, Ill.: Crossway, 1982), 41.

49. *Dennis* v. *United States*, 341 U.S. 494,508 (1951).

50. Dave Hunt and T. A. McMahon, *The Seduction of Christianity: Spiritual Discernment in the Last Days* (Eugene, Oreg.: Harvest, 1985), 89.

51. Herbert Schlossberg, *Idols for Destruction* (Nashville: Nelson, 1983), 40.

52. Goldenberg, *Changing of the Gods*, 94.

53. Daly, *The Church and the Second Sex*, xiii.

54. Douglass and Kay, *Women, Gender, and Christian Community*, 3.

CHAPTER 9
WHERE IS FEMINISM HEADED?

1. Friedan, *The Feminine Mystique*, jacket cover.

2. Ibid., 15.

3. Ibid., 385.

4. Ibid.

5. Ibid.

6. Ibid., 312–13.

7. Ibid., 32.

8. Letty M. Russell, *Household of Freedom* (Philadelphia: Westminster, 1987), 88.

9. Ibid.

10. Ruether, *Women and Redemption*, 213.

11. Daly, "Autobiographical Preface to the 1975 Edition," in *The Church and the Second Sex*, 5.

12. Ruether, *Women and Redemption*, 216.

13. See, for example, Daly, *Webster's First New Intergalactic Wickedary of the English Language* (Boston: Beacon, 1987).

14. Mary Daly, *Outercourse: The Be-Dazzling Voyage* (Boston: Beacon, 1992).

15. Ruether, *Women and Redemption*, 222.

16. Ibid., 223.

17. Ibid.

18. Carter Heyward, *A Priest Forever* (New York: Harper and Row, 1976).

19. Ruether, *Women and Redemption*, 226.

20. Ibid., 227.

21. Ibid., 231.

22. Delores Williams, "Black Women's Surrogacy Experience and the Christian Notion of Redemption," in *After Patriarchy: Feminist Transformations of the World Religions*, ed. Paul M. Cooey et al. (Maryknoll, N.Y.: Orbis, 1991), 1–14.

23. Jewett, *Man as Male and Female*, foreword.

24. Ibid., 134.

25. Ibid., 114.

26. Ibid., 134.

27. Mollenkott, *Sensuous Spirituality*, 16.

28. Scanzoni and Hardesty, *All We're Meant to Be*, 21.

29. Ibid., 24.

30. Ibid., 29.

31. Ibid., 2.

32. Ibid., 20.
33. Susan Starr Sered, *Priestess Mother Sacred Sister* (New York: Oxford University Press, 1994), 26.
34. Ibid.
35. Ibid.
36. Goldenberg, *Changing of the Gods*, 3.
37. Sered, *Priestess Mother Sacred Sister*. Estimates in 1990 indicated that there are about 100,000 members in the United States alone.
38. Goldenberg, *Changing of the Gods*, 89.
39. Sered, *Priestess Mother Sacred Sister*, 27.
40. Ibid.
41. Goldenberg, *Changing of the Gods*, 94.
42. Ibid.
43. Sered, *Priestess Mother Sacred Sister*, 27.
44. Margot Adler, quoted in *Priestess Mother Sacred Sister*, 27.
45. Sered, *Priestess Mother Sacred Sister*, 156.
46. Ibid., 157.
47. Miriam Simos, quoted in *Priestess Mother Sacred Sister*, 157.
48. Geela Raphael, quoted in *Priestess Mother Sacred Sister*, 157.
49. Miriam Simos (Starhawk), *The Spiral Dance: A Rebirth of the Ancient Religion of the Great Goddess*, 2d ed. (San Francisco: Harper & Row, 1979), 10–11.
50. Sered, *Priestess Mother Sacred Sister*, 171.
51. Mary E. Hunt wrote, "Virginia Ramey Mollenkott, trusted and beloved evangelical lesbian feminist, builds new bridges of intellect, spirit and psyche, helping everyone cross over from oppression to liberation" (Mollenkott, *Sensuous Spirituality*, back cover).
52. Sered, *Priestess Mother Sacred Sister*, 172.
53. Margot Adler, *Drawing Down the Moon: Witches, Druids, Goddess-Worshipers and Other Pagans in America Today*, 2d ed. (Boston: Beacon, 1986), quoted in Aida Besançon Spencer et al., *The Goddess Revival* (Grand Rapids: Baker, 1995), 23.
54. Sered, *Priestess Mother Sacred Sister*, 26–27.
55. Ibid.
56. Ibid.

57. Ibid., 28.
58. Goldenberg, *Changing of the Gods*, 89.
59. Ibid., 4.

CHAPTER 10
HELPING WOMEN LIVE LIFE TO THE FULLEST

1. Barna, *The Future of the American Family*, 50.
2. Ibid.
3. Ibid.
4. Trying to "cure" a person in isolation from his or her family is as misdirected as transplanting a healthy organ into a body whose imbalanced chemistry will destroy the new one just as it did the old one. It is easy to forget that the same "family" of organs that rejects a transplant contributed to the originally diseased part becoming "foreign" in the first place.

CHAPTER 11
HELPING WOMEN TAKE RESPONSIBILITY

1. *Random House Unabridged Dictionary*, 2119.
2. Ibid., 1641.
3. Jay Adams, *Competent to Counsel* (Grand Rapids: Baker, 1970), 93. He states that the most important aspect of counseling is to get counselees to change their behavior. "When a person feels depressed or high, or anxious, or hostile, there really is no problem with his emotions. . . . It is true that his emotions are not pleasant, but the real problem is not emotional, it is behavioral. . . . People feel bad because of bad behavior."

CHAPTER 12
MINISTERING TO WOMEN WHO HURT

1. Allan D. Wolfelt, *Understanding Grief; Helping Yourself Heal* (Bristol, Pa.: Accelerated Development, 1992), 2.

2. B. Clayton Bell and Peggy Bell, "A Look at Grief," *Leadership* 1 (fall 1980): 44–45.

3. Bertha Simos, *A Time to Grieve* (New York: Family Service Association, 1979), quoted in J. William Worden, *Grief Counseling and Grief Therapy*, 2d ed. (New York: Springer, 1991), 4.

4. J. Bowlby, *Attachment and Loss*, vol. 3 of *Loss, Sadness, and Depression* (New York: Basic, 1980), quoted in Worden, *Grief Counseling and Grief Therapy*, 4.

5. Worden, *Grief Counseling and Grief Therapy*, 10.

6. Ibid., 11.

7. Haddon W. Robinson, *Grief* (Grand Rapids: Zondervan, 1974), 13.

8. Worden, *Grief Counseling and Grief Therapy*, 11.

9. Ibid.

10. Ibid., 12.

11. Ibid.

12. Ibid., 13.

13. Ibid.

14. Ibid., 14.

15. Ibid., 15.

16. Ibid., 16.

17. S. R. Shuchter and S. Zisook, "Treatment of Spousal Bereavement: A Multidimensional Approach," *Psychiatric Annals* 16 (1986): 117.

18. Worden, *Grief Counseling and Grief Therapy*, 11.

19. Ibid.

20. E. L. Freud, ed., *Letters of Sigmund Freud* (New York: Basic, 1961), quoted in Worden, *Grief Counseling and Grief Therapy*, 19.

21. Fritz Rieneker, *A Linguistic Key to the Greek New Testament*, ed. Cleon L. Rogers, Jr. (Grand Rapids: Zondervan, 1980), 367.

22. Worden, *Grief Counseling and Grief Therapy*, 11.

23. Wolfelt, *Understanding Grief: Helping Yourself Heal*, 59.

24. Ibid., 49.

25. Worden, *Grief Counseling and Grief Therapy*, 23.

26. Wolfelt, *Understanding Grief: Helping Yourself Heal*, 64.

27. Worden, *Grief Counseling and Grief Therapy*, 30.

28. Sigmund Freud, *Mourning and Melancholia*, vol. 14 (London:

Hogarth, 1957), quoted in Worden, *Grief Counseling and Grief Therapy*, 30.

29. *Random House Unabridged Dictionary*, 638.

30. Worden, *Grief Counseling and Grief Therapy*, 32.

31. Bryron Calhoun, "Politicization of Medical Training: Coercing Abortion Training," *Journal of Biblical Ethics in Medicine* 8 (spring 1994): 36.

32. For more arguments against abortion see J. Kerby Anderson, *Moral Dilemmas*, Swindoll Leadership Library (Nashville: Word, 1998), chapter 1; and Roy B. Zuck, *Precious in His Sight: Childhood and Children in the Bible* (Grand Rapids: Baker, 1996), chapter 5.

CHAPTER 13
MINISTERING TO SINGLE WOMEN

1. Carolyn A. Koons and Michael J. Anthony, *Single Adult Passages* (Grand Rapids: Baker, 1991), 47.

2. *1998 Information Please Almanac*, 834.

3. Barna, *The Future of the American Family*, 130.

4. United States Census Bureau, *March 1996 Current Population Survey* (September 1996).

5. Barna, *The Future of the American Family*, 120.

6. Ibid.

7. Ibid., 51.

8. Ibid., 122.

9. Ibid.

10. Ibid.

11. Koons and Anthony, *Single Adult Passages*, 30.

12. Ibid., 68.

13. Barna, *The Future of the American Family*, 125.

14. Ibid., 124.

15. Ibid., 121.

16. Ibid., 123.

17. Ibid., 125.

18. Ibid., 130.

19. Koons and Anthony, *Single Adult Passages*, 67.
20. Barna, *The Future of the American Family*, 127.
21. Ibid., 137.
22. Ibid., 128.
23. Luci Swindoll, *Wide My World, Narrow My Bed* (Portland, Oreg.: Multnomah, 1982), 38.
24. Ibid., 37–38.
25. Ibid., 38.
26. Koons and Anthony, *Single Adult Passages*, 207.

CHAPTER 14
MINISTERING TO WOMEN WHO WORK AT HOME

1. Randy Frazee and Bill Donahue, Creative Leadership Ministries (CLM), Pantego Bible Church, 3302 West Park Row Drive, Arlington, TX 76013.
2. "The Creative Homemaker," by Randy and Rozanne Frazee, is currently used in twenty-five cities in twelve states.
3. Ibid.
4. Richard Simon, "Betty Friedan Takes On the Age Mystique," *Family Therapy Networker* (July–August, 1998): 42.
5. *1998 Information Please Almanac*, 840.

CHAPTER 15
MINISTERING TO WOMEN WHO WORK OUTSIDE THE HOME

1. Church Data Services, database, 1983.
2. Patricia Aburdene and John Naisbitt, *Megatrends for Women* (New York: Villard, 1992), 216.
3. Robert Famighetti, ed., *The World Almanac and Book of Facts 1998* (Mahwah, N.J.: World Almanac, 1997), 144.
4. Aburdene and Naisbitt, *Megatrends for Women*, 217.
5. John Naisbitt and Patricia Aburdene, *Megatrends 2000* (New York: William Morrow, 1990), 217.
6. Aburdene and Naisbitt, *Megatrends for Women*, 218.

7. *1998 Information Please Almanac*, 365.

8. Aburdene and Naisbitt, *Megatrends for Women*, 222

9. Ibid.

10. Ibid.

11. Ibid., 228–29.

12. Ibid., 229.

13. Ibid., 231.

14. Ibid., 232.

15. *1998 Information Please Almanac*, 132.

16. Aburdene and Naisbitt, *Megatrends for Women*, 64–67.

17. Ibid., 67–69.

18. Ibid., 72.

19. Ibid.

20. Ibid., 69.

21. Ibid., 73–74.

22. Ibid., 74–75.

23. Ibid.

24. Ibid., 77–78.

25. Ibid., 78–79.

26. *Encyclopedia Year Book 1998*, 577.

27. Aburdene and Naisbitt, *Megatrends for Women*, 82–83.

28. Juliet B. Schor, *The Overspent American* (New York: Basic, 1998), 72.

29. Ibid.

30. Randy Frazee and Bill Donahue, "Life Vision: A Tool for Developing a Vision for Your Life," Creative Leadership Ministries, 1988.

CHAPTER 16
MINISTERING TO WOMEN OF DIFFERENT CULTURES

1. Joseph F. Aponte, *Psychological Interventions and Cultural Diversity*, ed. Joseph F. Aponte, Robin Young Rivers, and Julian Wohn (Boston: Allyn and Bacon, 1995), ix.

2. U. S. Bureau of Census, 1992, quoted by Joseph F. Aponte and Ronald T. Crouch, "The Changing Ethnic Profile of the United States," in *Psychological Interventions and Cultural Diversity*, 3.

3. James and Lillian Breckenridge, *What Color Is Your God?* (Wheaton, Ill.: Victor, 1995), 61.
4. Ibid., 12.
5. Ibid., 14.
6. Ibid., 246.
7. Reuben H. Brooks, "Cross-Cultural Perspectives in Christian Education," in *Foundations of Ministry: An Introduction to Christian Education for a New Generation,* ed. Michael J. Anthony (Wheaton, Ill.: Victor, 1992), 107–8.
8. Breckenridge, *What Color Is Your God? 98.*
9. Lascelles Black, "Families of African Origin: An Overview," in *Ethnicity and Family Change,* ed. Monica McGoldrich, Joe Giordano, and John K. Pearce, 2d ed. (New York: Guilford, 1996), 57.
10. *1998 Information Please Almanac,* 829.
11. Black, "Families of African Origin: An Overview," 59.
12. Breckenridge, *What Color Is Your God?* 218.
13. Ibid., 219.
14. Black, "Families of African Origin: An Overview," 67.
15. *1998 Information Please Almanac,* 240.
16. Ibid., 823.
17. Nydia Garcia-Preto, "Latino Families: An Overview," in *Ethnicity and Family Change,* 141. By 1999 the number of Hispanics increased to almost forty million, nearly 14 percent of the population (Tad Szule, "The Fastest-Growing Minority in America," *Parade,* 3 January 1999, 6).
18. Breckenridge, *What Color Is Your God?* 110.
19. Ibid.
20. Garcia-Preto, "Latino Families: An Overview," 151.
21. Evelyn Lee, "Asian American Families: An Overview," in *Ethnicity and Family Change,* 229–30.
22. Ibid.
23. *1998 Information Please Almanac,* 823.
24. Breckenridge, *What Color Is Your God?* 130.
25. R. Berkhoffer, *The White Man's Indian: Images of the American Indian from Columbus to the Present* (New York: Vintage, 1978), quoted in Charles Etta T. Sutton and Mary Anne Broken Nose, "American

Indian Families: An Overview," in *Ethnicity and Family Therapy,* 31–32.

26. Sutton and Broken Nose, "American Indian Families: An Overview," 34.

27. Breckenridge, *What Color Is Your God?* 137.

28. *1998 Information Please Almanac,* 823.

CHAPTER 17
WOMEN IN MISSIONS

1. D. L. Cornell, "The Role of Single Women in Present Day Missions" (paper presented at the Worldwide Evangelization Crusade Mission Executive Retreat, October 1965), 1.

2. Ibid.

3. Roger Steer, "Pushing Inward," *Christian History* 15 (November 1996): 14.

4. Ibid., 16.

5. Ruth A. Tucker, "'Unbecoming' Ladies," *Christian History* 15 (November 1996): 28.

6. Kevin D. Miller, "Gritty Pioneers," *Christian History* 15 (November 1996): 36.

7. Fredrick Franson, quoted in Tucker and Liefeld, *Daughters of the Church,* 389–90.

8. Ibid., 309.

9. Ibid., 287.

10. A. B. Simpson, quoted in *Daughters of the Church,* 287.

11. Louise M. Johnson, "The Single Woman Missionary—An Undervalued Asset," *Trinity World Forum* 5 (Winter 1980): 2.

12. L. E. Maxwell with Ruth C. Dearing, *Women in Ministry* (Camp Hill, Pa.: Christian, 1987), 127.

13. Cornell, "The Role of Single Women in Present Day Missions," 1.

CHAPTER 18
DEVELOPING A WOMAN'S MINISTRY IN YOUR CHURCH

1. Jay Kesler, *Family Forum* (Wheaton, Ill.: Victor, 1984), 233.
2. Clark, *Man and Woman in Christ,* 480–81.
3. Bill Hybels, *Too Busy Not to Pray: Slowing Down to Be with God* (Downers Grove, Ill.: InterVarsity, 1988), 62.
4. Jill Briscoe, Laurie Katz McIntyre, and Beth Seversen, *Designing Effective Women's Ministries* (Grand Rapids: Zondervan, 1995), 24.
5. Ibid., 26.
6. Ibid., 27.
7. Vickie Kraft, *Women Mentoring Women* (Chicago: Moody, 1992), 116.
8. Ibid.
9. Ibid.
10. Ibid.
11. Ibid., 106.
12. Ibid.
13. Briscoe, McIntyre, and Seversen, *Designing Effective Women's Ministries,* 67.
14. Ibid.
15. Rienecker, *Linguistic Key to the Greek New Testament,* 518.
16. Ibid., 519.

CHAPTER 19
TEACHING WOMEN ABOUT LEADERSHIP

1. Ginia Bellafante, "Feminism: It's All about Me!" *Time,* 29 June 1998, 56.
2. Stephen Covey et al., *The Guru Guide: The Best Ideas of the Top Management Thinkers,* ed. Joseph Boyett and Jimmie Boyett (New York: John Wiley and Sons, 1998), 14.
3. Ibid., 16.
4. Paul A. Cedar, *Strength in Servant Leadership* (Waco, Tex.: Word, 1987), 34.
5. Ibid., 39.

6. John Haggai, *Lead On! Leadership That Endures in a Changing World* (Waco, Tex.: Word, 1986), 44–45.

7. Cedar, *Strength in Servant Leadership*, 36.

8. Allen P. Ross, "Spiritual Leaders" (unpublished paper, n.d.), 2.

9. Eugene H. Merrill, "Numbers," in *The Bible Knowledge Commentary, Old Testament*, 238.

10. Ross, "Spiritual Leaders," 3.

11. Ibid., 10.

12. Ibid.

13. Robert H. Gundry, *A Survey of the New Testament* (Grand Rapids: Zondervan, 1970), 10.

14. *Random House Unabridged Dictionary*, 1689.

15. Ross, "Spiritual Leaders," 18.

16. See Roy B. Zuck, *Teaching as Jesus Taught* (Grand Rapids: Baker, 1995), and *Teaching as Paul Taught* (Grand Rapids: Baker, 1997).

17. William D. Lawrence, "Distinctives of Christian Leadership," *Bibliotheca Sacra* 144 (July–September 1987): 317–29.

18. See Roy B. Zuck, *Spirit-Filled Teaching: The Power of the Holy Spirit in Your Ministry*, Swindoll Leadership Library (Nashville: Word, 1998).

19. Lawrence, "Distinctives of Christian Leadership," 323.

20. Ibid.

21. Kurt Aland et al., eds., *The Greek New Testament*, 3d ed. (New York: United Bible Societies, 1983), 151.

22. Kenneth O. Gangel, *So You Want to Be a Leader!* (Harrisburg, Pa.: Christian, 1973), 14.

23. Ibid., 16.

24. Ibid., 17.

25. Ibid., 20–21.

26. Kenneth O. Gangel, *Team Leadership in Christian Ministry* (Chicago: Moody, 1997), 250.

CHAPTER 20
DEVELOPING A PHILOSOPHY OF WOMEN'S MINISTRY

1. This program provides for the physical and emotional needs of terminally ill patients.
2. *Random House Unabridged Dictionary*, 1225.
3. J. Gary Inrig, "Called to Serve: Toward a Philosophy of Ministry," *Bibliotheca Sacra* 140 (October–December 1983): 336.
4. Ibid.
5. Ibid., 337.
6. Ibid., 338–42.
7. Ibid., 336.
8. Ibid., 339.
9. Ibid., 340.
10. Ibid., 344.
11. Ibid.
12. W. H. Griffith Thomas, *Ministerial Life and Work* (Grand Rapids: Baker, 1974), 82.
13. Inrig, "Called to Serve: Toward a Philosophy of Ministry," 347.
14. For discussions on spiritual gifts see Charles C. Ryrie, *Biblical Theology of the New Testament* (Chicago: Moody, 1959); Charles C. Ryrie, *Balancing the Christian Life* (Chicago: Moody, 1969); Leslie B. Flynn, *Nineteen Gifts of the Spirit* (Wheaton, Ill.: Victor, 1974); William J. McRae, *The Dynamics of Spiritual Gifts* (Grand Rapids: Zondervan, 1976); and Earl D. Radmacher, *Salvation*, Swindoll Leadership Library (Nashville: Word, 1999).
15. *The New International Dictionary of New Testament Theology*, ed. Colin Brown (Grand Rapids: Zondervan, 1971), 2544.
16. Inrig, "Called to Serve: Toward a Philosophy of Ministry," 347.

Bibliography

Aburdene, Patricia, and John Naisbitt. *Megatrends for Women*. New York: Villard Books, 1992.

Adeney, Miriam. *A Time for Risking*. Portland, Oreg.: Multnomah Publishers, 1986.

Barna, George. *The Future of the American Family*. Chicago: Moody Press, 1993.

———. *Absolute Confusion: How Our Moral and Spiritual Foundations Are Eroding in This Age of Change*. Vol. 3. Ventura, Calif.: Regal Book House, 1993.

Bilezikian, Gilbert. *Beyond Sex Roles: What the Bible Says about a Woman's Place in Church and Family*. Grand Rapids: Baker Book House, 1986.

Boldrey, Richard, and Joyce Bouldrey. *Chauvinist or Feminist: Paul's View of Women*. Grand Rapids: Baker Book House, 1976.

Breckenridge, James, and Lillian Breckenridge. *What Color Is Your God? Multicultural Education in the Church: Examining Christ and Culture in Light of the Changing Face of the Church*. Wheaton, Ill.: Victor Books, 1995.

Brisco, Jill, Laurie Katz McIntyre, and Beth Seversen. *Designing Effective Women's Ministries: Choosing, Planning and Implementing the Right Programs for Your Church.* Grand Rapids: Zondervan Publishing House, 1995.

Clark, Stephen B. *Man and Woman in Christ: An Examination of the Roles of Men and Women in Light of Scripture and the Social Sciences.* Ann Arbor, Mich.: Servant Books, 1980.

Cook, Kaye, and Lance Lee. *Man and Woman: Alone and Together.* Wheaton, Ill.: Victor Books, 1992.

Clouse, Bonnidell, and Robert G. Clouse, eds. *Women in Ministry.* Downers Grove, Ill.: InterVarsity Press, 1989.

Elliott, Elizabeth. *Let Me Be a Woman.* Wheaton, Ill.: Tyndale House Publishers, 1976.

Evans, Mary J. *Women in the Bible: An Overview of All the Crucial Passages on Women's Roles.* Downers Grove, Ill.: InterVarsity Press, 1983.

Foh, Susan T. *Women and the Word of God: A Response to Biblical Feminism.* Nutley, N.J.: Presbyterian and Reformed Publishing Co., 1980.

Grenz, Stanley J. *Women in the Church: A Biblical Theology of Women in Ministry.* Downers Grove, Ill.: InterVarsity Press, 1995.

Groothuis, Rebecca Merrill. *Good News for Women: A Biblical Picture of Gender Equality.* Grand Rapids: Baker Books, 1997.

Hurley, James B. *Man and Woman in Biblical Perspective.* Grand Rapids: Zondervan Publishing House, 1981.

Jewett, Paul K. *Man as Male and Female.* Grand Rapids: Wm. B. Eerdmans Publishing Co., 1975.

Kassian, Mary A. *Women, Creation and the Fall.* Westchester, Ill.: Crossway Books, 1990.

Kessler, Jay. *Family Forum*. Wheaton, Ill.: Victor Books, 1984.

Koons, Carolyn A., and Michael J. Anthony. *Single Adult Passages: Uncharted Territories*. Grand Rapids: Baker Book House, 1991.

Köstenberger, Andreas J., Thomas R. Schreiner, and H. Scott Baldwin, eds. *Women in the Church: A Fresh Analysis of 1 Timothy 2:9–15*. Grand Rapids: Baker Books, 1995.

Kraft, Vickie. *Women Mentoring Women: Ways to Start, Maintain, and Expand a Biblical Women's Ministry*. Chicago: Moody Press, 1992.

Luter, Boyd, and Kathy McReynolds. *Women as Christ's Disciples*. Grand Rapids: Baker Books, 1997.

Maxwell, L. E., with Ruth C. Dearing. *Women in Ministry: An Historical and Biblical Look at the Role of Women in Christian Leadership*. Camp Hill, Pa.: Christian Publications, 1987.

McGoldrick, Monica, Joe Giordano, and John K. Pearce, eds. *Ethnicity and Family Therapy*. 2d ed. New York: Guilford Press, 1996.

Mickelsen, Alvera, ed. *Women, Authority and the Bible*. Downers Grove, Ill.: InterVarsity Press, 1986.

Nicholas, David R. *What's a Woman to Do . . . in the Church?* Scottsdale, Ariz.: Good Life Productions, 1979.

Piper, John, and Wayne Grudem, eds. *Recovering Biblical Manhood and Womanhood: A Response to Evangelical Feminism*. Wheaton, Ill.: Crossway Books, 1991.

Reed, Bobbie, ed. *Baker Handbook of Single Parent Ministry*. Grand Rapids: Baker Book House, 1998.

Sue, Derald Wing, and David Sue. *Counseling the Culturally Different: Theory and Practice*. 2d ed. New York: John Wiley and Sons, 1990.

Swindoll, Luci. *Wide My World, Narrow My Bed: Living and Loving the Single Life.* Portland, Oreg.: Multnomah Press, 1982.

Tucker, Ruth A., and Walter L. Liefeld. *Daughters of the Church: Women and Ministry from New Testament Times to the Present.* Grand Rapids: Zondervan Publishing House, 1987.

Van Leeuwen, Mary Stewart. *Gender and Grace: Love, Work and Parenting in a Changing World.* Downers Grove, Ill.: InterVarsity Press, 1990.

Wolfelt, Alan D. *Understanding Grief: Helping Yourself Heal.* Bristol, Pa.: Accelerated Development, 1992.

Worden, J. William. *Grief Counseling and Grief Therapy: A Handbook for the Mental Health Practitioner.* 2d ed. New York: Springer Publishing Co., 1991.

Scripture Index

Subject Index

Additional books from the Swindoll Leadership Library

MORAL DILEMMAS
J. Kerby Anderson

Should biblically informed Christians be for or against capital punishment? How should we as Christians view abortion, euthanasia, genetic engineering, divorce, and technology? In this comprehensive, cutting-edge book, J. Kerby Anderson challenges us to thoughtfully analyze the dividing issues facing our age, while equipping believers to maneuver through the ethical and moral land mines of our times.

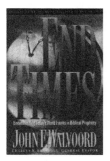

END TIMES
Dr. John F. Walvoord

Long regarded as one of the top prophecy experts, Dr. John F. Walvoord now explores world events in light of biblical prophecy. By examining all of the prophetic passages in the Bible, Walvoord clearly explains the mystery behind confusing verses and conflicting viewpoints. This is the definitive work on prophecy for Bible students.

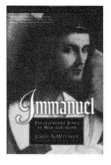

IMMANUEL
Dr. John A. Witmer

Dr. John A. Witmer presents the almighty Son of God as a living, breathing, incarnate man. He shows us a full picture of the Christ in four distinct phases: the Son of God before He became man, the divine suffering man on Earth, the glorified and ascended Christ, and the reigning King today.

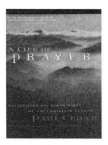

A LIFE OF PRAYER
Dr. Paul Cedar

Dr. Paul Cedar explores prayer through three primary concepts, showing us how to consider, cultivate and continue a lifestyle of prayer. This volume helps readers recognize the unlimited potential and the awesome purpose of prayer.

ANGELS, SATAN, AND DEMONS
Dr. Robert Lightner

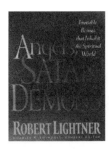

The supernatural world gets a lot of attention these days in books, movies and television series, but what does the Bible say about these other-worldly beings? Dr. Robert Lightner answers these questions with an in-depth look at the world of the "invisible" as expressed in Scripture.

COLOR OUTSIDE THE LINES
Dr. Howard G. Hendricks

Just as the apostle Paul prodded early Christians "not to be conformed" to the world, Dr. Howard Hendricks vividly—and unexpectedly—extends that biblical theme and charges us to learn the art of living creatively, reflecting the image of the Creator rather than the culture.

SPIRIT-FILLED TEACHING
Dr. Roy B. Zuck

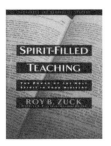

Whether you teach a small Sunday school class or a standing-room-only crowd at a major university, the process of teaching can be demanding and draining. This lively book brings a new understanding of the Holy Spirit's essential role in teaching.

TALE OF THE TARDY OXCART AND 1501 OTHER STORIES
Dr. Charles R. Swindoll

In this rich volume, you'll have access to resourcing Dr. Charles Swindoll's favorite anecdotes on prayer or quotations for grief. In *The Tale of the Tardy Oxcart,* thousands of illustrations are arranged by subjects alphabetically for quick-and-easy access. A perfect resource for all pastors and speakers.

THE CHURCH
Dr. Ed Hayes

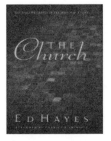

In this indispensable guide, Dr. Ed Hayes explores the labyrinths of the church, delving into her history, doctrines, rituals and resources to find out what it means to be the Body of Christ on earth. Both passionate and precise, this essential volume offers solid insights on worship, persecution, missions and morality: a bold call to unity and renewal.

EMPOWERED LEADERS
Dr. Hans Finzel

What is leadership really about? The rewards, excitement and exhilaration? Or the responsibilities, frustrations and exhausting nights? Dr. Hans Finzel takes readers on a journey into the lives of the Bible's great leaders, unearthing powerful principles for effective leadership in any situation.

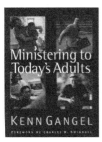

MINISTERING TO TODAY'S ADULTS
Dr. Kenn Gangel

After 40 years of research and experience, Dr. Kenn Gangel knows what it takes to reach adults. In an easy-to-grasp, easy-to-apply style, Gangel offers proven systematic strategies for building dynamic adult ministries.

HUMANITY AND SIN
Dr. Robert A. Pyne

Sin may seem like an outdated concept these days, but its consequences remain as destructive as ever. Dr. Robert A. Pyne takes a close look at humankind through the pages of Scripture and the lens of modern culture. As never before, readers will understand sin's overarching effect on creation and our world today.

THE FORGOTTEN BLESSING
Dr. Henry Holloman

For many Christians, the gift of God's grace is central to their faith. But another gift—sanctification—is often overlooked. *The Forgotten Blessing* clarifies this essential doctrine, showing us what it means to be set apart, and how the process of sanctification can forever change our relationship with God.

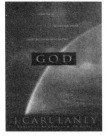

GOD
Dr. J. Carl Laney

With tenacity and clarity, Dr. J. Carl Laney makes it plain: it's not enough to know about God. We can know God better. This book presents a practical path to life-changing encounters with the goodness, greatness and glory of our Creator.

(21)

E 10972

|145|